'This book is perfect for anyone studying or considering a career in organisational psychology. It really is the essential guide. Read this book and learn from expert academics and practitioners. I wish a book like this had existed when I did my own MSc!'

Martin Greaves, *Business Partner, BBC*

'Accessible, comprehensive and relevant. A must-read for students wanting to grasp the essentials of organisational psychology and practitioners keen to benefit from the latest thinking in the field.'

Dr Phillipa Coan, *Psychologist,*
Coach and Behaviour Change Specialist

'*Organisational Psychology: An Essential Guide* offers a captivating and practical introduction to the intricate world of humans at work. It delves into work dynamics and provides guidance on optimising organisations for enhanced effectiveness for both employers and individual workers. What sets this book apart is its applicability, regardless of whether you're a student, professional, or just keen on knowing more about thriving organisations. It's an easy-to-read resource packed with evidence-based insights. I highly recommend it.'

Dr Antonio Pangallo,
Principal Researcher, Qualtrics

'This book has it all – from the theory and research to the application of organisational psychology. What makes it truly unique is that it acts as a guide to the core research areas and offers real-world application to prepare you for the many careers and routes available within the field. If you are looking to either study or work in OP, then put this book on your essential-reading list!'

Lucy Gallagher, *Group People Programmes*
Manager, Endava

Organisational Psychology

Organisational Psychology offers an accessible, engaging and practical introduction to this fascinating discipline. It explores the latest thinking, reveals surprising truths about the way we work, and explains how to craft a successful and fulfilling career in the field.

Organisational psychology is a complex and dynamic field that focuses on human behaviour in the workplace, and explores how individuals, groups and organisations function. Structured in three parts, the book combines an overview of the field with effective advice on how to become a successful organisational psychologist. It offers a deep-dive into the British Psychological Society's five core areas of organisational psychology: Psychological Assessment at Work; Learning, Training and Development; Leadership, Engagement and Motivation; Well-being and Work; and Work Design, Organisational Change and Development. Chapters include key academic and theoretical concepts, practical applications, future directions for the field, key learning points, and further reading.

Written by highly qualified experts in the field, this text is ideal for both undergraduate and postgraduate students taking programmes or modules in organisational psychology or related topics, including work and business psychology and human resources, as well as human resources practitioners. This text will also be valuable for anyone interested in understanding how organisations function and the best ways to allow individuals and organisations to survive, thrive and flourish.

Julia Yates is Chartered Psychologist and Associate Professor at City, University of London where she teaches career development and coaching on the MSc in Organisational Psychology. Before moving into academia, Julia spent 15 years working as a career coach and trainer, supporting individuals and organisations with their career-development planning.

Lara Zibarras is Reader in Organisational Psychology at City, University of London and teaches the Psychological Assessment module. Her key research areas are employee selection (where she particularly focuses on fairness, diversity, unconscious bias and applicant reactions) and pro-environmental behaviour in the workplace and she has published widely in academic journals. She is also a Chartered Psychologist and HCPC Registered Occupational Psychologist.

Lynsey Mahmood is Chartered Psychologist working in academia and practice. She is currently Lecturer in Business and Organisational Psychology at the University of Kent. Working as a practitioner she helps organisations with team development and behaviour-change implementation and has spent the last four years working in the Fire and Rescue Service to deliver behaviour-change interventions and evaluate their impact.

Organisational Psychology

An Essential Guide

Edited by Julia Yates, Lara Zibarras and
Lynsey Mahmood

Routledge
Taylor & Francis Group

LONDON AND NEW YORK

Designed cover image: © Getty Images

First published 2024
by Routledge
4 Park Square, Milton Park, Abingdon, Oxon OX14 4RN

and by Routledge
605 Third Avenue, New York, NY 10158

Routledge is an imprint of the Taylor & Francis Group, an informa business

British Library Cataloguing-in-Publication Data
A catalogue record for this book is available from the British Library

Library of Congress Cataloging-in-Publication Data
Names: Yates, Julia, editor. | Zibarras, Lara, editor. | Mahmood, Lynsey, editor.
Title: Organisational psychology : an essential guide / edited by Julia Yates, Lara Zibarras and Lynsey Mahmood.
Other titles: Organisational psychology (Routledge)
Description: Abingdon, Oxon ; New York, NY : Routledge, 2024. |
Includes bibliographical references and index. |
Summary: "Organisational Psychology offers an accessible, engaging and practical introduction to this fascinating discipline. It explores the latest thinking, reveals surprising truths about the way we work, and explains how to craft a successful and fulfilling career in the field"– Provided by publisher.
Identifiers: LCCN 2023030762 (print) | LCCN 2023030763 (ebook) |
ISBN 9781032286365 (paperback) | ISBN 9781032295480 (hardback) |
ISBN 9781003302087 (ebook)
Subjects: LCSH: Psychology, Industrial. | Organizational behavior.
Classification: LCC HF5548.8 .O6953 2024 (print) |
LCC HF5548.8 (ebook) | DDC 158.7–dc23/eng/20230629
LC record available at https://lccn.loc.gov/2023030762
LC ebook record available at https://lccn.loc.gov/2023030763

ISBN: 978-1-032-29548-0 (hbk)
ISBN: 978-1-032-28636-5 (pbk)
ISBN: 978-1-003-30208-7 (ebk)

DOI: 10.4324/9781003302087

Typeset in Sabon
by Newgen Publishing UK

Contents

Figures

Tables

Boxes

Contributors

Jennifer Gerson works at City, University of London, where she specialises in research methods teaching on both the MSc in Organisational Psychology and the MSc in Behavioural Economics. Jennifer's particular research interests are in cyberpsychology – specifically, the use of social media and its impact on well-being and happiness, and in 2019 she won an award for her research from the International Society of Quality of Life Studies. She is involved in research into workplace well-being, exploring the mental health and well-being of post graduate research students and academia as a workplace.

Shannon Horan is a Workforce Science Consultant within the People Analytics team at a Fortune 100 organisation based in the United States. Within her role, Shannon facilitates the measurement for all employee surveys and listening efforts, leads employee research which focuses mainly on employee sentiment, and consults with HR executives and senior leaders to enable decisions that are data-driven and employee-focused. Shannon completed her PhD in Organisational Psychology at City, University of London in 2020, where her research focused on employee well-being, perfectionism in the workplace, and recovering from work-related stress.

Hayley Lewis is a Chartered Psychologist, Registered Occupational Psychologist and Associate Fellow of the British Psychological Society, and an honorary lecturer at City, University of London. Hayley started her career 25 years ago, first working at the BBC and then in a variety of management and leadership roles in local government. She now works as an independent coach, consultant and trainer, specialising in leadership and management behaviour. Hayley is also joint programme director for the first part of the Professional Doctorate in Occupational Psychology, at Birbeck, University of London. Hayley is well known for her use of social media as a way to make psychology more accessible and she has made *HR Magazine*'s Most Influential Thinkers in HR list.

Lynsey Mahmood is a Chartered Psychologist working in academia and practice. She is currently a Lecturer in Business and Organisational Psychology at the University of Kent. Working as a practitioner she helps organisations with team development and behaviour-change implementation, and has spent the last four years working in the Fire and Rescue Service to deliver behaviour-change interventions and evaluate their impact. Lynsey is passionate about helping organisations ensure they are taking an evidence-based approach, focusing on embodying the role of a scientist-practitioner.

Suchi Pathak is a leader on the E-Assessment Team at Hogrefe Publishing the leading provider of assessments, books and journals for psychology in Europe. Suchi is passionate about leveraging psychometric data alongside AI and machine learning to ensure organisations select, develop and promote people with high predictability and less bias. She is a Visiting Lecturer at City University and has been a leader in the behavioural assessment and consulting industries for over a decade – she was the Head of Psychology for a global assessment provider and was responsible for research and product development initiatives for over 60 countries. She has designed selection, assessment and development solutions for clients worldwide in the commercial, military, education and sports sectors.

Jane Stewart is a Founder and Director at World of Work Project CIC and Principal Consultant at Mint Decisions where she specialises in supporting non-profit organisations and SMEs with people and leadership development. Before moving into consultancy, Jane spent 20 years leading teams and change in UK sports development organisations. After becoming increasingly frustrated with people's experience of work and volunteering in the sports sector, she returned to education to help organisations create change by completing her MSc in Organisational Psychology and her Psychology conversion, and is currently working towards her Professional Doctorate. She lives with her partner and border terrier in Edinburgh and in her spare time she is a trustee of LEAP Sports and Personal Best Foundation and co-hosts the World of Work Podcast.

Claire Stone is a Chartered Member of the CIPD and a Visiting Lecturer at City, University of London, contributing to the Work Design, Organisation Change and Development module on the MSc in Organisational Psychology. During 22 years in the energy industry, Claire specialised in gathering employee engagement data; developing engagement and well-being initiatives, and supporting people through change. Claire uses dialogic organisation development techniques, such as The World Café, to enable teams to adapt and determine their own direction for change. She is also a research evaluation enthusiast, having helped colleagues to produce successful Impact Case Studies for the Research Excellence Framework (REF) 2021.

Jutta Tobias Mortlock is a Social Psychologist with 25 years of work experience in capacity-building in six countries on three continents. Her research and public outreach is focused on the link between well-being and sustainable performance at work, especially in high-stakes settings such as in the Armed Forces and in extreme poverty contexts. Jutta co-directs City University's Centre for Excellence in Mindfulness Research (mindfulness-science.com) and serves as advisor to The Mindfulness Initiative, a non-profit mindfulness thinktank. Her work has been published in leading academic journals as well as in popular media including in *The Times* and on the BBC.

Julia Yates is a Chartered Psychologist and an Associate Professor at City, University of London where she teaches career development and coaching on the MSc in Organisational Psychology. Before moving into academia, Julia spent 15 years working as a career coach and trainer, supporting individuals and organisations with their career development planning. Julia is passionate about making stronger links between research and practice, and writes and speaks widely about the practical application of theories in practice. She has written more than 50 articles and four books including *The Career Coaching Handbook* and *The Career Coaching Toolkit.*

Lucie Zernerova is currently a Post-doctoral Researcher with the Institute of Psychology at the Czech Academy of Sciences and a Lecturer in Organisational Psychology at Charles University in Prague in the Czech Republic. In her work, Lucie focuses on research, development and application of individual and organisational interventions to promote employee health, well-being and behavioural effectiveness using mindfulness-informed approaches and contextual behavioural science. Lucie completed her PhD in Organisational Psychology at City, University of London in 2020, where she researched mindfulness as a personal resource in context of work-related stress and motivation.

Lara Zibarras is a Reader in Organisational Psychology at City, University of London and teaches the Psychological Assessment module. Her key research areas are employee selection (where she particularly focuses on fairness, diversity, unconscious bias and applicant reactions) and pro-environmental behaviour in the workplace and she has published widely in academic journals. She is also an HCPC registered Chartered Occupational Psychologist and has consulted for a range of public and private sector organisations in the areas of selection, training, development and psychometric assessment. This is her third edited book.

Acknowledgements

First and foremost, we would like to thank all of our students, past, present and future, for galvanising us into action. We have written this book for you and because of you. We thank you for your enthusiasm and engagement, and for making our jobs so much fun and so stimulating. You inspire us, you teach us and we are very optimistic of the future of our profession in your hands.

We also owe a huge debt of gratitude to our wonderful chapter authors, who have each generously shared their considerable expertise with us and with our readers. Suchi, Claire, Jane, Lucie, Shannon and Hayley, you are fantastic colleagues to work with and we are very grateful for your contributions to this book, to our programme and to the whole field.

Closer to home, we would like to thank our own team. Jenny and Jutta: thank you for your brilliant chapters and Paul for your expert advice, and to all of you for your endless, unwavering support, advice and camaraderie.

Chapter 1

Introduction

Julia Yates, Lara Zibarras and Lynsey Mahmood

Overview

This chapter will offer you an introduction to the book and an introduction to organisational psychology. We will explain what organisational psychology is, its purpose, and
how it works in practice and will also offer a brief history of the discipline. We then move
on to introducing the book itself, explaining why we decided to write it, and why you
might want to read it. We end with an introduction to each of the chapters ahead.

The book is divided into three parts. In Part I there are chapters which map the British
Psychological Society's core areas of organisational psychology – together these give a
comprehensive overview of the discipline, covering psychological assessment, learning
training and development, leadership engagement and motivation, well-being and work,
and work design, organisational change and development. In Part II we take these five
core areas and pick one aspect of each of them for a more in-depth discussion. Within
psychological assessment, we focus on psychometrics; for learning training and development, we explore coaching psychology; within leadership engagement and motivation,
the focus is on team dynamics; for well-being and work we examine mindfulness, and for
work design and organisational change we look at some of the future trends in organisational psychology. In the final part of the book we turn our attention towards the more
practical aspects of working in this field. The chapters in Part III focus on ethical and
reflective practice and research in organisations, and we finish with a chapter that offers
an overview of career paths in this field, and some useful practical tips for carving out a
fulfilling career in the field.

Learning outcomes

By the end of the chapter you will:

- understand what organisational psychology is and where it comes from;
- be aware of the purpose of the book and what you will gain from reading it;
- have a clear sense of the structure of the book and the topics covered.

DOI: 10.4324/9781003302087-1

Introduction

Box 1.1 What's in a name?

There are several terms used to refer to this field of applied psychology. Within the UK, the term *Occupational Psychology* is often used. This is the official and 'protected title', meaning that you can't call yourself an 'occupational psychologist' even if you have finished an MSc course in 'occupational psychology'. To use the title Occupational Psychologist, you need to complete specific, accredited training through the British Psychological Society (BPS) and register with the Health Care Professional Council (HCPC). But many people working in this field don't call themselves occupational psychologists and you may also come across the terms *organisational psychologist*, *business psychologist* and *work psychologist*. Roles with these different titles are generally quite similar, focusing on the same sorts of issues, but held by people who have slightly different qualifications. If you are based in the US you may use the term *industrial and organisational psychology*. The terms *business*, *industrial* and *work* psychology are more or less interchangeable and, in the UK, you are more likely to find *'business psychology'* courses housed within a business school with a commensurate business focus.

The most commonly used term is probably *'organisational psychology'*. Arguably, this is a more accurate reflection of what people in our field do – we don't just focus on occupations, but tend to work with, for, and inside organisations. For that reason, in this chapter and throughout the book, we refer to *organisational psychology*.

What is organisational psychology?

Organisational psychology is an area of applied psychology that focuses on human behaviour at work. It uses theories and ideas from other areas of psychology (such as social and health psychology) to improve the lives of people within organisations. A good way to think about the ways in which organisational psychology can help, is to think about an employee's lifecycle (see Figure 1.1).

From the individual's perspective, before an employee starts working at an organisation, they must be **attracted** to an organisation. As organisational psychologists we can ensure that the right people are **recruited** into the organisation, and **onboarded** effectively. We would aim to support their mental and physical health during their time as employees, to ensure that they **learn** and **develop** the right skills and use the best ways to **motivate** and **reward** them. As employees **progress** through the organisation, their **performance** will be measured, and organisations will attempt to **retain** them. At some point they (may) **leave** and then the cycle starts all over again.

At the organisational level, organisational psychology can focus on strategies to improve efficiency and innovation, and to prepare for and cope with change. More widely, organisational psychology can be used to help with workforce planning at a national level.

Figure 1.1 The employee lifecycle.

Organisational psychologists are employed in every sector and every kind of business – public, private and charity sectors, small, medium and large organisations, in-house and consultancies; they can also work as freelancers, working with several different organisations. As an organisational psychologist, you will never be bored. The evidence base that underpins your work is always developing and new research, ideas and approaches are published every week. It is important for practitioners to keep up with the shifting landscape (as you will learn in Chapter 13) so whatever your specialism and whatever your industry, you will always be learning.

The workplace lies at the heart of our lives and our society, and organisational psychologists are therefore well placed to use their expertise to make a real difference, helping people to be happier, more skilled and more suited to their jobs, to make organisations more creative, fairer and more effective, and to have a significant and positive impact on people's lives. No wonder then that the field of organisational psychology is growing as fast as it is.

A brief history of organisational psychology in the UK

Although organisational psychology emerged soon after the turn of the 20th century, its notable expansion didn't occur for some decades. During the Second World War psychological assessments were used to assess military recruits. Vernon and Parry (1949) give a detailed outline of the use of psychological assessments in the Army, Navy and Air Force and the use of follow-up data to demonstrate effectiveness. This is thought to be one of the earliest accounts of the use of differential psychology in the UK.

After the Second World War, psychologists started practising within Government and in 1950, a separate 'Psychologist' job title was created (Shimmin & Wallace, 1994). These psychologists were important in helping the country navigate post-war workplace changes, reintegrating those who had fought in the war into civilian life, and capitalising on technological advancements (Shimmin & Wallace, 1994). Indeed, some of their work laid foundations for aspects of today's occupational psychology, such as modern-day assessment centres (Murray, 1990).

Occupational psychology was developed as a 'science', with the aim of developing universal theories and research (Herriot & Anderson, 1997). Much of the early work focused on the study of individual differences (such as traits, abilities and personality), underpinned by the assumption that individual differences are the main predictor of job performance. This perspective grew in popularity at this time because it aligned with the development of the bureaucratic model of organisations where stable jobs in large numbers were common (Herriot & Anderson, 1997; McCourt, 1999).

In the 1960s, occupational psychology started to move away from the idea of being a 'pure' science in part as a result of an influx of ideas from social psychology. The organisational context was seen as a dynamic and social environment, changing over time (Anderson et al., 2004; Herriot, 1993), and this led to a shift of approach in how job performance was considered, acknowledging wider team, organisational, social and economic factors.

In 1971, the Division of Occupational Psychology within the BPS was founded, and later that decade in 1977, the *Journal of Occupational and Organisational Psychology* was established, publishing high quality research to increase our understanding of people and organisations at work. It is still an important journal in the field today. The 1980s saw a rise in opportunities for Occupational Psychologists. Many new consultancies were founded and grew, including Saville & Holdsworth (SHL) and Pearn Kandola. The term 'Occupational Health Psychology' was coined at this time, reflecting the rise in interest of the mental health of workers, and a focus on the factors that influence their stress and well-being (Shimmin & Wallace, 1994). There has since been increased interest in psychological well-being and in the relationships between well-being and performance. This highlights a broader focus in the field, as it moved beyond performance issues. The 90s – the 'information age' – saw a huge increase in globalisation, the introduction and then widespread use of the Internet, and the idea of the War for Talent which described the increased competition between employers to attract the best recruits (Michaels et al., 2001).

There have been significant changes in the workplace over the last two decades, which have had a dramatic impact on the way we work and communicate.

Technological changes have been wide-ranging. There has been increased automation in jobs across all sectors and growth in the use of artificial intelligence. New technologies are now widely used across organisations, for example there has been increased use of asynchronous video interviewing within the recruitment process, and workplace training is now often delivered via asynchronous online courses. With the enormous rise in smartphone use, people have access to more information than ever before and a proliferation of new ways to communicate with people worldwide through emails, video, text messaging and social media. People can literally run businesses from the palm of their hands. The advantages that come with this technology are clear but there are also drawbacks, including rising levels of burnout and the inability to switch off, unhealthy phone addictions and a reduction in face-to-face communication, which can impact relationship building in the workplace.

Technology has enabled dramatic changes in working patterns. We now have more flexible working hours and contracts, opportunities for side hustles and the convenience of remote working. But these benefits have come at a cost, with more zero hours contracts, an increase in working hours and blurred boundaries between home and working life.

There has been a huge increase in globalisation with a seismic shift in the workforce, creating multicultural workplaces and increased diversity. Yet there is still work to do to improve equality, diversity and inclusion. We need better ways to manage bias, both conscious and unconscious, to increase gender and ethnic diversity, and to manage generational issues at work and the differences in (or perceptions of) work ethic and commitment.

There have been rapid changes in the economy, financial crises across the world, the impact of Brexit in the UK, and the unprecedented disruption from the Covid-19 pandemic, with the sudden and unexpected requirement for home-working. Organisations by and large showed remarkable resilience and creativity during the pandemic, but we also saw more loneliness, disconnection and mental ill-health. Many of us liked the flexibility and autonomy that working from home brought and have chosen to continue working flexibly, but maintaining a positive organisational culture whilst employees work remotely is not easy. Some organisations are now trying to entice people back into offices and others are looking for ways to improve the commitment and engagement of remote workers. These crisis-driven changes will, without doubt, have a lasting impact on the way we work, but it will take time to determine the most effective ways to incorporate these developments into our workplaces permanently.

Since the Covid-19 pandemic, we have also been witnessing changes in attitudes to work. The term the 'great resignation' was coined to describe the large numbers of people who left their jobs in the months after the lockdowns. The reasons for this are not entirely clear, but it may be that they felt undervalued at work, or perhaps because the unusual circumstances allowed them to better understand their own limits and to become more aware of their own needs. Then there's the so-called 'quiet quitting' – where employees do just the work that they're paid to do, rather than getting involved in extracurricular activities at work or taking on extra duties, which has perhaps gained in popularity due to pandemic-induced burnout.

Organisational psychology can and should be at the forefront of supporting employees and organisations through these changes. We are well placed to help people adapt to a rapidly changing landscape and it is encouraging to see that employers are becoming well aware of the value that organisational psychology can bring.

Why read this book?

We want to inspire others to reap the rewards of a career in organisational psychology, but (as we discuss in Chapter 3) making a career choice is a significant and often difficult task. Training as an organisational psychologist is time consuming and costly, but you can minimise the risks involved by learning as much as you can about the field before you commit. That is what this book is all about. In the pages that follow, we will give you an overview of the different aspects of the discipline. If you enjoy reading the book, this might well be a good career direction for you. If you find that you aren't wholly engaged, then maybe it's worth exploring further afield. Either way, this book is going to be a useful investment and even if you don't pursue organisational psychology professionally, we hope the book offers you insights about your own work and career, and the organisations you have been involved with.

Of course most jobs in organisational psychology won't incorporate all aspects of the discipline. One appealing feature of working in this field is that you can find jobs that are either highly specialised or broadly generalist – as well as everywhere in between. Dr Hayley Lewis talks more about this in Chapter 14. You may find that there are one or two chapters that captivate you, where others are less inspiring, and that can help you start to clarify your own career goals.

Who will benefit from this book?

This book is an introductory guide. It's aimed at anyone who is considering studying or working in the field of organisational psychology. You may have a background in psychology and are thinking about what to study next. You may be working in HR already and are considering a shift in emphasis; perhaps you are contemplating your first career choice or perhaps you are a bit further down your career journey and are considering a whole new direction.

Wherever you are, the book will offer you an overview of the whole field that doesn't assume any previous knowledge. We have tried to avoid too much technical language, and explained any terms we think you may not have come across before. We have also included a comprehensive glossary at the end which should help to clarify any of the more discipline-specific terms.

How this book is structured

One of the strengths of this book is that it is structured around the British Psychological Society's (BPS) framework. The BPS is the professional body in the UK which has a Royal Charter mandating it to oversee the academic discipline of psychology and the various professions within it, promoting the application of psychology for the public good. The division of occupational psychology oversees the training of organisational psychologists in the UK, and has identified certain standards which together constitute a comprehensive overview of the discipline. The BPS identifies five core areas: (1) psychological assessment at work; (2) learning, training and development; (3) leadership, engagement and motivation; (4) well-being and work; and (5) work design, organisational change and development.

The rest of the book is divided into three sections. In Part I we offer a set of overview chapters, summarising the latest thinking in each of the five core areas. In Part II we delve a bit deeper, choosing one aspect from each of the five core areas to describe in detail. Finally, in Part III we consider the practice of organisational psychology, looking at what you need to carve out a career in the field.

Part I: The Core Areas of Organisational Psychology

Chapter 2: Psychological Assessment, by Dr Lara Zibarras

This chapter provides an overview of various aspects and stages of assessing people in work settings. It focuses on how to design a selection process, what methods can be used and how to judge the quality of a selection process.

Chapter 3: Learning Training and Development, by Dr Julia Yates

In this chapter we focus on occupational choices and introduce some of the theories that underpin career choice and development. We then go on to look at learning and training within organisations, describing some of the research that identifies good practice in this field and highlighting the factors that too often mean that training in organisations is less than optimal.

Chapter 4: Leadership, Engagement and Motivation, by Dr Jutta Tobias Mortlock

This chapter offers an overview of the rich history of leadership scholarship, summarising some of the key theories of leadership that were popular in the 20th century, before addressing the contemporary literature and highlighting some of the leadership theories and practices that have emerged more recently. The chapter then turns its attention to practical applications of these ideas, looking at some evidence-based approaches to leadership development.

Chapter 5: Well-Being and Work, by Dr Lara Zibarras, Dr Julia Yates, Dr Shannon Horan and Dr Lucie Zernerova

This chapter explores the increasingly important field of workplace well-being. The chapter explores exactly what we mean by well-being and how it relates to stress, and gives some compelling reasons for organisations to engage with it. The chapter describes some of the key causes of workplace stress and gives some examples of some evidence-based interventions aimed at boosting well-being in organisations.

Chapter 6: Work Design, Organisational Change and Development, by Dr Claire Stone

This is the core area that that is probably the broadest in scope, covering a number of fundamental aspects of organisational behaviour. The chapter offers an introduction to this area, providing insights into the evolution and theoretical underpinnings of both traditional and contemporary organisation development, and describing the relevance of these change approaches to different organisational structures, cultures and needs.

Part II: Core Areas in Focus

Chapter 7: Psychological Assessment in Focus: Psychometrics, by Suchi Pathak

Within Psychological Assessment, psychometric assessments are used in every part of the employee lifecycle, from selection and development through to succession planning. This chapter explores the history and use of psychometric assessments in today's workplace.

Chapter 8: Learning, Training and Development in Focus: Coaching Psychology, by Dr Julia Yates

Within the area of Learning, Training and Development, coaching psychology is one of the most popular and effective approaches to development, and in this chapter we look at what we know about why and how coaching works, and introduce some key coaching approaches.

Chapter 9: Leadership, Engagement and Motivation in Focus: Groups and Teams, by Dr Lynsey Mahmood

As part of the core area of Learning, Engagement and Motivation, this chapter focuses on groups and teams in the workplace, and specifically on the application of social identity theory to team behaviour at work. The chapter offers an overview of this theory and then unpicks what it means for organisations and the people within them. The chapter ends with a brief look hybrid or remote teams, and the implications of these new ways of working on groups, leaders and organisations.

Chapter 10: Well-Being and Work in Focus: Mindfulness at Work, by Dr Jutta Tobias Mortlock

As part of Well-Being and Work we delve deep into the area of mindfulness. The chapter offers an introduction to what exactly mindfulness is and how it works, and offers a summary of the evidence about its not altogether straightforward relationship with well-being. The chapter ends with some practical examples and a case study showing how mindfulness is used in organisations.

Chapter 11: Work Design, Organisational Change and Development in Focus: Latest Developments in Organisational Psychology, by Jane Stewart

As part of Work design, Organisational change and Development, this chapter identifies a number of key trends in the contemporary workplace and offers an analysis of where we are and where we might be going with them.

Part III: Organisational Psychology in Practice

Chapter 12: Professionalism in Organisational Psychology: Ethical and Reflective Practice, by Dr Julia Yates

This chapter offers an introduction to these two important professional skills, explaining the importance of ethical and reflective practice. The chapter offers some useful frameworks for enhancing good practice and suggests some practical steps that psychologists can take to maintain and enhance their professional standards.

Chapter 13: Research Design and Evidence-Based Practice, by Dr Jennifer Gerson, Dr Lynsey Mahmood and Dr Lara Zibarras

One philosophy that is core to the identity of organisational psychologists is the notion of being scientist practitioners. Our work always aims to be grounded in evidence and we often need to generate this evidence ourselves by conducting research in organisations. In this chapter we offer an overview of the whole research process, introducing the basics of good research design and some key methods of quantitative and qualitative research.

Chapter 14: Working in Organisational Psychology, by Dr Hayley Lewis

In this chapter we unpick some of the complexities involved in carving out a career in the field and offer some practical tips for those of you keen to take this further.

We have been fortunate to work with a superb collection of chapter authors. They are all experts in their fields, with both in-depth understanding of the academic literature and practical knowledge about how their topics are applied in the workplace. They have also all been involved in training organisational psychology students, so have a clear sense of what is easy to understand and what may need more explaining. We, the book editors, have also had the pleasure of writing some of the chapters, in our own fields of expertise, and sincerely hope that from start to finish, we have managed to share some of our passion for the academic subject and the profession with you.

References

Anderson, N., Lievens, F., van Dam, K. & Ryan, A.M. (2004). Future perspectives on employee selection: Key directions for future research and practice. *Applied Psychology*, 53(4), 487–501.

Herriot, P. (1993). A paradigm bursting at the seams. *Journal of Organizational Behavior*, 371–375.

Herriot, P. & Anderson, N. (1997). Selecting for change: How will personnel and selection psychology survive. *International Handbook of Selection and Assessment*, 1–34.

McCourt, W. (1999). Paradigms and their development: The psychometric paradigm of personnel selection as a case study of paradigm diversity and consensus. *Organization Studies*, 20(6), 1011–1033.

Michaels, E., Handfield-Jones, H. & Axelrod, B. (2001). *The war for talent*. Harvard Business Press.

Murray, H. (1990). The transformation of selection procedures: The War Office Selection Boards. In E. Trist & H. Murray (Eds.), *The Social Engagement of Social Science* (pp. 45–67). London: Tavistock Institute.

Shimmin, S. & Wallis, D. (1994). *Fifty years of occupational psychology in Britain*. Division and Section of Occupational Psychology, British Psychological Society.

Vernon, P.E. & Parry, J.B. (1949). *Personnel selection in the British forces*. London: University of London Press.

Part I

The core areas of organisational psychology

Chapter 2

Psychological assessment

Lara Zibarras

Overview

This chapter explores how selection processes are designed, from job analysis and selection method choice, through to evaluation. This chapter provides you with an understanding about how selection methods are created and how selection decisions are made about individuals in the workplace. You'll be introduced to selection theories, different selection methods and issues to consider in designing a selection process, such as fairness, diversity, the candidate's perspective and the use of technology and social media.

Learning outcomes

By the end of this chapter you will:

- understand how selection and assessment processes fit within the context of an organisation;
- appreciate how selection processes are designed and implemented;
- understand which methods can be used to assess and then select candidates, and their relative strengths and weaknesses;
- appreciate the importance of fairness, diversity and inclusion within selection and assessment;
- recognise the applicant's involvement in the selection process.

Introduction: why should we select people into organisations?

Why is it necessary to select people into organisations? Why can't we just offer a job to anyone who applies?

To consider these questions, let's start with a thought experiment. Imagine a medium-sized marketing company; what kinds of job roles do you imagine there would be?

Within marketing-related roles, you might have considered:

- marketing manager
- market research analyst

DOI: 10.4324/9781003302087-3

- graphic designer
- social media manager.

Thinking more widely within the organisation, you might have considered the following roles:

- finance manager
- bookkeeper
- HR manager
- office manager.

Taking a look at all the roles outlined above, what kind of knowledge, skills, abilities and other attributes (KSAOs) do you imagine someone would need to perform these roles?

Take the marketing and finance managers for example, they would need different skills and abilities to perform these roles effectively. A marketing manager might need excellent communication, proactivity, customer service and leadership skills. Conversely, the finance manager might need business acumen, a high level of numeracy, excellent attention to detail and organisational skills. Furthermore, job holders probably studied different degrees in higher education and developed different skills throughout their career. Using this scenario, it's possible to see why finding the right person for the job might be important.

As illustrated by this thought experiment, there are two main principles that underpin selection assessment methods (Patterson, 2018):

1 there are individual differences between people in knowledge, skills, abilities and other attributes, so that people are not equally suited to specific roles; and
2 future behaviour is (at least partly) predictable. Therefore, a primary goal of selection methods is to find the best person for a role.

Designing a selection process

Figure 2.1 outlines the main steps in designing and implementing a selection process. The process starts with an analysis of the job role to identify what work is done (i.e. tasks, responsibilities), along with the KSAOs needed in order to be successful in the role.

Once the KSAOs are identified, a competency model and person and job specifications can be created and the selection criteria can be identified. The person and job specifications describe the tasks and person requirements necessary for the role. These are used during the recruitment process, where organisations advertise the job role and attract candidates to apply. In deciding to apply for a job role, applicants will also *self-select* to make an informed decision as to whether they feel they are suitable for the role.

Selection methods are chosen, or designed, based on the KSAOs needed to perform the role. Essentially you are considering, *will this selection method help me identify the knowledge, skills or abilities needed in this role?*

Selection processes involve several stages. Some selection methods are used earlier in the selection process, and some are used later on. The earlier methods are often referred to as 'short-listing' methods where candidates are rejected on the basis that they don't meet some minimum requirement such as educational qualifications. Short-listing methods

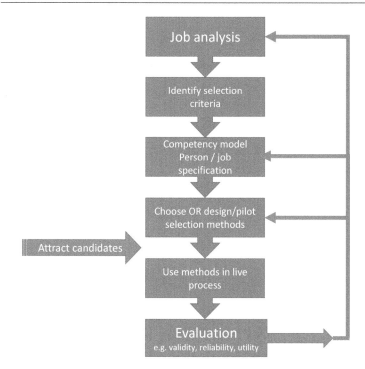

Figure 2.1 Designing a selection process.

may include CVs, application forms, references, situational judgement tests, psycho-metric tests and sometimes interviews.

The later methods are often referred to as 'long-listing' methods, used to identify the top performing candidates and offer them a job. This decision is informed by several selection methods. Long-listing methods may also include situational judgement tests, and interviews and assessment centres.

Once selection decisions are made, applicants' performance on the selection methods can be examined to evaluate the selection process. Here, a validity study would be con-ducted to examine the extent to which scores during selection are associated with later, on-the-job performance (explained in more detail later in the chapter).

Job (or role) analysis

The first step in designing a selection process is a job analysis, used to generate the KSAOs required to perform a particular job.

As we explored above in the marketing company example, each of the roles considered would require different knowledge, skills, attitudes and other attributes. Identifying the correct KSAOs allows the organisation to create a person and job specification in order to target the right kind of person (Breaugh, 2017). In addition, job analysis allows ana-lysts to obtain job-related samples of behaviour which can be used to develop the content of a selection method (Campion et al., 2011) and increase its job-relatedness.

Methods of job analysis

There are two broad approaches to job analysis. The first is task or job oriented which aims to describe the tasks or work actually being done. The other is a worker-oriented approach, where the focus is determining what KSAOs the job holder requires in order to perform the role effectively (Morgeson et al., 2019).

Examples of task-oriented approaches are as follows:

Questionnaire/survey

Questionnaires or surveys (completed by job holders) can be used to understand job-relevant information and can elicit information such as physical activities, relationships and the context of the role. Although easy to administer, they can lack a level of nuance about the role.

Observation

This is when the job holder is directly observed carrying out their role. It's useful for jobs where the behaviours are clearly observable, such as a machine operator or a surgeon. Observations can be a useful way of gaining first-hand knowledge of the tasks, along with the work environment and the equipment used for the role. However, observations cannot give information about the cognitive element of the job, and it's often not possible to identify the importance or difficulty of a specific task.

Task analysis

A task analysis breaks the job down into components to examine how it is performed, including duration, frequency and complexity. Often a task analysis results in a hierarchical representation of the steps needed to perform a specific task (known as a hierarchical task analysis). A task analysis is a structured technique that can be relatively easy to carry out, and is a useful way to understand how jobs are performed. However, it can be time consuming to create a detailed task analysis.

Work diaries

These are self-reported diaries where job holders consider what tasks they performed throughout the day. This offers insight into the common tasks and their duration. Work diaries can be inexpensive to use, and are flexible and therefore relevant for a variety of jobs. However, work diaries depend on accurate recall of events and some people keep incomplete diaries, or miss out important items.

Some examples of worker-oriented job analysis methods are as follows:

Interviews and/or focus groups

Interviews and focus groups are conducted with job holders, supervisors and other members of the team. Typically, respondents are asked questions about tasks, responsibilities and the KSAOs needed to perform competently in the role. The advantage of this approach is the input from relevant staff. However, job holders may be prone to some exaggeration or distortion, and it relies to some extent on the interviewer's skill.

Critical incident technique (CIT) (Flanagan, 1954)

This is a widely used approach to obtain behavioural descriptions of the job and relevant activities. A *critical incident* is viewed as an extreme behaviour that is either effective or ineffective in achieving a particular outcome. CIT is often used during interviews or focus groups and the interviewer asks job holders to describe incidents of (in)effective performance, relating to the role in question. For example, you might ask: '*Tell me about a time when you successfully closed a sale*'.

CIT is useful in identifying critical tasks, flexible to use for different levels and roles, and useful for job tasks that are not easily observed. However, CIT might not give a complete picture of the job role, and can be subjective and time consuming to analyse.

When conducting job analyses in practice, it is useful to examine the validity of the results. This can be done by triangulating findings from several different job analysis methods, and by using subject matter experts to confirm them. For example, in research by Patterson and colleagues (2013) to design a competency model for General Practitioners (GPs), three different job analysis methods were used. These were stakeholder interviews; focus groups and behavioural observation which allowed for triangulation of findings across three different methods and perspectives. The study also used a validation questionnaire to gain feedback from a different group of stakeholders to allow comment and critique on the competency domains. In addition, an expert panel was used to review findings from the job analysis and validation questionnaire. The process adopted by these researchers ensured that the findings were relevant to the role of GP.

As cautioned by several researchers (Prien et al., 2009; Voskuijl, 2017) there are some caveats to the use of job analysis which fall under two categories – **accuracy** and **stability** (Sanchez & Levine, 2012).

In terms of accuracy, not all respondents will be equally familiar with the role, especially if information is gathered from several sources like supervisors, direct reports and clients. Furthermore, people may inflate the importance of their role, or certain elements of their job; and finally, *time spent* on a task does not necessarily indicate how *important* it is.

In terms of stability, the nature of work is changing rapidly and as such, competencies and job descriptions won't be relevant forever (Pereira et al., 2021). Indeed, for some roles there is natural seasonal variation (e.g.. fruit pickers and Christmas jobs). Technological changes may reduce skills that employees need due to automation, but might also increase skills needed such as autonomy and decision making. Furthermore, there are employee-determined changes where job holders change and improve their role.

Box 2.1 Selection paradigms

The traditional perspective that has dominated research and practice in selection takes a rationalistic and scientific approach and has been termed the 'psychometric' paradigm.

This dominant paradigm evolved during an era of the bureaucratic work organisation, where stable jobs in large numbers were common (e.g. public sector and military organisations). There are certain assumptions that underly this perspective:

- work is performed by individuals;
- jobs rarely change;
- job performance can be assessed and credited to individuals;
- individual attributes can be measured and don't really change over time;
- selection is by the organisation only and not vice versa (Herriot & Anderson, 1997; Searle, 2003).

But we know from other areas of organisational psychology (such as learning and development) that these assumptions don't always hold. And further, the context within which the psychometric paradigm flourished is disappearing with an emergence of small- to medium-sized companies, sub-contracted labour, and the trend towards more flexible, changeable work roles (Santana & Cobo, 2020).

A more critical social-interactionist perspective challenges the psychometric approach (Anderson, 2001; Searle, 2003). Its assumptions are:

- people can and do change;
- work behaviour is part of a process and involves social interactions between people;
- jobs are a changing set of role expectations and relationships;
- selection is by *both* organisation *and* candidate and each can influence the outcome.

The social process paradigm suggests that one-way assessment (i.e. selection of the applicant by the organisation) is not the only purpose of selection. It is the first step in a continuing relationship and may be the start of the formation of the psychological contract (Anderson, 2001).

It's worth considering these assumptions when you are exploring research and practice in this area.

Selection methods

In this section, a review of the different types of selection methods will be presented, followed by some guidance on how to judge the quality of selection methods.

Curriculum vitae (CVs), application forms and biodata

CVs (or résumés) are viewed as a major tool in selection (Furnham, 2017) and are often the first contact between the applicant and the organisation. CVs are positively perceived by applicants because candidates can create a positive impression, market themselves and indicate their fit to the job or organisation (Searle, 2003). CVs include both 'hard' verifiable items (e.g. education qualifications), as well as 'soft' and less verifiable items (e.g. hobbies).

CVs are a popular selection method (Zibarras & Woods, 2010), but despite this, there is limited research evidence supporting their use. CVs are considered unreliable, especially since candidates are likely to exaggerate on their CV and screening can be subject to biases (Derous & Ryan, 2019).

Application forms are more standardised than CVs because they ask candidates a specific set of questions relating to education, experience and competencies. Although the information may be similar to a CV, organisations have more control over what information candidates can submit, and since the information is collected in a standardised way, it's likely to be easier for recruiters to shortlist candidates.

Within Application Forms, a growing practice is to include items relating to 'biographical data' or biodata. This includes previous experience, education and hobbies which have been shown to predict performance in a variety of job roles (Bret Becton et al., 2009).

References

References are used to obtain further information about applicants and allow organisations to check with past supervisors to determine if the applicant is suitable for the role. Although they are widely used, their validity is relatively low (Robertson & Smith, 2001) and may not be a true reflection of the candidate.

Psychometrics – ability and personality

Psychometrics are designed to assess aspects of a person such as their intelligence or personality traits like extraversion. Psychometrics are commonly used earlier in the selection process and generally show good to moderate levels of validity and reliability (Robertson & Smith, 2001). Chapter 7 is entirely dedicated to exploring the use of psychometrics in the selection context and as such we won't delve into detail here.

Situational judgement tests (SJTs)

SJTs are hypothetical job-related scenarios that refer to a problem or dilemma faced at work and candidates are asked to choose an appropriate response from a list of options. SJTs are referred to as a measurement methodology (Lievens et al., 2008; Patterson et al., 2016) rather than a single method, because SJTs can be designed to measure multiple constructs.

SJTs can be presented to candidates in different ways including written or video formats, and response instructions are generally either KNOWLEDGE BASED (i.e. *what is the best option?*) or BEHAVIOURAL TENDENCY (i.e. *what would you most likely do?*). There are several different response formats that are used including multiple choice (i.e. *choose the best option from four options*); rank order (i.e. *rank all the responses in order of appropriateness*); rating (i.e. *rate the appropriateness of each option*); and best / worst choice (i.e. *choose the best and worst response option*). Unlike other psychometric tests, SJTs are designed to be bespoke to the organisation and therefore created to fit the requirements of the role (Christian et al., 2010).

SJTs are developed based on a job analysis to ensure that they reflect the role in question (Patterson et al., 2016). Research generally shows that SJTs can be reliably used in selection to identify a range of professional attributes in different settings, e.g. recruitment (Wyatt et al., 2010), engineering (Jesiek et al., 2020), teaching (Chao et al., 2020), and medicine (Patterson et al., 2009). SJTs are useful in high volume selection since they are completed online and this can reduce the time taken to shortlist candidates compared to reading hundreds of CVs and/or application forms.

Interviews

Employment interviews can be structured or unstructured. Unstructured interviews have no format or fixed questions and as such, interviewers are likely to ask different applicants different questions. Further, there is no fixed way of scoring responses.

In a structured interview, the questions are derived from a job analysis, and there is a fixed set of questions that are asked in the same order for each applicant. Although more costly to create, structured interviews are less subject to bias (Levashina et al., 2014) and generally have much higher validities than unstructured interviews (McDaniel et al., 1994; Thorsteinson, 2018).

Interviews can be further distinguished between behavioural based interviews and situational interviews. Behavioural based interview questions ask candidates how they have behaved in the past, for example '*Tell me about a time when you experienced conflict with a team member and how you handled it*'.

Situational based interview questions present hypothetical job-related situations to a candidate and ask them how they would behave, for example '*You are working on a tight deadline, but you find you are unable to complete your part because a co-worker hasn't answered some questions. How would you deal with this situation?*'

Assessment centres

The concept 'assessment centre' refers to a process as opposed to a place. Assessment centres (ACs) take place over one or a few days where candidates are observed taking part in several different selection methods that simulate job-relevant tasks. This could include work samples, such as presentation, group or written exercises, role plays, ability tests and in-depth structured interviews. Candidates are then rated on a range of different competencies. As such, ACs are known to be multi-trait, multi-method approaches.

Ratings from the different selection methods are combined, resulting in an overall rating for each competency, which can be totalled for an overall AC score. This represents the candidate's overall performance across all the different selection methods and competencies.

ACs can be used for a wide range of different jobs, tend to be one of the final stages of the selection process and can be costly to develop and time intensive to run. They also require several trained assessors to observe and then record candidates' behaviour during the process. Research shows that ACs predict future job performance and have incremental validity beyond cognitive ability and personality (e.g. Sackett et al., 2017).

Historically, concerns were raised regarding the construct validity of ACs; however, more recent research views them as a measurement method since different ACs can be designed to measure different constructs (Lievens et al., 2009; Wirz et al., 2020). In addition, selection methods may activate competencies differently – for example assessing 'communication skills' via a role-play is different to assessing communication skills during an interview. Construct validity is explored in more detail later in this chapter.

Box 2.2   Fidelity of selection methods

Fidelity is the extent to which a selection method mirrors the types of tasks and the context found on the job (Callinan & Robertson, 2000; Lievens, De Corte & Westerveld, 2015). A high fidelity selection method presents job-related situations to candidates and requires *actual* behavioural response (examples would be a role-play exercise or group exercise). On the other hand, a low fidelity selection method offers written, or video-based *descriptions* of job-related situations and candidates must state how they would react, or how they reacted in the past. Examples would be an interview, situational judgement test or psychometric test.

Case study:

Developing a role-play exercise and competency-based interviews for underwriters in a micro-lending company

The managing director of a medium-sized micro-lending company wanted to have a more rigorous selection process for underwriters, since they had ambitious growth targets in the following two years.

The first step of this project was to conduct a job analysis for the role of underwriter. The occupational psychologists sought input from several sources and interviewed underwriters, team leaders and clients to get a broad picture of what the role entailed.

The output of the job analysis led to the development of a competency framework. Based on this framework, competency-based interview questions were developed, along with marking criteria for the assessors.

To create the role play, critical incident technique was used during the job analysis in order to identify possible scenarios to be used in the role-play exercise. When an appropriate scenario was identified, this was developed into a role-play exercise along with a relevant scoring key.

Before implementing the role play and interviews into the live selection process, they were piloted on current employees to ensure (1) they elicited the correct competencies; (2) that exercises were relevant for the role; (3) that the marking criteria were appropriate.

Although it wasn't possible to include a formal validation process (since the organisation only had 20 underwriters), their pilot scores were checked against current performance to show a positive correlation between the two – higher performers scored higher on the interview and role play.

How do you choose the correct selection methods to use?

It is important that the selection methods chosen can help you identify the relevant KSAOs (outlined in the competencies) for the role. You should also consider whether the method is reliable (i.e. consistent or stable); valid (i.e. relevant / accurate); and objective, standardised and administered by trained professionals. It is also useful to consider whether the method is fair, legally defensible and cost effective. It is therefore important for organisations to seek feedback and evaluate their selection methods and processes in order to continually improve. Taken together, these elements help you choose the correct methods for a specific role.

Two important concepts to consider in choosing selection methods – reliability and validity – are explored in further detail below.

Reliability

Reliability is the extent to which a selection method is free from error (Rust & Golombok, 2014). There are several different types of reliability to consider when examining selection methods. These are:

Internal consistency

This is considered for ability tests, personality questionnaires, and situational judgement tests and often referred to as Cronbach's alpha reliability (Bland & Altman, 1997). This measures how closely related items are to the overall scale.

Test-retest reliability

This examines the consistency of test results over time, by correlating test results from a group of candidates at Time 1 (e.g. today) with the same group of candidates at Time 2 (e.g. 3 months later).

Parallel forms

This examines the consistency between two different versions of the same test, where you'd expect a high correlation between the two. An example would be exploring the relationship between an online and a mobile-based version of the same psychometric test.

Inter-rater reliability

This measures the extent to which two or more people agree on a rating (for example, the degree of agreement between two assessors who are rating one candidate in an interview).

Validity

Validity refers to the extent to which a selection method measures what it claims to measure (Rust & Golombok, 2014). There are several different types of validity that are important to understand when considering employee assessment and selection. These are:

Face validity

The candidate's subjective opinion of whether the selection method or process looks job relevant.

Content validity

A subject matter expert's perception of whether the selection method or process is job relevant.

Note that Face and Content validity are subjective perceptions by two different groups of people (applicants and experts). The follow types of validity are quantitative and objective:

Construct validity

This is the extent to which the selection method measures the construct in question – for example, does the interview actually measure *team work* or *leadership skills?*

Criterion-related validity

Criterion-related validity examines the extent to which the predictor (i.e. a selection method) is related to a criterion (i.e. an output such as job performance). You are asking the question: does this selection method predict job performance? There are two ways to answer this question:

- **Predictive validity:** Take a group of candidates who complete a selection method during the selection process (e.g. SJT) and then correlate their score with their performance once they are on the job. You would hope for a high correlation between the SJT and job performance and you could say: *this situational judgement test predicts who WILL perform well.*
- **Concurrent validity:** Take a group of current employees and ask them to complete the SJT, and then correlate this score with their current job performance. Again, you would hope for a high correlation between the two scores and you could say: *this situational judgement test predicts who IS performing well.*

Incremental validity

Incremental validity is a type of validity that is used to understand whether a specific selection method increases predictive validity beyond an already-established method. For example, imagine you wanted to explore whether it's useful to add a situational judgement test to a selection process, alongside a cognitive ability test that is already being used. You would first explore the extent to which the cognitive ability test predicts job performance, and then you would examine how much further variance in performance that the SJT predicts *over and above* the cognitive ability test. A good example of how this can be done in practice is research conducted by Koczwara and colleagues (2012), where the validities of two cognitive ability tests were explored, alongside a problem solving test and a situational judgement test.

Utility

A selection process can be costly to design and implement and therefore it's important for organisations to show that they are cost effective (Schmidt & Hunter, 1998). When you consider the utility of a selection process, it assumes that there is variability in job performance. That is, at one extreme if there was no variability in job performance, then all applicants who were hired would have the exact same level of job performance. If this was the case, then there is no practical value or utility of the selection method. Conversely, if performance variability is large, that is, once hired, applicants have very different levels of performance, then it's important to hire the best-performing applicants. Therefore, the practical utility of the selection methods is large.

Another determinant of utility is the selection ratio – the proportion of applicants who are hired. At one extreme if all applicants who apply for a job are hired, the selection method has no practical utility. At the other extreme, if the organisation only selects the top-scoring 5% of applicants, the practical utility of the selection methods is large.

A traditional utility analysis calculates the value of a specific selection method over random selection and would consider several factors such as the number of employees impacted, validity, costs and legal ramifications (Macan et al., 2013).

How effective are selection methods?

When reviewing the literature, there are some clear messages about the effectiveness of various selection methods. This is outlined briefly in Table 2.1.

Validity studies in practice

Whilst it is considered 'best practice' to evaluate selection processes, conducting validation studies in practice can present various problems.

1 Identifying an appropriate criterion (outcome) in order to evaluate the selection methods.

Many validation studies use supervisor ratings as a way to measure 'job performance', yet these are known to be problematic. For example, a supervisor might not be directly aware of a job holder's performance or might avoid low ratings because it reflects badly on them; additionally, these types of ratings are subject to certain stereotypes and biases (Yam et al., 2014).

2 'Restriction of range' in validation studies

Range restriction happens because the validation study sample has less variability on a score than the full population. Consider a scenario where scores on an SJT are used to

Table 2.1 Brief summary of the effectiveness of selection methods

Selection Method	Summary of Evidence
Short-listing methods	
CVs and application forms	Although widely used and favoured by candidates, there is little evidence for their validity and reliability. When biodata is used on application forms, there is more validity evidence.
References	References are widely used, despite there being little evidence of their validity or reliability.
Psychometric tests	Research shows good reliability and validity for some ability-type tests, although some concerns with adverse impact.
Personality	Research shows moderate validity evidence for personality.
Situational judgement interviews	Evidence shows that SJTs are both valid and reliable methods of selection. Although costly to design, they can be cost-saving in large-scale recruitment.
Long-listing selection methods	
Interviews	Unstructured interviews show poor reliability and validity evidence. When interviews are structured, based on a job analysis, and interviewers are trained, they can be both valid and reliable.
Assessment centres	Assessment centres are costly and candidates generally like them. They show moderate validity and reliability evidence.

predict job performance after 6 months. The candidates on the job after 6 months will be a restricted sample (i.e. the ones who were offered the job) rather than the full population of all candidates who completed the SJT. Restricted range underestimates the validity coefficient between the selection method and the outcome (Sackett et al., 2002). This is why in research you sometimes see a 'corrected' validity coefficient which has taken into consideration this range restriction.

Fairness and diversity in selection and assessment

In the UK, recruitment and selection adheres to the terms outlined in the Equality Act 2010. This Act legally protects people from both direct and indirect discrimination at work. Direct discrimination relates to being treated less favourably than others due to being a member of a certain group (e.g. age, gender, ethnicity). Indirect discrimination is much harder to spot because it is subtler. This is when a requirement is applied equally to different groups (and therefore on the surface of it, may seem fair). However, the proportion of people within a certain group who can comply is much smaller than the proportion of people in another group. For example, let's say that an organisation stipulates *supervisory experience* in order to be promoted – a requirement that is equally applied to men and women. However, the proportion of women that can be promoted is smaller than men. This is because more women work part-time hours in junior roles and therefore have had less supervisory experience than men. As a result, this might be classified as indirect discrimination.

It's worth noting that discrimination is the necessary point of selection. After all, we are trying to determine who will be best for the job role by discriminating between different people. However, this discrimination can be either fair or unfair. It is fair when you are choosing between people based on job-relevant criteria (i.e. the KSAOs). It is unfair when the distinction is made based on criteria that have no relevance to the role (e.g. hair colour or sports team preference).

In rare situations, organisations can justify discriminating between individuals on the grounds of race, religion or gender; for example:

- **Authenticity** (e.g. theatrical role or provision of food in particular setting)
- **Preservation of decency or privacy** (e.g. working in areas where people are in 'state of undress' or using sanitary facilities)
- Where language or knowledge and **understanding of cultural and religious backgrounds** needed (e.g. a social worker in certain ethnically populated areas)

That said, there are several strategies that organisations can use in order to ensure fairness in their selection process.

1 Use fair and objective criteria

This relies on using a job analysis to determine the relevant KSAOs necessary to perform the role, along with ensuring that the chosen selection methods can accurately assess these. It's also important to consider barriers to entry, for example using broad educational requirements such as 'A levels *or equivalent*'.

2 Decisions based on several selection methods

A range of different selection methods should be used in order to select people into the role. Selection methods should be chosen because they can assess the relevant KSAOs and chosen based on validity, reliability and other evidence.

3 Reasonable adjustments

Employers have a legal responsibility to ensure that people with a disability are not disadvantaged during the selection process. Therefore, organisations must make reasonable adjustments. For example, hearing impaired candidates may require different modes of communication, visual impaired might need text alterations (larger font, braille etc.).

4 Monitor outcomes

Monitoring the outcome of selection processes promotes objectivity and good practice, and may also be used as evidence in legal proceedings. The process should be checked for adverse impact to see whether the process unfairly impacts certain groups of candidates.

The candidate perspective of the selection process

Historically, selection was viewed as assessing an individual's suitability for a job with little acknowledgement of the applicant's part in the process. However, candidates are not just passive recipients of the selection process, instead they actively present themselves in favourable ways (Burgess et al., 2014). As such, since the 1990s an increasing applicant-focused research agenda has grown, along with a body of literature examining the attitudes, affect and cognitions applicants have about a selection process (Anderson et al., 2010; Gilliland, 1994; Zibarras & Patterson, 2015). The main premise being that applicants' reactions to selection will influence personal and organisational outcomes including decision-making, organisation attractiveness and possible litigation (Gilliland, 1993; Patterson et al., 2012; Patterson et al., 2011; Zibarras & Patterson, 2015).

Applicant perceptions are considered important during a selection process for several reasons:

1 Good applicants can remove themselves from the selection process (McLarty & Whitman, 2016), which can have a negative impact on its utility (Murphy, 1986);
2 If a candidate feels unfairly treated, they may legally challenge the process, which is costly (Schmitt & Chan, 1999); and
3 If disgruntled, applicants may actively dissuade other applicants, or spread negative opinions about the organisation (McCarthy et al., 2009; Patterson et al., 2011).

Several studies have explored fairness perceptions of different selection methods (Anderson et al., 2010; Anderson & Witvliet, 2008) and on the whole findings suggest that interviews, CVs and work samples are rated most favourably by candidates whilst personal contacts, graphology and honesty tests are rated least favourably.

Technology and web-based selection

Over the last two decades the Internet has become an integral part of the recruitment and selection process, from pre-selection, online applications, mobile-based psychometric tests, complex and interactive work sample tasks, and asynchronous video interviews (Konradt et al., 2013; Zibarras et al., 2018).

For example, artificial intelligence techniques have been used to streamline recruitment activities such as using text mining to screen application forms (Acikgoz et al., 2020); the use of game-based assessments for employee selection (Weiner & Sanchez, 2020); and asynchronous video interviews to improve the efficiency of the selection processes and allow more flexibility for applicants (Langer et al., 2021). There has also been a rise in the use of the 'video résumé' (or CV) where the candidate tapes a short message presenting themselves to recruiters and elaborating on their competencies (Apers & Derous, 2017).

However, research is still in its infancy in this area, and mixed findings for candidate acceptance have been found. For example, asynchronous video interviewing appears to lead to negative applicant perceptions, due to the lack of social presence during the interview (Zibarras et al., 2018), and the lack of transparency by which algorithms make decisions (Gonzales et al., 2019); yet Langer and colleagues (2021) found that providing applicants with information about an automated interview improved certain applicant reactions, but negatively impacted others.

Social media use in selection

Social networking (SNW) sites have become a major way to communicate, share content and connect with others. One by-product of SNW sites is that communication is less private and more accessible by others (Tews et al., 2020).

Given the ease of access to this information, employers are increasingly using SNW sites to gather information about employees. Hartwell and Campion (2020) found that SNW sites were used during the recruitment process by almost half of the HR professionals they surveyed, whilst only 18% did not use SNW sites at all. Furthermore, the HR professionals considered the information gathered from SNW sites to be useful.

It could be argued that SNW sites contain valuable information to an employer that isn't otherwise available about candidates (such as political affiliation, hobbies and perceptions about social issues; Roth et al., 2016). Ethics aside, SNW sites may be a way to obtain a broader and more realistic picture of candidates. Indeed, the potential to obtain negative information about candidates may be a strong motivator for using SNW sites, for example negative content such as self-absorption and alcohol and drug use can lead to worse candidate evaluations (Tews et al., 2020).

However, there are several drawbacks in using SNW as part of a selection process. First, selection decisions may be based on non-relevant criteria (e.g. marital status or affiliations); second, candidates have no control about what others post about them (Hartwell & Campion, 2020); and third, the use of information obtained via SNW sites may be seen as an invasion of privacy. Furthermore, the use of SNW may impact applicant reactions, especially since some searches lead to disqualifying applicants based on content found (Berger & Zickar, 2016; Zeidner, 2007).

Conclusion

Selection and assessment practices are widely used within organisations and therefore designing valid and reliable processes is important. Designing a selection process should start with a thorough analysis of the job to identify the KSAOs required to competently perform the role. There are many ways to assess candidates during the selection process, including both short-listing methods (e.g. application forms, psychometrics and SJTs) and long-listing methods (e.g. interviews and assessment centres). In choosing selection methods, the reliability and validity evidence should be considered, along with fairness and diversity issues. Wherever possible, selection processes should be evaluated so that they can continuously improve and add value to the organisation.

There are some emerging issues to consider in the area of selection and assessment. Given the increase in use of technology, it's likely that selection processes will become increasingly sophisticated in line with future technology. Applicants who have limited access to computer technology may be disadvantaged. Careful design of methods is necessary to ensure that technical issues aren't experienced by candidates. In addition, organisations should consider ethical issues around data privacy. It will be vital for research to keep up with trends in practice. Furthermore, as organisations become more globalised and engage in international recruitment, organisational psychologists will have to ensure that certain candidates aren't unfairly disadvantaged due to cultural differences.

Explore further

- See Morgeson et al. (2019) for a more in-depth analysis of different job analysis methods.
- For an in-depth review on interviews, see both Huffcutt (2011) and Macan (2009).

- Professor Filip Lievens' website (www.filiplievens.com/overview) includes all his published work on situational judgement tests, assessment centres and more.
- See this working paper (Schmidt et al., 2016), prepared as an update to Schmidt and Hunter's (1998) seminal research on the validity and utility of selection methods. https://home.ubalt.edu/tmitch/645/session%204/Schmidt%20&%20Oh%20validity%20and%20util%20100%20yrs%20of%20research%20Wk%20PPR%202016.pdf

References

Acikgoz, Y., Davison, K.H., Compagnone, M. & Laske, M. (2020). Justice perceptions of artificial intelligence in selection. *International Journal of Selection and Assessment, 28*(4), 399–416.

Anderson, N. (2001). Towards a theory of socialization impact: Selection as pre-entry socialization. *International Journal of Selection and Assessment, 9*(1–2), 84–91.

Anderson, N. & Witvliet, C. (2008). Fairness reactions to personnel selection methods: An international comparison between the Netherlands, the United States, France, Spain, Portugal, and Singapore. *International Journal of Selection and Assessment, 16*(1), 1–13.

Anderson, N.R. (2011). Perceived job discrimination (PJD): Toward a model of applicant propensity to case initiation in selection. *International Journal of Selection and Assessment, 19*(3), 229–244.

Anderson, N.R., Salgado, J.F. & Hülsheger, U.R. (2010). Applicant Reactions in Selection: Comprehensive meta-analysis into reaction generalization versus situational specificity. *International Journal of Selection and Assessment, 18*(3), 291–304.

Apers, C. & Derous, E. (2017). Are they accurate? Recruiters' personality judgments in paper versus video resumes. *Computers in Human Behavior, 73*, 9–19.

Berger, J. & Zickar, M. (2016). Theoretical propositions about cybervetting: A common antecedents model. In R.N. Landers & G.B. Schmidt (Eds.) *Social media in employee selection and recruitment* (pp. 43–57).

Bland, J. M. & Altman, D. G. (1997). Statistics notes: Cronbach's alpha. *BMJ, 314*(7080), 572.

Breaugh, J. A. (2017). The contribution of job analysis to recruitment. In H.W. Goldstein, E.D. Pulakos, J. Passmore & C. Semedo (Eds.). *The Wiley Blackwell Handbook of the psychology of recruitment, selection and employee retention* (pp. 12–28). Wiley Blackwell.

Bret Becton, J., Matthews, M. C., Hartley, D. L. & Whitaker, D. H. (2009). Using biodata to predict turnover, organizational commitment, and job performance in healthcare. *International Journal of Selection and Assessment, 17*(2), 189–202.

Burgess, A., Roberts, C., Clark, T. & Mossman, K. (2014). The social validity of a national assessment centre for selection into general practice training. *BMC Medical Education, 14*, 261.

Callinan, M. & Robertson, I. T. (2000). Work sample testing. *International Journal of Selection and Assessment, 8*(4), 248–260.

Campion, M.A., Fink, A.A., Ruggeberg, B.J., Carr, L., Phillips, G.M. & Odman, R.B. (2011). Doing competencies well: Best practices in competency modeling. *Personnel Psychology, 64*(1), 225–262.

Chao, T.Y., Sung, Y.T. & Huang, J.L. (2020). Construction of the situational judgment tests for teachers. *Asia-Pacific Journal of Teacher Education, 48*(4), 55–374.

Christian, M., Edwards, B. & Bradley, J. (2010). Situational judgement tests: constructs assessed and a meta-analysis of their criterion-related validities. *Personnel Psychology, 63*, 83–117.

Derous, E. & Ryan, A.M. (2019). When your resume is (not) turning you down: Modelling ethnic bias in resume screening. *Human Resource Management Journal, 29*(2), 113–130.

Flanagan, J.C. (1954). The critical incident technique. *Psychological Bulletin, 51*(4), 327–358. https://doi.org/10.1037/h0061470

Furnham, A. (2017). The contribution of others' methods in recruitment and selection: Biodata, references, résumés and CVs. In H.W. Goldstein, E.D. Pulakos, J. Passmore & C. Semedo (Eds.), *Handbook of the psychology of recruitment, selection and employee retention* (pp. 202–225). Wiley Blackwell.

Gilliland, S.W. (1993). The perceived fairness of selection systems: An organizational justice perspective. *The Academy of Management Review*, 18(4), 694–734.

Gilliland, S.W. (1994). Effects of procedural and distributive justice on reactions to a selection system. *Journal of Applied Psychology*, 79(5), 691–701.

Gonzalez, M.F., Capman, J.F., Oswald, F.L., Theys, E.R. & Tomczak, D.L. (2019). 'Where's the IO?" Artificial intelligence and machine learning in talent management systems. *Personnel Assessment and Decisions*, 5(3), 5.

Hartwell, C.J. & Campion, M.A. (2020). Getting social in selection: How social networking website content is perceived and used in hiring. *International Journal of Selection and Assessment*, 28(1), 1–16.

Herriot, P. & Anderson, N. (1997). Selecting for change: How will personnel and selection psychology survive. *International Handbook of Selection and Assessment*, 1–34.

Huffcutt, A.I. (2011). An empirical review of the employment interview construct literature. *International Journal of Selection and Assessment*, 19(1), 62–81.

Jesiek, B.K., Woo, S.E., Parrigon, S. & Porter, C.M. (2020). Development of a situational judgment test for global engineering competency. *Journal of Engineering Education*, 109(3), 470–490.

Kelly, M.E., Gallagher, N., Dunne, F.P. & Murphy, A.W. (2014). Views of doctors of varying disciplines on HPAT-Ireland as a selection tool for medicine. *Medical Teacher*, 36(9), 775–782.

Koczwara, A., Patterson, F., Zibarras, L., Kerrin, M., Irish, B. & Wilkinson, M. (2012). Evaluating cognitive ability, knowledge tests and situational judgement tests for postgraduate selection. *Medical Education*, 46(4). https://doi.org/10.1111/j.1365-2923.2011.04195.x

Konradt, U., Warszta, T. & Ellwart, T. (2013). Fairness perceptions in web-based selection: Impact on applicants' pursuit intentions, recommendation intentions, and intentions to reapply. *International Journal of Selection and Assessment*, 21(2), 155–169.

Langer, M., Baum, K., König, C.J., Hähne, V. Oster, D. & Speith, T. (2021). Spare me the details: How the type of information about automated interviews influences applicant reactions. *International Journal of Selection and Assessment*, 29(2), 154–169.

Levashina, J., Hartwell, C.J., Morgeson, F.P. & Campion, M.A. (2014). The structured employment interview: Narrative and quantitative review of the research literature. *Personnel Psychology*, 67(1), 241–293.

Lievens, F., De Corte, W. & Westerveld, L. (2015). Understanding the building blocks of selection procedures: Effects of response fidelity on performance and validity. *Journal of Management*, 41(6), 1604–1627.

Lievens, F., Peeters, H. & Schollaert, E. (2008). Situational judgment tests: a review of recent research. *Personnel Review*, 37(4), 426–441.

Lievens, F., Tett, R.P. & Schleicher, D.J. (2009). Assessment centers at the crossroads: Toward a reconceptualization of assessment center exercises. *Personnel and Human Resources Management*, 28, 99–152.

Macan, T. (2009). The employment interview: A review of current studies and directions for future research. *Human Resource Management Review*, 19(3), 203–218.

Macan, T., Lemming, M.R. & Foster, J.L. (2013). Utility analysis: Do estimates and format matter? *Personnel Review*, 42(1), 105–126.

McCarthy, J., Hrabluik, C. & Jelley, B. (2009). Progression through the ranks: Assessing employee reactions to high-stakes employment testing. *Personnel Psychology*, 62(4), 793–832.

McDaniel, M., Whetzel, D.L., Schmidt, F. & Maurer, S.D. (1994). The validity of employment interviews: A comprehensive review and meta-analysis. *Journal of Applied Psychology*, 79(4), 599–616.

McLarty, B.D. & Whitman, D.S. (2016). A dispositional approach to applicant reactions: Examining core self-evaluations, behavioral intentions, and fairness perceptions. *Journal of Business and Psychology, 31*(1), 141–153.

Morgeson, F.P., Brannick, M.T. & Levine, E.L. (2019). *Job and work analysis: Methods, research, and applications for human resource management.* Sage Publications.

Murphy, K.R. (1986). When your top choice turns you down: Effect of rejected offers on the utility of selection tests. *Psychological Bulletin, 99*(1), 133–138.

Patterson, F. (2018). Designing and evaluating selection and recruitment in healthcare. In F. Patterson & L.D. Zibarras (Eds.), *Selection and recruitment in the healthcare professions.* Palgrave Macmillan.

Patterson, F., Ashworth, V., Zibarras, L., Coan, P., Kerrin, M. & O'Neill, P. (2012). Evaluations of situational judgement tests to assess non-academic attributes in selection. *Medical Education, 46*(9). https://doi.org/10.1111/j.1365-2923.2012.04336.x

Patterson, F, Carr, V., Zibarras, L., Burr, B., Berkin, L., Plint, S., ... Gregory, S. (2009). New machine-marked tests for selection into core medical training: evidence from two validation studies. *Clinical Medicine, 9*(5), 417–420.

Patterson, F, Tavabie, A., Denney, M., Kerrin, M., Ashworth, V., Koczwara, A. & MacLeod, S. (2013). A new competency model for general practice: implications for selection, training, and careers. *The British Journal of General Practice: The Journal of the Royal College of General Practitioners, 63*(610), e331–338. https://doi.org/10.3399/bjgp13X667196

Patterson, F., Zibarras, L. & Ashworth, V. (2016). Situational judgement tests in medical education and training: Research, theory and practice: AMEE Guide No. 100. *Medical Teacher, 38*(1). https://doi.org/10.3109/0142159X.2015.1072619

Patterson, Fiona, Zibarras, L., Carr, V., Irish, B. & Gregory, S. (2011). Evaluating candidate reactions to selection practices using organisational justice theory. *Medical Education, 45*(3), 289–297.

Pereira, V., Hadjielias, E., Christofi, M. & Vrontis, D. (2021). A systematic literature review on the impact of artificial intelligence on workplace outcomes: A multi-process perspective. *Human Resource Management Review*, 100857.

Prien, E.P., Goodstein, L.D., Goodstein, J. & Gamble Jr, L.G. (2009). *A practical guide to job analysis.* John Wiley & Sons.

Robertson, I.T. & Smith, M. (2001). Personnel selection. *Journal of Occupational and Organizational Psychology, 74*(4), 441–472.

Roth, P.L., Bobko, P., Van Iddekinge, C.H. & Thatcher, J.B. (2016). Social media in employee-selection-related decisions: A research agenda for uncharted territory. *Journal of Management, 42*(1), 269–298.

Rust, J. & Golombok, S. (2014). *Modern psychometrics: The science of psychological assessment (Vol. 3rd).* London: Routledge.

Sackett, P.R., Laczo, R.M. & Arvey, R.D. (2002). The effects of range restriction on estimates of criterion interrater reliability: Implications for validation research. *Personnel Psychology, 55*(4), 807–825.

Sackett, P.R., Shewach, O.R. & Keiser, H.N. (2017). Assessment centers versus cognitive ability tests: Challenging the conventional wisdom on criterion-related validity. *Journal of Applied Psychology, 102*(10), 1435.

Sanchez, J.I. & Levine, E.L. (2012). The rise and fall of job analysis and the future of work analysis. *Annual Review of Psychology, 63*, 397–425.

Santana, M. & Cobo, M.J. (2020). What is the future of work? A science mapping analysis. *European Management Journal, 38*(6), 846–862.

Schmidt, F. & Hunter, J.E. (1998). The validity and utility of selection methods in personnel psychology: Practical and theoretical implications of 85 years of research findings. *Psychological Bulletin*, 124(2), 262–274.

Schmitt, N. & Chan, D. (1999). The status of research on applicant reactions to selection tests and its implications for managers. *International Journal of Management Reviews*, 1(1), 45–62.

Schmidt, F.L., Oh, I.S. & Shaffer, J.A. (2016). The validity and utility of selection methods in personnel psychology: Practical and theoretical implications of 100 years. *Fox School of Business Research Paper*, 1–74.

Searle, R.H. (2003). *Selection and recruitment: a critical text*. Milton Keynes: The Open University.

Tews, M.J., Stafford, K. & Kudler, E.P. (2020). The effects of negative content in social networking profiles on perceptions of employment suitability. *International Journal of Selection and Assessment*, 28(1), 17–30.

Thorsteinson, T.J. (2018). A meta-analysis of interview length on reliability and validity. *Journal of Occupational and Organizational Psychology*, 91(1), 1–32.

Voskuijl, O.F. (2017). Job analysis: Current and future perspectives. In H.W. Goldstein, E.D. Pulakos, J. Passmore & C. Semedo (Eds.) *The Wiley Blackwell handbook of the psychology of recruitment, selection and employee retention* (pp. 25–46). Wiley Blackwell.

Weiner, E.J. & Sanchez, D.R. (2020). Cognitive ability in virtual reality: Validity evidence for VR game-based assessments. *International Journal of Selection and Assessment*, 28(3), 215–235.

Wirz, A., Melchers, K.G., Kleinmann, M., Lievens, F., Annen, H., Blum, U. & Ingold, P.V. (2020). Do overall dimension ratings from assessment centres show external construct-related validity? *European Journal of Work and Organizational Psychology*, 29(3), 405–420.

Wyatt, M.R.R., Pathak, S.B. & Zibarras, L. (2010). Advancing selection in an SME: Is best practice methodology applicable? *International Small Business Journal*, 28(3), 258–273. https://doi.org/10.1177/0266242609350815

Yam, K.C., Fehr, R. & Barnes, C.M. (2014). Morning employees are perceived as better employees: Employees' start times influence supervisor performance ratings. *Journal of Applied Psychology*, 99(6), 1288.

Zeidner, R. (2007). How deep can you probe? *HR Magazine, 52 (10)*, 57–60.

Zibarras, L. & Woods, S.A. (2010). A survey of UK selection practices across different organization sizes and industry sectors. *Journal of Occupational and Organizational Psychology, 83*, 499–511.

Zibarras, Lara D. & Patterson, F. (2015). The role of job relatedness and self-efficacy in applicant perceptions of fairness in a high-stakes selection setting. *International Journal of Selection and Assessment*, 23(4), 332–344. https://doi.org/10.1111/ijsa.12118

Zibarras, L.D., Patterson, F., Holmes, J., Flaxman, C. & Kubacki, A. (2018). An exploration of applicant perceptions of asynchronous video MMIs in medical selection. *MedEdPublish.*, 7(4), 64.

Chapter 3

Learning, training and development

Julia Yates

Overview

This chapter focuses on the British Psychological Society's (BPS's) areas of Learning, Training and Development, exploring career development, occupational choice and workplace learning and development. Underpinning this aspect of organisational psychology is a desire for workers to develop what De Vos et al. (2020) describe as a 'sustainable career', one that allows us to be happy, healthy and productive. A sustainable career is important both for the good of the individual, whose life will be better for being in a career they find fulfilling and which makes use of their strengths, and for the organisation, which will reap the rewards of workers who are engaged and productive. We approach the sustainable career, in this chapter, in two ways. We will look first at how to help people to make good occupational choices – to increase their chances of ending up in careers that make use of their strengths, align with their values, and allow them to lead the lives they want to outside of work. We then turn to the idea of productive workers, exploring how organisations can best equip workers with the skills they need to do their jobs well. But first, we start the chapter reflecting on the nature of contemporary career paths.

Learning outcomes

By the end of this chapter, you will:

- understand the nature of contemporary career paths;
- be aware of the complexities of career choice;
- recognise the challenges of running effective training;
- understand the factors that facilitate effective training;
- know about the key learning theories.

Contemporary career paths

It is often declared that a job for life is a thing of the past (for example, Future Learn 2021). The assumptions behind this assertion are twofold. First, it assumes that traditional

DOI: 10.4324/9781003302087-4

career paths used to be stable and linear, with most workers sticking with their first employer until they retired, and job changes rare; and second, that modern careers are quite different, with workers changing jobs and industries frequently. In truth, both sets of assumptions are somewhat overstated and the reality is that the number of job and career changes an individual is likely to make has not shifted very much at all over the last 50 years: careers in the past weren't always stable, and careers now often are (OECD, 2020). Any changes we have seen, have generally followed economic cycles, with more job changes observed, as one might predict, during times of economic prosperity.

It is unclear why the myth of the change in working patterns has been so widespread, but one explanation could be the number of high-profile career theories supporting these assumptions, which were developed at the turn of the century, and which have found significant popularity in the academic and popular press. One such example is Arthur and Rousseau's idea of the Boundaryless Career (2001). This theory holds that careers no longer need to conform to the traditional boundaries of the past, and workers can and should take advantage of the new flexible labour market, crossing geographical, organisational, industrial, occupational and psychological boundaries, to create more fluid, and ultimately, more fulfilling, work lives. Although the idea of a boundaryless career is appealing to many, the evidence suggests that whilst we may have become a little more psychologically flexible in our attitudes towards careers, most of us would still prefer a stable and predictable path. It seems that those whose careers are boundaryless are more often forced into this position, making their non-linear career choices as a result of job loss, discrimination, or to accommodate family demands, rather than choosing a boundaryless career path voluntarily (Rodrigues & Guest, 2010).

Whilst the overall pattern of careers has not changed very much over the last few decades, there have been changes in the way we work. Although we generally prefer to stick with a good organisation, we no longer expect our employers to manage our careers for us (Savickas, 2011). Traditionally, employers had something of a paternalistic attitude towards their employees' career paths, making choices about the training an employee needed and promoting them when they were considered ready for the next step. These days the psychological contract between the individual and their employer has shifted. It is now more often the responsibility of the individual worker to manage their own career, choosing and often funding their own training, negotiating pay rises when they feel the time is right, identifying and requesting new projects or challenges to broaden their own skillset, and indeed, sometimes leaving one organisation to apply for a promotion elsewhere (Savickas, 2011).

Another development which has had considerable impact is the pace of change within the labour market. Whilst people may not be moving from one organisation to another as often as we might imagine, their jobs are nevertheless changing rapidly, and even if you stay in the same role for some time, your day-to-day duties might look quite different a few years down the line. The combination of these rapid changes and the shift of career ownership mean that individuals need to engage with their own employability, harnessing psychological resources such as resilience and adaptability in order to stay relevant and attractive to employers throughout their careers (Bimrose & Hearn, 2012).

The rapid changes that we see in the labour market also make occupational choices difficult, as people looking to start a new career or a new chapter in their career may struggle to keep up with the rapid changes in the labour market, and find it hard to gain a good understanding of the realities of the options open to them. Let us move on now to explore what the literature can tell us about career decision making.

Career choice

Career choices are amongst the most significant decisions that we make in life (Bimrose & Mulvey, 2015; Lent & Brown, 2020) and a good career choice can have a broad and long-lasting positive impact on an individual's job satisfaction and life happiness (Rath & Harter, 2010). But making a career choice is not easy. The vast number of possible occupations open to us is one key challenge. Research tells us that we are happiest with our decisions when we have six or so options to choose from (Iyengar & Lepper, 2000) but the UK government recognises an eye-watering 29,554 different occupations – far too many for any of us to even imagine, let alone weigh-up thoughtfully (ONS, 2020).

Then there is the challenge of researching these occupations. Some information about a particular job or occupation, such as the salary, location or duties, may be easy to find, but some of the information that is going to have the biggest impact on job satisfaction, such as the nature of your colleagues, or the amount of autonomy a manager will allow, is more difficult to gauge before you start work. Finally, most people are expected to make career choices when they are young – as they leave school or university and before they have any significant experience of working at all: it is quite a task to identify an occupation you might enjoy before you have had the chance to learn much about yourself in a work context. Taken together, it is a wonder that any of us ends up in a role that is at all suitable!

Happily there is a wealth of theory and research that can help us to understand how it works. We will turn to this topic now looking at the factors that people base their career choices on, and the process of career decision making.

There is a bewildering array of factors that influence career choice. Patton and McMahon (2015, 2021) in their Systems Theory Framework of Career Development, offer a comprehensive account of the key factors, noting that they are all underpinned by the role of chance and the impact of time. Their model incorporates both individual and external factors. Individual factors include demographic characteristics such as ethnicity, gender, sexual orientation and age; physical attributes including health and disability; individual differences such as personality, ability, aptitudes, interests and beliefs and knowledge about the world of work. External influences include other people (peers, family, community groups), society-wide factors (political decisions, media, employment market) and bigger issues such as historical trends and globalisation.

The Systems Theory Framework offers an overview of all the factors that may have an impact, but we also know something about the factors that people say are the most influential. People generally report that their decisions have been most influenced by their belief in their ability to get the job (Rousseau & Ventner, 2009), the views of their family and friends (Chope, 2005; de Magakhaes & Wilde, 2015), and how successful they think they might be in the role (Abrahams et al., 2015).

As well as the factors that influence our choices, it is useful to understand something about the process of career choice. The first career decision making model was proposed by Parsons in 1909, who suggested choices should be made through developing self-awareness, learning about occupations and then applying what he described as 'true

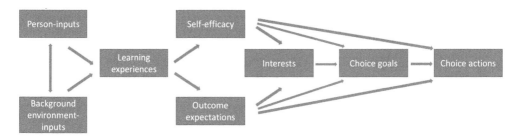

Figure 3.1 The Social Cognitive Career Model (based on Lent et al., 1994).

reasoning' to identify a perfect match between the two. Over a hundred years on, this early model still resonates with many of us, but the dominant narrative in the vocational psychology literature now acknowledges that rational decision making or Parsons' idea of 'true reasoning' may simply not be possible, and recent models of career decision making incorporate the influence of a more intuitive approach (Gati & Kulcsas, 2021; Hennessy & Yip, 2021; Lent & Brown 2020).

Arguably, the most influential career choice process model comes from Lent, Brown and Hackett, originally developed in 1994. Based on Bandura's social cognitive theory (1986), this model highlights the role of self-efficacy (a person's belief in themselves) and outcome expectations (their idea of how likely particular actions are to lead to particular outcomes) and shows how some of the influences, identified in the Systems Theory Framework interact. The model suggests that individual and environmental factors both influence learning experiences, which in turn have an impact on self-efficacy and outcome expectations. These then influence career interests, goals and actions. Figure 13.1 offers an overview of the key elements of the model, and the case study below describes how Jeremy ended up as a social worker, through the lens of this theory.

Box 3.1 Case study: Jeremy's career choice

Jeremy was enjoying studying History at university but had no idea what to do after graduation. He had been quite keen on the idea of publishing, but having looked into it, it seemed like a dauntingly difficult industry to break into, and he wasn't sure he wanted it that much *[outcome expectations]*.

Back at home during the university holidays, his mother mentioned an opportunity she had heard about from a friend, to volunteer for a holiday scheme her friend was running, supporting young people with learning difficulties *[background factors leading to learning experiences]*. Jeremy found the idea quite appealing *[personal inputs leading to learning experiences]* and as he had no other plans for the summer, decided to give it a go. The holiday scheme turned out to be a great success and a significant turning point for Jeremy. He loved the young people, loved the fellow volunteers, and most of all, loved the idea of trying to help disadvantaged people to a better future *[learning experiences leading to interests]*. He also found that it was something that he was quite naturally good at – he was able to use his communication skills and creative problem solving to communicate with people who struggled to talk, and found that his empathy and patience were very well suited to working in this environment. These successes made him enjoy his experience all the more *[personal inputs and experiences leading to self-efficacy]*.

He decided that in some way, shape or form, he wanted to spend his working life in this field *[experiences and self-efficacy leading to interests]*. Researching into jobs in this field, he learnt more about the role of a social worker, and found an MA course that looked appealing *[interests leading to choice goals]* and found out that once qualified, there was a high chance that he would be able to find a job in this field *[outcome expectations leading to goals]*. It was clear that he would need to gain more experience in social care and then it would take two years to qualify *[interest leading to learning experiences]*, but he was fortunate enough to be able to live rent-free with his parents during this time, so it was at least financially viable *[background inputs facilitating experiences]*. He volunteered at a local children's charity alongside his studies for the duration of his degree and worked in a residential home when he graduated. Armed with the confidence in his own skills that he had gained from the experience, he applied for his MA in Social Work *[self-efficacy and choice goals leading to action]* and started his training the following year.

The chapter started with a mention of De Vos et al.'s (2020) idea of a 'sustainable career' – one in which a person can be happy, healthy and productive. We have looked so far at the way that people choose a particular occupation, and we know that a good choice can certainly go some way towards ensuring a happy, healthy and productive career, but organisations can play their part too. We will now turn to the multi-billion-dollar learning and development industry, and see what the literature can tell us about how to make this more effective.

Learning and development

Learning and Development is big business. Organisations are very aware that training is important and are prepared to spend enormous sums of money ensuring that their staff are suitably equipped to do their jobs. In 2020 $358 billion was spent on training globally (Statista, 2021) and in the UK alone the government estimates that there are around 100 million training days in the workplace each year (Department for Education, 2020).

Training has benefits at the societal, organisation and individual levels. For society, it leads to an upskilled workforce, which makes a positive contribution to growth at a national level; for organisations it leads to better performance and a competitive edge, and all the benefits that come from a satisfied workforce; and for individuals, it increases individual employability and their sense of agency (Aguinis & Kraiger, 2009). Indeed, access to educational opportunities (formal and informal) is one of the six work features that is most associated with job satisfaction (Roelen et al., 2008).

Notwithstanding the importance of training, and the tangible benefits it brings, there seems to be a lot that is wrong with workplace training. The main issue is that, to a large degree, formal training simply does not work. Skills and knowledge taught through training programmes are not transferred to the workplace, leading to a huge waste of money and risking sub-optimal workforce performance. An article by Steve Galevski in the Harvard Business Review (2019) reports that only 25% of people think that training improves performance, and only 12% of employees apply their newly acquired skills to their job, and these kinds of figures are widely replicated (for example, Cromwell & Kolb, 2004; Lim & Morris, 2006).

These statistics make for quite shocking headlines, but they do mask significant variation in the effectiveness of training courses. Whilst some studies even show a negative return on investment (Percival et al., 2013) others show that training can be hugely beneficial, *if the conditions are right* (Lacerenza et al., 2017). Let us now look more closely at some of these conditions.

Box 3.2   Learning that won't work

Learning for the wrong reasons.

It is not uncommon for a trainer to face a room full of delegates who are not there because of an inherent interest in the topic itself, but for some other, external reason. If your trainees have been forced to attend, or have signed up simply because they want to impress their boss, they are far less likely to absorb the information or apply it in their work (Kodwani & Prashar, 2019). Spending some time at the start of a course focusing on the relevance and value of the training for delegates' individual circumstances can be time well spent.

Learning at the wrong time

People learn best when they have a real and immediate need for the new information or skills – just think about how quickly employees learnt to use Zoom and MS Teams when the UK went into lockdown during the Covid-19 pandemic in March 2020. Learning will be more effective if delegates can see the contribution that their new skills can make to a project they are working on at the time.

Failure to apply the learning

A key message that runs strongly throughout the learning and development literature is the importance of applying new knowledge as soon as possible. Ebbinghaus (1880) identified the 'Forgetting Curve' which suggests that 75% of what we learn is forgotten if we don't apply it, and studies have replicated this more recently with similar results (Murre & Dros, 2015).

Learning the wrong things

A good learning and development offer will always start with a training needs analysis, in which time is spent trying to identify what skills or knowledge may be missing, and designing training courses that will be relevant to workers (Denby, 2010). Sadly, in most cases, organisations don't feel that this is a good use of resources, instead offering a more generic programme of training courses that may not be quite what the workers need.

Existing literature seems to have reached a consensus that the chances of achieving a good level of training transfer are dependent on three elements: trainee characteristics, work characteristics and training design (Blume et al., 2019; Ford et al., 2018). We will now take each of these in turn.

Trainee characteristics

In a large meta-analysis, Blume and colleagues identified the characteristics of what they described as 'transfer-ready' trainees (Blume et al., 2010, p. 1090). They found several individual characteristics within trainees themselves which seem to lead to a higher chance of training transfer, the most significant of which was cognitive ability. Other important factors included high levels of conscientiousness, low levels of neuroticism, learning goal orientation, and strong motivation. One other characteristic which emerges consistently in the literature is self-efficacy – your confidence in your ability to succeed in a particular endeavour. Blume et al. (2010) noted the importance of levels of pre-training self-efficacy; Velada et al. (2007) highlight the value of performance self-efficacy; and Chiaburu and Lindsay (2008) found that training self-efficacy is particularly useful. The importance of self-efficacy is a useful one to understand, as trainers can design their courses to include some activities intended to boost trainees' confidence in their new knowledge or skills, such as positive feedback, learning from others and actual experience of putting their new skills into practice (Bandura, 1986).

Work characteristics

Trainees will only put their new learning into practice if there is a positive 'transfer climate' (Mathieu et al., 1992). The transfer climate is one of the most widely discussed and intensively studied environmental factors in training transfer research, and it seems that a good positive climate is, in essence, about having the right support in the workplace. An environment that is conducive to training transfer includes support from the organisation as a whole, from supervisors and from peers (Hughes et al., 2020). These three kinds of support are each important in their own different ways. Peer support has been shown to be the most important of the three, as peers spend so much time with an individual on a day-to-day basis, and their support can help with the regular consolidation of the new learning. A manager or supervisor can support training transfer by adding a layer of accountability to the trainee, inviting them to show what they have gained from their training course. Organisations can support training by creating a positive learning culture (e.g. Egan et al., 2004), by introducing measures to boost workers' motivation to transfer such as reward schemes and through on-going support activities such as coaching and mentoring (Schindler & Burkholder, 2016).

Training design

This is the one of the three that you are most likely to have some control over, and it also seems to be the most complicated of the three aspects so it may be useful to delve a bit deeper here. The literature suggests that a well-designed session includes a range of characteristics. Holton (2005) focuses on the notion of relevance, highlighting that for training to be effective, it needs not only to be relevant, but to be *perceived* as relevant. Chukwu (2016) identifies factors that keep trainees engaged, including facilitator disposition (conviction and enthusiasm), interaction and group work; factors that help participants to see how the ideas apply in the real world include stories and illustrations, real life examples and demonstrations.

One other aspect of the training design that has been shown to lead to more effective training and more chance of training transfer, is a session that is based on theoretically derived principles (Kahlil & Elkhider, 2016), and it is to this that we turn now, looking at the three key groups of learning theories: behaviourism, cognitivism and constructivism.

Learning theories

The theoretical basis of learning is probably the aspect of learning and development which is least understood, and least often considered (Ertmer & Newby, 2013), but it is a crucial element of evidence-based practice in this field. Many of the traditional learning theories can be grouped into behaviourist, cognitivist or constructivist learning theories. All three offer useful suggestions and guidelines for training, but as you will see, each takes quite a different position, and will be appropriate in different situations – depending on what is being learnt, the context in which the learners will be operating and the nature of the learners themselves.

Behaviourism

Behaviourism is a school of psychology which focuses exclusively on observable behaviour, paying no attention to the cognitive processes which may be involved, but examining which context leads to which outcomes. Two important elements of behavioural learning are repetition and reinforcement. Learning can be cemented through repetition which makes a particular act become an automatic habit (this is how rote learning works). Learning can be reinforced through a 'carrot and stick' approach in which positive behaviour is rewarded and negative behaviour punished. If a behaviour is rewarded, an individual will be encouraged to repeat that behaviour, at first to reap that particular reward again, later because the positive behaviour is associated with a positive outcome, and eventually because it has become a habit. Conversely, if a behaviour is punished, the individual will link the behaviour with a negative experience and eventually stop the behaviour because they want to stop the unpleasant associated feeling. Early promoters of this theory included Skinner (1938) and Pavlov (1897), who conducted experiments on rats and dogs, and Watson (1913). More recently, Bandura further developed the theory, identifying the impact that vicarious learning can have (i.e. learning by watching others) and highlighting the importance of self-efficacy – one's belief in one's own ability, which has been shown to be an important condition for learning (Bandura, 1986).

A behavioural approach is widely used with children, as pupils in schools are given plus points and minus points to encourage certain behaviour, and parenting guides are full of suggestions of how to reward good behaviour and punish negative behaviour. It works well with young children who are not able to understand the reasons behind various rules, and in contexts where rules are non-negotiable and imposed. There are also numerous examples of this kind of learning theory applied within the workplace, specifically with the reward systems of appraisals and performance-related pay, and can be of great value where workers have to behave in highly prescribed ways, for example during a fire alarm.

Cognitivism

In the mid-20th century, and in part linked to the development of computers, psychologists started to think in more depth about the role the brain plays in learning. Theorists (for example, Bruner et al., 1956) began to conceptualise the brain as an information processing system, and focused on processes such as memory and organisation. Learning was understood as a process of information transfer – from the mind of the trainer to the mind of the trainee – and the goal of learning was to help learners to create their own hypotheses from the information they were taught, which they could then apply to other contexts. To help this process the cognitive trainer needs to break complex concepts down into bite sized, manageable chunks that can be learnt individually and then put back together or manipulated into different configurations. Knowledge is assumed to be right or wrong, and the trainer's role is to know and impart the right information. This approach underpins most training courses, and you will no doubt recognise it from your own experiences, when you were asked to absorb knowledge from reading text (as you are right now!) and from listening to lecturers or trainers.

Constructivism

This is the last of the big three, and the most recent. Up to this point, theorists had assumed that knowledge of the world was something objective that existed outside the mind of the learner, and that knowledge was objective and true. Constructivism instead assumes that knowledge is co-created between the individual and their experiences – knowledge is constructed by the individual, within their own minds, based on their experiences and their reflections on those experiences. Constructivists suggest that learning happens best when individuals are allowed to build on their existing knowledge and find solutions to problems on their own.

In practice, this means that a learner might be introduced to a concept or idea at the start of a training course, and then would be given a real-world scenario or problem to think about. The learner would be encouraged to collaborate and experiment, discover their own solutions and develop their understanding. Because knowledge is constructed by the individual, there is no assumption that knowledge is right or wrong and it is thought that learning is enhanced by listening to different perspectives, through collaboration or debate. The role of the trainer in constructivist learning is one of a facilitator – guiding and supporting the learning, but not giving the answers.

One specific branch of constructivism, particularly relevant for organisational training, is andragogy (Knowles & Associates, 1984). Knowles wanted to develop a learning theory which was tailored to the needs of adults, and developed his idea of andragogy (from the Greek meaning teaching adults) in contrast to the more traditional pedagogy (from the Greek meaning teaching children). Andragogy is a constructivist approach which aims to encourage learners to build their own understanding of reality, but, acknowledging that adults bring significant experience to any learning situation, emphasises the role of the learner's existing knowledge.

Constructivist training is not suitable for all kinds of topics. It works best when trainees are developing the skills they will need to handle novel or unclear situations and will need to identify a solution that is tailored to the particular context. It is particularly well suited to learning how to handle complex or uncertain situations or problems and doesn't work so well for situations in which a consistent response is needed every time. Constructivist learning also relies on the engagement and intellectual capacity of learners and can take some time – it's not a quick fix, although can lead to deep level learning, so the time may be considered well spent. Constructivism is the dominant approach in the learning literature at the moment, and has spawned a number of other popular approaches (including situated learning, problem based learning, collaborative learning and heutagogy).

Trainers need to understand all three of these approaches to learning, and make choices in their training about which to choose and when. A single training course could encompass all three, as complex cognitive ideas are broken down into simple ideas and then explained (cognitivism), trainees are given ill-defined real-world problems to discuss collaboratively (constructivism) and rules and regulations are drummed into them through regular repetition (behaviourism).

Box 3.3   The enduring myth of learning styles

Learning styles are widely understood and often applied within training courses. There is evidently something appealing or intuitive in the idea of learning styles, and people seem to be able to relate to these ideas easily, but the evidence behind their value in training is less compelling than their widespread popularity might imply.

Learning styles assume that people have different preferences for how they like to learn. These differences have been described in many different ways. One of the most widely used is Honey and Mumford's Learning Styles (Honey and Mumford, 1982) which groups people into activists, reflectors, pragmatists and theorists. Another popular one is the VAK (Barbe, 1961) which suggests that people are either visual, auditory or kinaesthetic learners. It is important to remember that these are not about ability – learning styles explain how people learn, not how well or how much they learn.

The theories suggest that individuals will learn better if information is presented to them in a way that chimes with their preferred learning style. Educators and trainers are advised that they should use this information to help them deliver more effective training sessions – identifying which pedagogical approaches are going to work best with which trainees. The literature on learning styles assumes that preferences are stable and have an impact on learning.

It is fairly well established that people seem to relate more to one style than another, although the reliability of the inventories calls the stability of these styles into question (Peterson et al., 2009). But the claim that students or trainees learn better when they are trained in their preferred style is not borne out in the literature and review after review concludes that people do not learn more, or more easily, when teaching styles reflect preferred learning styles (Willingham et al., 2015). As

Reiner and Willingham state (Riener & Willingham, 2010, p. 36) 'Students may have preferences about how to learn, but no evidence suggests that catering to those preferences will lead to better learning'.

Learning styles do exist – people do often prefer one type of approach to another but, despite their popularity, but there is no compelling evidence that they have an impact on learning (Lethaby & Harries, 2016; Rohrer & Pashler, 2012), so a trainer looking to design a session underpinned by robust theory should look elsewhere for guidance.

Online learning

In this final section of the chapter, we will explore what makes good online learning. Distance learning of course has been around for decades – the Open University has been changing people's lives through distance education since the 1970s, and in the form of correspondence courses, distance learning has been around since the early 18th century.

More recently, and certainly since the Covid-19 lockdown, online learning has become more common, and is now perhaps the most popular method of professional training: individuals like the accessibility and convenience of the approach and organisations appreciate the low cost and high participation (Haley, 2008). The last few years have, inevitably, seen a proliferation of papers published about online learning – trying to find out whether it is as good, worse or better than learning 'in real life'; whether asynchronous learning (i.e. online training materials that learners can engaged with in their own time, such as podcasts, online quizzes) enhances synchronous delivery (i.e. live webinars) and what trainers need to do to optimise the online experience. The headline findings are that online learning can be as effective as in-person learning, but is less enjoyable because there is less of a focus on the relationships developed (Burklund, 2020; Ebner & Gegenfurtner, 2019). In terms of the quality of the learning, itself, one important message is that synchronous online training needs to be designed specifically with the medium in mind – we can't simply take an in-person course and transfer it to an online context. It seems to be particularly important to set clearer expectations of online learners, specifically to discourage learners from multi-tasking, as trainees logging in to training from a computer at home have easy access to emails and other distractions. Interaction can be more difficult to manage online, so trainers might need to consider strategies for plenary discussion – for example, warning trainees that they may be asked to contribute, or making use of technology such as the chat function, breakout rooms and online polls, and it can be useful to offer more deliberate opportunities for informal interaction between delegates, and between delegates and trainers.

Conclusion

The benefits of a workforce well suited to their jobs and well-trained to perform are manifold. Yet they are not always easy to achieve. Occupational choice is enormously complex and difficult to research, and it seems to be surprisingly difficult to run a training course that actually has an impact on how well people perform at work. Thankfully there is a significant body of literature within this field that can help us, and we can draw on models, theories and research to help us to understand how to work towards the goal of a career that is fulfilling and productive.

Explore further

Burns, M. & Griffith, A. (2018). The learning imperative: Raising performance in organisations by improving learning. Crown House Publishing Ltd. This offers a practical, evidence-based overview of both formal and informal learning in organisations.

Kahneman, D. (2012). Thinking Fast and Slow. New York: MacMillan. This book dives into the research behind decision making – it's not specific to organisations, but makes for very interesting reading.

Willingham, D.T., Hughes, E.M. & Dobolyi, D.G. (2015). The scientific status of learning styles Theories. Teaching of Psychology, 42(3), 266–271. https://doi.org/10.1177/0098628315589505. This one will give you a bit more detail about the evidence behind learning styles

Yates, J. (2022) The Career Coaching Handbook. Hove: Routledge. This has a good overview of a range of career theories as well as some ideas for using them in practice.

References

Abrahams, F., Jano, R. & van Lill, B. (2015). Factors influencing the career choice of undergraduate students at a historically disadvantaged South African university. *Industry and Higher Education, 29*(3), 209–219.

Aguinis, H. & Kraiger, K. (2009). Benefits of training and development for individuals and teams, organizations, and society. In *Annual Review of Psychology*. https://doi.org/10.1146/annurev.psych.60.110707.163505

Arthur, M.B. & Rousseau, D.M. (Eds.). (2001). *The boundaryless career: A new employment principle for a new organizational era*. Oxford University Press on Demand.

Bandura, A. (1986). *Social foundations of thought and action: a social cognitive theory / Albert Bandura*. New Jersey: Prentice-Hall.

Barbe, W.B. (1961). Slow learner: a plea for understanding. *Education*.

Bimrose, J. & Hearne, L. (2012). Resilience and career adaptability: Qualitative studies of adult career counseling. *Journal of Vocational Behavior, 81*(3), 338–344.

Bimrose, J. & Mulvey, R. (2015). Exploring career decision-making styles across three European countries. *British Journal of Guidance & Counselling, 43*(3), 337–350.

Blume, B.D., Ford, J.K., Baldwin, T. T. & Huang, J. L. (2010). Transfer of training: A meta-analytic review. *Journal of Management, 36*, 1065–1105.

Blume, B.D., Ford, J.K., Surface, E.A. & Olenick, J. (2019). A dynamic model of training transfer. *Human Resource Management Review, 29*(2), 270–283.

Bruner, J., Goodnow, J. & Austin, G. (1956). *A study of thinking*. New York. Science Editions.

Burklund, A.S. (2020). Synching up on a satisfaction: A mixed methods study exploring synchronous online classroom learning satisfaction in the corporate training environment. *The Interactive Journal of Global Leadership and Learning, 1*(1), 1

Chiaburu, D.S. & Lindsay, D.R. (2008). Can do or will do? The importance of self-efficacy and instrumentality for training transfer. *Human Resource Development International, 11*(2), 199–206.

Chope, R.C. (2005). Qualitatively assessing family influence in career decision making. *Journal of Career Assessment, 13*(4), 395–414.

Chukwu, G.M. (2016). Trainer attributes as drivers of training effectiveness. *Industrial and Commercial Training. 48*(7)

Cromwell, S.E. & Kolb, J.A. (2004). An examination of work-environment support factors affecting transfer of supervisory skills training to the workplace. *Human Resource Development Quarterly.* https://doi.org/10.1002/hrdq.1115

de Magalhaes, J.R.A. & Wilde, H. (2015). An exploratory study of the career drivers of accounting students. *Journal of Business & Economics Research (Online), 13*(4), 155.

De Vos, A., Van der Heijden, B.I. & Akkermans, J. (2020). Sustainable careers: Towards a conceptual model. *Journal of Vocational Behavior, 117*, 103196.

Denby, S. (2010). The importance of training needs analysis. *Industrial and Commercial Training, 42*(3), 147–150.

Department of Education (2020). *Employer Skills Survey, 2019.* London: Department of Education. https://assets.publishing.service.gov.uk/government/uploads/system/uploads/attachment_data/file/936487/ESS_2019_Training_and_Workforce_Development_Report_Nov20.pdf

Ebbinghaus, H. (1880) *Urmanuskript "Ueber das Gedächtniß".* Passau: Passavia Universitätsverlag.

Ebner, C. & Gegenfurtner, A. (2019, September). Learning and satisfaction in webinar, online, and face-to-face instruction: a meta-analysis. *Frontiers in Education, 4*, 92.

Egan, T.M., Yang, B. & Bartlett, K.R. (2004). The effects of organizational learning culture and job satisfaction on motivation to transfer learning and turnover intention. *Human Resource Development Quarterly, 15*, 279–301

Ertmer, P.A. & Newby, T.J. (2013). Behaviorism, cognitivism, constructivism: Comparing critical features from an instructional design perspective. *Performance Improvement Quarterly.* https://doi.org/10.1002/piq.21143

Ford, J.K., Baldwin, T.T. & Prasad, J. (2018). Transfer of training: The known and the unknown. *Annual Review of Organizational Psychology and Organizational Behavior, 5*, 201–225

Future Learn (2021). *Global Report.* FutureLearn.Com www.futurelearn.com/info/press-releases/global-report-suggests-job-for-life-a-thing-of-the-past

Galevski, G. (2019). Where companies go wrong with learning and development. *Harvard Business Review.* https://hbr.org/2019/10/where-companies-go-wrong-with-learning-and-development

Gati, I. & Kulcsár, V. (2021). Making better career decisions: From challenges to opportunities. *Journal of Vocational Behavior, 126*, 103545.

Haley, C.K. (2008). Online workplace training in libraries. *Information Technology and Libraries, 27*(1), 33–40.

Hennessy, G. & Yip, J. (2021). Career decision making. In W. Murphy & J. Toski-Kharas (Eds.) *Handbook of research methods in careers.* Edward Elgar Publishing.

Holton III, E.F. (2005). Holton's evaluation model: New evidence and construct elaborations. *Advances in Developing Human Resources, 7*(1), 37–4.

Honey, P. & Mumford, A. (1992) *The Manual of learning styles,* 3rd Edition. Maidenhead: Honey.

Hughes, A.M., Zajac, S., Woods, A.L. & Salas, E. (2020). The role of work environment in training sustainment: A meta-analysis. *Human Factors, 62*(1), 166–183.

Iyengar, S.S. & Lepper, M. (2000) When choice is demotivating: Can one desire too much of a good thing? *Journal of Personality and Social Psychology, 76*: 995–1006.

Khalil, M.K. & Elkhider, I.A. (2016). Applying learning theories and instructional design models for effective instruction. *Advances in Physiology Education, 40*(2), 147–156.

Knowles, M.S. & Associates (1984). *Andragogy in action.* San Francisco: Jossey-Bass.

Kodwani, A.D. & Prashar, S. (2019). Assessing the influencers of sales training effectiveness before and after training: Mediating role of motivation to learn and moderating role of choice. *Benchmarking: An International Journal. 26*(4)

Lacerenza, C.N., Reyes, D.L., Marlow, S.L., Joseph, D.L. & Salas, E. (2017). Leadership training design, delivery, and implementation: A meta-analysis. *Journal of Applied Psychology*. https://doi.org/10.1037/apl0000241

Lent, R.W. & Brown, S.D. (2020). Career decision making, fast and slow: Toward an integrative model of intervention for sustainable career choice. *Journal of Vocational Behavior, 120*, 103448.

Lent, R.W., Brown, S.D. & Hackett, G. (1994). Toward a unifying social cognitive theory of career and academic interest, choice, and performance. *Journal of Vocational Behavior, 45*(1), 79–122.

Lethaby, C. & Harries, P. (2016). Learning styles and teacher training: Are we perpetuating neuromyths? *ELT Journal*. https://doi.org/10.1093/elt/ccv051

Lim, D.H. & Morris, M.L. (2006). Influence of trainee characteristics, instructional satisfaction, and organizational climate on perceived learning and training transfer. *Human Resource Development Quarterly*. https://doi.org/10.1002/hrdq.1162

Mathieu, J.E., Tannenbaum, S.I. & Salas, E. (1992). Influences of individual and situational characteristics on measures of training effectiveness. *Academy of Management Journal, 35*(4), 828–847.

Murre, J.M. & Dros, J. (2015). Replication and analysis of Ebbinghaus' forgetting curve. *PloS One, 10*(7), e0120644.

OECD (2020). *Employment by job tenure*. Organisation for the Economic Cooperation and Development https://stats.oecd.org/Index.aspx?DataSetCode=TENURE_FREQ

Office for National Statistics. (2020) *Standard Occupational Classification 2020*. London: ONS.

Parsons, F. (1909). *Choosing a vocation*. Brousson Press.

Patton, W. & McMahon, M. (2015). The systems theory framework of career development: 20 years of contribution to theory and practice. *Australian Journal of Career Development, 24*(3), 141–147.

Patton, W. & McMahon, M. (2021). The systems theory framework of career development. In J. P. Sampson, E. Bullock-Yowell, V. C. Dozier, D. S. Osborn & J. G. Lenz (Eds.), *Integrating theory, research, and practice in vocational psychology: Current status and future directions*. Tallahassee, FL: Florida State University. http://doi. org/10.17125/svp2016.ch4 P50–62

Pavlov, I.P. (1897). *The work of the digestive glands*. London: Griffin.

Percival, J.C., Cozzarin, B.P. & Formaneck, S.D. (2013). Return on investment for workplace training: The Canadian experience. *International Journal of Training and Development*. https://doi.org/10.1111/ijtd.12002

Peterson, E.R., Rayner, S.G. & Armstrong, S.J. (2009). Researching the psychology of cognitive style and learning style: Is there really a future? *Learning and Individual Differences*. https://doi.org/10.1016/j.lindif.2009.06.003

Rath, T., Harter, J.K. & Harter, J. (2010). *Wellbeing: The five essential elements*. Simon and Schuster.

Riener, B.Y.C. & Willingham, D. (2010). The Myth Of Learning. *Change Magazine*.

Rodrigues, R. A. & Guest, D. (2010) Have careers become boundaryless? *Human Relations, 63*(8): 1157–1175.

Roelen, C.A.M., Koopmans, P.C. & Groothoff, J.W. (2008) Which work factors determine job satisfaction? *Work, 30*: 433–439.

Rohrer, D. & Pashler, H. (2012). Learning styles: Where's the evidence? *Medical Education*. https://doi.org/10.1111/j.1365-2923.2012.04273.x

Rousseau, G.G. & Venter, D.J. (2009). Investigating the importance of factors related to career choice. *Management Dynamics: Journal of the Southern African Institute for Management Scientists, 18*(3), 2–14.

Savickas, M.L. (2011). New questions for vocational psychology: Premises, paradigms, and practices. *Journal of Career Assessment, 19*(3), 251–258.

Schindler, L.A. & Burkholder, G.J. (2016). A mixed methods examination of the influence of dimensions of support on training transfer. *Journal of Mixed Methods Research, 10*(3):292–310.

Skinner, B.F. (1938). *The behavior of organisms: An experimental analysis.* New York: Appleton-Century.

Statista (2021). Size of the global workplace training market. www.statista.com/statistics/738399/size-of-the-global-workplace-training-market/

Velada, R., Caetano, A., Michel, J. ., Lyons, B.D. & Kavanagh, M.J. (2007). The effects of training design, individual characteristics and work environment on transfer of training. *International Journal of Training and Development, 11*(4), 282–294.

Watson, J.B. (1913). Psychology as the behaviorist views it. *Psychological Review, 20,* 158–178.

Willingham, D.T., Hughes, E.M. & Dobolyi, D.G. (2015). The scientific status of learning styles theories. *Teaching of Psychology, 42*(3) 266–271. https://doi.org/10.1177/0098628315589505

Leadership, engagement and motivation

Jutta Tobias Mortlock

Overview

This chapter offers an introduction to the science and practice of leadership in organisations. It starts by outlining the evolution of leadership since the early 20th century, and presents the theoretical underpinnings of the science of leadership and its development. It explains how leadership science can be applied by organisational psychologists in workplaces, to help grow leadership in organisations today. This chapter offers several frameworks for the practical application of leadership science to workplaces and concludes with practical recommendations for designing effective leadership development programmes and what the future for leadership may mean for our global society.

Learning outcomes

By the end of this chapter, you will:

- understand what leadership means in organisations
- recognise how the concept of leadership has evolved since the early 20th century
- know key features of emerging leadership theories in the 21st century
- gain an insight into the practical application of leadership development for people at work
- realise that leadership is for everyone, not merely for top managers.

Key concepts

Leadership vs management

What is leadership, and how does it differ from management? Management is a social process that involves creating plans, control systems and coordination, and motivating people at work (Brech, 1957): managers manage human and other resources. The aim of management is 'to achieve organisational goals efficiently and effectively' (Jones & George, 2018, p. 5), while leadership is more difficult to define.

DOI: 10.4324/9781003302087-5

This is not for lack of trying: leadership is a vast area of study, and scholars have identified at least 66 distinct leadership theory domains (Dinh et al., 2014). Still, there is no universal consensus on what leadership is, and no unified theory of leadership currently exists. On the one hand, this is because the literature includes a diverse set of antecedents and outcomes of leaders' attitudes and actions, and on the other because leadership relates to behaviours and events that apply at different levels of analysis: individuals, dyads, groups, entire organisations, even political systems. In short, the study of leadership ranges from investigating the thoughts, words, and actions of individual *leaders* to examining the causes and various effects of collective *leadership* in a variety of contexts.

However, scientists today do agree that leadership in the 21st century revolves around three core properties:

1 It is aspirational (defined as 'the art of mobilising others to want to struggle for shared aspirations'; Kouzes & Posner, 2002, p. 24);
2 It is future-oriented (defined as 'the capacity of a human community to share its future, and specifically to sustain the significant processes of change required to do so'; Senge et al., 1999); and
3 It revolves around collective responsibility (defined as 'persuading the collective to take responsibility for collective problems'; Grint, 2010).

Leadership, motivation, and engagement

Scientists and practitioners are interested in leadership because of its outcomes, particularly its effect on employee engagement and motivation.

Work motivation has been studied since the early 20th century (Maier 1955). Early scientific debates on motivation deliberated the extent to which workers' performance derived from their capacity to act (i.e. their ability) vs. their willingness to engage in the task at hand (motivation), suggesting that individual ability and perceived future benefits would generate motivation (c.f. Vroom 1964).

More recently, work motivation includes a broader understanding of workers' basic psychological needs, outlined in Deci and Ryan's (2000) Self-Determination Theory (SDT). Individuals seek to satisfy three fundamental psychological needs – (1) autonomy, a person's need to self-regulate their experience and action; (2) competence, an individual's need to perform tasks deemed important effectively; and (3) relatedness, the perception of being socially connected.

SDT distinguishes between three types of motivation: *autonomous motivation*, *controlled motivation*, and *amotivation*. When people find an activity intrinsically enjoyable or inherently valuable, they experience *autonomous* motivation. In contrast, when people engage in an activity because they feel pressure or to pursue an extrinsic reward or avoid punishment, they experience *controlled* motivation. Finally, *amotivation* is about the absence of either autonomous or controlled motivation: people lacking in any motivation to engage in an activity because they cannot see why this would be useful.

SDT can help explain work motivation by linking leadership and subordinate behaviours. Specifically, research has shown that a leader's autonomous work motivation is mirrored by their subordinates, who also tend to be autonomously motivated at work – while leaders who demonstrate controlled motivation or even amotivation tend to lead subordinate teams marked by the same motivation type (Kanat-Maymon et al., 2020).

Kahn (1990, p. 694) coined the term 'engagement', defining it as 'the harnessing of organisation members' selves to their work roles; in engagement people employ and express themselves physically, cognitively, and emotionally during role performances'. Work engagement is an important construct because it predicts both mental health and performance at work (Bakker & Demerouti, 2017). Engagement is also defined as a 'positive motivational state', suggesting that engaged workers meet work demands with vigour, dedication, and absorption (Schaufeli & Bakker, 2004). Vigour relates to an employee's perceived energy and mental resilience at work; dedication refers to a sense of pride, inspiration, and enthusiasm; absorption is about being fully immersed in a task, often related to losing track of time. Vigour has been shown to help employees translate thought into action, which may explain why engagement is linked to job performance (Demerouti & Cropanzano, 2010).

It seems that employee engagement may be a key driver of job performance. One study demonstrated that more engaged workers perform better at work, and an open-minded attitude explains the link between engagement and performance (Reijseger et al., 2017).

Leadership theorising in the 20th century

There are five general 'waves' of leadership theory that dominated thinking on leadership in the 20th century. Today, these schools of thought are supplemented by new waves of leadership scholarship emerging in the 21st century (see University of Cambridge Institute for Sustainability Leadership, 2017; Dinh et al. 2014). We start with a discussion of 20th-century leadership theorising; emerging 21st-century leadership theorising will be covered later.

The most important 'traditional' or established leadership theories created in the 20th century (some of which are still attracting considerable researcher and practitioner attention today) are summarised in Table 4.1.

The scientific study of leadership started with the *Great Man* school of leadership in the first half of the 20th century. The Great Man Theory promoted the view that leaders are born, not made and suggested that certain individuals may possess innate characteristics that predispose them to lead others – however, more recent leadership theories suggest that leadership is learned even if some individuals are more inclined to lead (Burgoyne, 2010).

In the second wave of leadership theorising, the *Behavioural* or *Styles* School, the focus was on leadership effectiveness. This literature started to differentiate leadership from management and shifted the focus from leaders' traits and characteristics onto leader behaviours, especially in relation to followers. Lewin et al. (1939) identified three leadership styles – autocratic, democratic, and laissez-faire leadership, and found that a democratic leadership style was most strongly associated with overall group performance. One insight from this perspective was that leaders should not focus merely on the tasks at hand, but that great leaders inspire the heads and hearts of those around them (Kouzes & Posner, 1991).

In the third wave, the *Situational* or *Contingency* School of leadership, scholars focused on the importance of situational factors and how understanding follower characteristics can improve leaders' impact. The consensus was that the 'best' way to lead depends on the situation at hand. Leaders were encouraged to align their decision-making to the situation and level of involvement of followers: autocratic, consultative, or based on group consensus (Vroom & Yetton, 1973). One of the most prominent typologies in this wave was Hersey and Blanchard's (1969; 1974) *Situational Leadership* matrix, which stipulated that how directive or supportive leaders should be towards their followers would depend on the relationship quality and on followers' maturity levels.

Today, behavioural and situational approaches to studying leadership are comparatively less popular, and so research is not growing significantly in these areas (Dinh et al., 2014).

The fourth wave of studying leadership, the *Social exchange* or *Relational* School, further examined leaders in relation to their followers, and focused on the two-way relationship between a leader and followers. According to Social Exchange Theory (Blau, 1964), social behaviour between leader and follower depends on an exchange process whereby both aim to maximise benefits and minimise costs. For example, if people perceive their

Table 4.1 Five waves of leadership theorising in the 20th century

Theory / School	Description	Key References
Great Man / Trait	Celebrates outstanding individual leaders and studies their traits or characteristics to understand their accomplishments as leaders.	Stodgill (1948); Tannenbaum & Schmidt (1973)
Behavioural / Styles	Describes leadership in terms of people- and task-orientation, creating leadership behaviour taxonomies, and suggesting that different combinations of these produce different styles of leadership.	Lewin et al. (1939); Kouzes & Posner (1991)
Situational / Contingency	Specifies situations in which the leader adjusts to the situation or the followers' needs and capabilities. Leaders' decisions may be more authoritative or consultative, contingent on context.	Hersey & Blanchard (1969); Vroom & Yetton (1973)
Social exchange / Relational	Examining leadership with a relational focus, including vertical leader-follower dyads such as the Leader-Member Exchange (LMX) theory of leadership, and 'social exchanges' whereby leaders' perceived morality is reciprocated by subordinates' support and motivation	Blau (1964); Dansereau et al. (1975)
Transactional vs Transformational	Contrasts leadership as a negotiated cost-benefit exchange with an appeal to charismatic leaders and self-transcendent values of pursuing shared goals for the common good.	House (1976); Burns (1978); Mumford et al. (2008)

Adapted from University of Cambridge Institute for Sustainability Leadership (2017) and Dinh et al. (2014).

leader to be ethical, they 'repay' the leader for this perceived benefit with positive attitudes and motivated work behaviours (Kacmar et al., 2011).

One popular leadership theory created during this wave is the Leader-Member Exchange (LMX) which explores relationship quality of leader-follower dyads (c.f. House and Aditya, 1997). LMX originates from the vertical dyad linkage theory (VDL; Dansereau et al., 1975), stipulating that a relationship develops depending on how competent, trustworthy, and loyal the subordinate appears to the leader. This creates a series of in-group and out-group relationships between subordinates and the leader, based on the nature of the dyad. The quality of this relationship determines the subordinate's opportunities to succeed and grow (Liden et al., 1997). In addition, positive LMX relationships significantly predict objective performance, job satisfaction, and organisational commitment (Gerstner & David, 1997). The relationship between leaders and followers may also influence a variety of group-level organisational phenomena, such as Organisational Citizenship Behaviours (OCBs), justice perceptions, and turnover intentions (Graen & Uhl-Bien, 1995).

The final wave of theorising on leadership is the *Transactional vs Transformational School*. This final wave incorporates a new focus on self-transcendental motivations in leadership. The most prominent debate has been the dichotomy between transactional leadership and transformational leadership. Transactional leadership involves leaders and followers interacting based on cost-benefit calculations, which often leads to adaptive, reciprocal relationships which have no enduring purpose that binds leaders and followers together (Burns, 1978). By contrast, transformational leadership includes a focus on improving the status quo, with leaders capable of generating higher levels of motivation and inspiration among their followers.

While scholars continue to debate what exactly a leader's moral purpose is (or should be), a consensus has emerged that transformational leadership is more effective than transactional leadership (Bass & Avolio, 1990). Transactional leadership is analogous to how we understand 'management'; a transactional process of controlling and managing resources. According to Bass and Avolio (1990), the more involved a leader is with their followers, the more inspirational, intellectually stimulating, and effective their leadership.

The context of leadership today

Leadership today is a *contextual* science: the context in which leadership occurs dramatically impacts the leadership attitudes and actions we see in organisations. 'Context' in organisational psychology refers to the surroundings and boundaries in which phenomena are situated, and context often helps explain how and why these phenomena occur (Cappelli & Sherer, 1991).

Ever since social psychologist Kurt Lewin equated behaviour to the product of the person and their situation (Lewin, 1947), the study of leadership has sought to include the role of context and how this influences both leaders and their leadership styles (Fiedler, 1967).

However, when social scientists and workplace managers think of leadership, they often have *individual* characteristics in mind: a leader's charisma, personality traits, gender, culture, style, and so on. This is problematic because context matters for understanding leadership and leaders' behaviour. Today's specific leadership context is marked by 'VUCA': Volatility, Uncertainty, Complexity, and Ambiguity. The term VUCA was originally coined by Bennis and Nanus (1985) and originally applied to warfare in the 20th century, specifically by the United States Army War College. VUCA became associated with the reality that certain warfare tactics were no longer reliable because the context in which 20th-century US-American soldiers found themselves was increasingly volatile, uncertain, complex, and ambiguous.

More than ever, the term VUCA is used to describe today's world of work. Organisations are increasingly forced to consider their clients' or customers' wants and needs and balance these with their internal resources, and the wants and needs of their own employees. Nowadays an increasingly complex set of geopolitical challenges impacts the world of work for leaders in organisations daily: we live in a world where global pandemics, polarised public opinion, and the climate catastrophe are a reality. In other words, VUCA describes the *new normal* for leadership and all the stakeholders touched by it today.

Paradigm shifts in understanding the meaning of 'leadership'

Clarifying how leadership is understood in the 21st century is important for *science* and *practice* to develop, shape, and improve leadership in organisations.

There are three important paradigm shifts for making sense of leadership in the 21st century:

1 From traits to shared qualities
2 From leaders to leadership networks
3 Towards complexity leadership

Each of these helps to build and grow leadership in 21st-century organisations.

Paradigm shift 1: from traits to shared qualities

Recall that people traditionally imagine 'leader' when thinking 'leadership', often associating masculine traits with effective leaders: 'strong', 'directive', or 'visionary' (Schein, 1973).

However, this view reflects a certain naivete about the power of prominent leaders in organisations, politics, and society in making effective leadership 'happen' by itself.

We know that human behaviour is highly variable and changeable depending on context: human behaviour is a function of both the person *and* the situation (Lewin, 1943). Thus, focusing on individual leaders' traits only addresses one of several parts involved in the challenge of generating effective leadership.

This explains the shift towards understanding and developing leadership as an exercise in developing shared qualities between different stakeholders in an organisation. Leadership becomes effective 'by building a common purpose and bridging the different and sometimes conflicting objectives of the various stakeholders' (Buytendijk, 2008, p. 61).

Moreover, this change in thinking moves the focus of leadership research from an individual level of analysis towards interpersonal or more collective analysis levels (e.g. exploring the dynamic nature of interpersonal relationship quality, the evolution of trust among leadership teams).

Returning to Grint's (2010) seminal definition of leadership as the act of generating collective responsibility for collective problems, this indicates that leadership today is co-constructed between different leadership agents, in a process that inevitably needs to be shared by multiple stakeholders. It may be seductive to view leadership as an attractive quality of a minority of outstanding individuals, yet this view is unworkable in today's connected world and networked economies (Raelin, 2018).

Paradigm shift 2: from leaders to leadership networks

To find leadership in an organisation today, where would you look for it? Would you ask for the organisation chart and study the relational hierarchy of the positions you find there, and work out who reports to whom? Would you find the organisation's leadership there, and get a sense of how effective it is? Pearce and Conger (2003) argue that you would not find meaningful answers because leadership in the 21st century is not accurately represented in formal organisational charts. Instead, anyone intent on *finding* leadership in organisations needs to determine who the key stakeholders are that help the organisation achieve its goals, and how they work together. In other words, to understand real leadership today, we need to know who workers go to for advice, who they seek out to brainstorm different perspectives, and who relates to whom. The visual image of this leadership activity is therefore a social network map of relationships and communication flows between networked agents.

Understanding leadership as an act of creating and maintaining networks of actors communicating and collaborating effectively has created a significant shift in how scientists conceptualise leadership, from a role-focused description of the traditional 'leadership tripod' (Bennis, 2007) of leader / followers / shared goals towards a more collective notion of leadership. Thus, leadership today is often seen as the outcome of collective action, not based on individual agency.

Drath et al. (2008) explain that leadership today emerges because of three socially focused actions:

1 **Direction**: Widespread agreement in a group or organisation about overall goals, aims, and mission.
2 **Alignment**: Effective coordination of knowledge and work in a group or organisation.
3 **Commitment**: Willingness of members of a group or organisation to subsume their personal interests and benefits within the collective interest and benefit.

This conceptual shift is graphically illustrated in Figure 4.1.

If leadership is indeed to emerge as the outcome of social and collectively focused action, then teamwork and effective team building are becoming more important.

Of relevance here is Edmondson and Lei's (2014) work on psychological safety, as a key driver of team effectiveness. Psychological safety is a group's shared perception that team members can speak their mind freely and safely. It consists of two parts; (1) interpersonal trust: team members trust that they can contribute freely without feeling vulnerable; and (2) mutual respect: all team members' contribution is equally valuable independent of rank or seniority. As Edmondson and her colleagues have demonstrated (Edmondson &

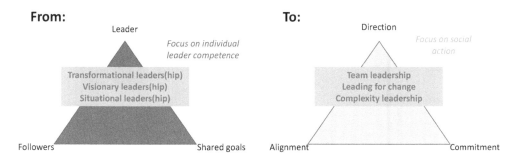

Figure 4.1 Conceptual shift from individual leader competence towards social action in leadership.

Lei, 2014), psychological safety is particularly important for high performance in complex, ambiguous work situations.

But what does psychological safety look and sounds like, in real-world organisations? It looks like symmetric and proportional interpersonal communication in a team. Pentland (2012) mapped interpersonal communication flows between members of thousands of effective and ineffective teams. Teams operating as symmetric networks of equally empowered 'leaders' who can speak up without fear of being shamed or ridiculed, and who take turns so that team members speak and listen in equal proportion, are more effective than teams led by a single leader who directs communication flows. Most notably, team effectiveness is linked to symmetric and proportional team communication, which in turn is based on strong social relationships between all members of the social network (Pentland, 2012).

Leaders must therefore shift their focus away from themselves and their own actions towards attending to who speaks up, or dominates, in team conversation and who remains silent. In addition, leaders need to focus away from role-based communication in the team and towards ensuring that all team members feel empowered to freely share ideas and information, and foster trust-based relationships among all team members. This is especially important in virtual work teams (Lechner & Tobias Mortlock, 2021).

Paradigm shift 3: towards complexity leadership

Grint's (2010) complexity leadership theory proposes that leadership success in an organisation depends much more on learning, knowledge exchange, and creativity than on the coordination of material and human resources (Uhl-Bien et al., 2007). Put simply, complexity leadership shifts leaders' actions from managing human capital towards generating social capital (Arena & Uhl-Bien, 2016).

Grint is also known for his typology of three interrelated constructs: leadership problems, power, and leadership authority (2005). He mapped these interconnected concepts to explain why 75% of all change programmes today fail. This illustrated the complexities involved in addressing different leadership challenges, traced across two axes: (1) increasing levels of uncertainty; and (2) increasing need for collaboration. This typology shows how leadership challenges can be categorised into three key problems, at increasing levels of uncertainty, and addressed via three key leadership authority styles,

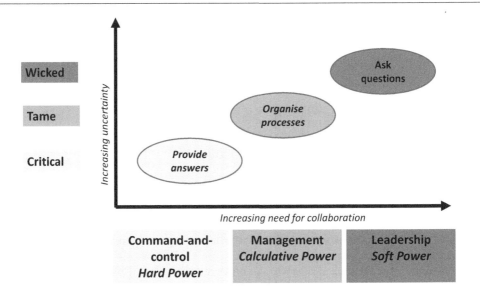

Figure 4.2 A typology of leadership challenges and types of leadership power.
Adapted from Grint (2005).

each of which requires increasing levels of collaboration between stakeholders. The three typologies (see Figure 4.2) consist of the three different leadership problems: (a) critical; (b) tame; and (c) wicked, addressed by the corresponding leadership authority types: (a) command and control; (b) management; and (c) leadership, and types of authority (a) hard power; (b) calculative power; and (c) soft power.

At the lowest levels of uncertainty and need for collaboration, leadership challenges are 'critical' in nature. A critical leadership challenge is a crisis that requires traditional leadership in the form of an identified individual or group to provide clear answers to an identified threat – for example, military aggression from another nation. In such situations, stakeholders typically accept a command-and-control leader style and the use of coercion or physical force by leaders.

A tame leadership problem requires leaders to serve as managers of a coordinated response to the leadership challenge. Typical examples of tame leadership challenges are natural disasters, for example a flash flood requiring evacuation. While this type of leadership challenge is marked by higher levels of both uncertainty and need for collaboration, it is possible to calculate the risks involved in resolving the problem, hence the use of a calculated, *rational* response is acceptable by the stakeholders.

The final category of leadership challenge in Grint's (2005) typology is called a wicked challenge, which applies to situations marked by high uncertainty as well as a high need for collaboration between stakeholders. Wicked leadership challenges are those where there is no easy definition of right or wrong and where risks are difficult to quantify. A pertinent example of a wicked leadership challenge is the Covid-19 pandemic. In wicked leadership challenges, leaders add value by asking questions (not providing answers or issuing orders). The type of leadership required here is predominately normative or emotional in quality; this type of leadership power is also called *soft power*.

How does this typology shift our paradigm of leadership in the 21st century?

First, it shows that traditional, authority-based leadership exerting 'hard power' is appropriate for 'critical' leadership challenges. Second, when addressing 'tame' leadership challenges, leaders can act as managers, organising processes and resources. Finally, and most importantly, for 'wicked' leadership challenges, leaders increasingly need to use 'soft power': asking questions and encouraging those in their care to co-create solutions for today's VUCA problems. This last type of leadership challenge tends to be increasingly prevalent in our world today, because contemporary organisations operate in a complex interdependent system of geopolitical, societal and environmental challenges.

This creates a certain paradox in leadership theory, and in the debate around how to develop leaders effectively in our organisations. While some may *want* strong, decisive leaders, who create and communicate simple messages, what we *need* is effective leadership from many individuals and stakeholders across all levels in an organisation. We need collective action to build creative solutions for the complex problems of today, rather than leaders barking out orders.

Emerging 21st century leadership theories

Leadership theory – and its practice in organisations across the globe – is changing in the 21st century. Dinh et al. (2014) found that at least seven new leadership schools of thought have emerged since the new millennium and ranked these according to how frequently peer-reviewed articles have been published in top leadership journals since 2000. All of these are summarised in Table 4.2 in descending order of top journal publication frequency and outlined in the text below.

The most prolific leadership literature since 2000, Strategic Leadership, concerns how top executives' choices and their context shape the emergence and evolution of leadership in organisations. Organisational psychology studies in this field focus either on the chief executive officer (CEO) or on the entire top management team. For example, researchers have linked mindfulness and neuroscience insights to the decision patterns of individual top managers (Kleiner et al., 2019). The second most influential leadership theory since 2000 is Team Leadership which focuses on the dynamics of leadership and the routines and processes in teams and decision groups. Team leadership scholars explore the link between team leadership and performance-related outcomes (Rahmani et al., 2018; Ali et al., 2020). More recent research has included a focus on leadership dynamics in virtual teams (Purvanova et al., 2021; Bell et al., 2023).

The third most popular emerging leadership theory is Complexity Leadership, outlined previously.

Ranked fourth is Leadership Development, the study of approaches through which organisations can increase leadership capacity among its employees (McCauley et al., 1998). This literature is particularly relevant in organisational psychology as research topics include the design and evaluation of leadership training programmes, developmental activities for leaders and leadership teams, and the conditions under which leadership development is most successful. Of note here is the Leadership as Practice Development (LaDP) movement among leadership scholars (Crevani et al., 2010), outlined in detail below. The future of leadership development involves increased integration with 'megatrends' (trends impacting people on a global scale) and further disruption of the field (Hieker & Pringle, 2021).

Table 4.2 Emerging leadership theories in the 21st century, ranked by top journal publication frequency

Rank	Theory / School	Description	Key References
1	Strategic Leadership	Focus on top management leaders and teams in organisations including public leadership (of politicians, senior executives)	Boal & Hooijberg (2000)
2	Team Leadership	Focal level of analysis is team- or group-level leadership at middle- or lower-level echelons in organisations.	Mehra et al. (2006)
3	Complexity Leadership	Draws on complexity theory and social network analysis to describe how leadership may succeed in turbulent contexts.	Lichtenstein et al. (2006); Uhl-Bien et al. (2007)
4	Leadership Development	Prescriptive research on processes to develop leadership capacity and development including effective training.	Day (2001); Chia & Holt (2006)
5	Ethical / Moral Leadership	Focus is on altruistic and moral leadership behaviours, including authentic leadership.	Avolio & Gardner (2005); Lemoine et al. (2019)
6	Leading for Change	Examines the role of leadership in organisational learning and change in organisations and in society or government.	Denis et al. (2001)
7	Identity-based Leadership	Explores a social identity approach to leadership including leader categorisation theory.	Hogg (2001)

Based on Dinh et al. (2014).

Ranked fifth among emerging leadership theories is the study of Ethical / Moral leadership. This area came about because scholars suggested that most existing leadership theories (including transformational leadership) ignored the behaviour of altruistic leaders (Bass, 1999), and because extant leadership theorising implied that leaders were hedonistic, not altruistic (House & Aditya, 1997). A popular ethical leadership literature today is Authentic Leadership (Avolio & Gardner, 2005), exploring the impact of self-awareness, a balanced mindset, transparency in relationships, and a moral perspective on leaders' effectiveness.

Leading for Change is the next most popular emerging leadership literature. This literature is concerned with the role of leadership in organisational learning and change (Denis et al., 2001), or with larger societal changes. For example, recent research in this field includes an examination of how political leaders contribute to societal destabilisation (Maskor et al., 2020), and the role of leadership in mobilising collective action in society (Subašić et al., 2022).

Finally, Identity-based leadership, in particular focusing on the Social Identity Theory of leadership (Hogg, 2001), also emerged at the turn of the new millennium. According to Social Identity Theory of leadership, any given group (for example an organisation) is more likely to select as leaders those individuals who are most prototypical of the group norms. This literature is discussed in detail in Chapter 9 in this book.

In sum, the emphasis in studying leadership in the 21st century has broadened, from examining leaders and their interactions with individual followers or teams of subordinates towards exploring leadership in a more holistic way; as a multifaceted endeavour permeating individuals, teams, and entire workplaces.

Box 4.1   Leadership and mindfulness

Over the last 20 years, leadership experts and mindfulness scholars have started collaborating, spurred on by the collaboration between The Dalai Lama and van den Muyzenberg. The Dalai Lama famously said that he is not interested in creating more Buddhists; instead, his interest in engaging with world leaders is to help them draw on mindfulness to make better decisions, for their organisations and for the world at large (Dalai Lama & van Muyzenberg, 2009). Leadership and mindfulness may seem an unlikely pairing – yet mindfulness in the contemplative traditions is concerned with reducing suffering and improving life satisfaction, and the task of leadership is essentially that.

Langer and colleagues have also studied the link between mindfulness and leadership. They suggest that mindful leadership is about focusing on creating shared meaning to build capacity to address contentious challenges and about creating a culture of respect, authenticity, and trust in organisations – by proactively noticing new perspectives, new meaning, and information in work situations (Dunoon & Langer, 2011). Numerous practitioners today offer mindful leadership courses and examine the impact of these courses on leaders and their work cultures. An example of this is a study on a three-day mindful leadership programme for senior executives (Tobias Mortlock & Robinson, 2019). The authors lean on Drath et al.'s (2008) direction, alignment, and commitment leadership practice trilogy and suggest that mindful leadership as a practice may be culture-changing, specifically by prompting improved alignment and commitment before shaping up direction in the leader's work culture.

Practical applications

Leadership as practice development (LaPD)

In a VUCA world, leadership scientists and practitioners need to create compelling visions for workers yet at the same time engage their stakeholders at all levels of their organisation (and their community) to become empowered in taking collective action to address the important leadership challenges at hand. They need to manage the tension between people's traditional need to see strong leaders taking decisive action during times of crisis and nurturing new leadership to emerge from unexpected places so as to co-create adaptive solutions for an ever-changing world.

Leadership as Practice Development (LaPD) is based on Practice Theory, highlighting the importance of *practice* and metacognition in developing organisational routines and processes that accurately describe how workers process information and adjust action accordingly (Fernandez-Duque et al., 2000). It is a highly practical school of leadership development that assumes that leadership consists of 'dynamic changing networks of informally interacting agents' (Uhl-Bien et al., 2007, p. 302) and that leadership occurs in the *space between* individuals (Lichtenstein et al., 2006). LaPD is focused on producing leadership, negotiating how goals are to be accomplished, and the practices – actions and interactions – that create *the work* of leadership (Chia & Holt, 2006).

Applying LaPD to real-life leadership challenges moves the needle of action away from individual action and towards acknowledging the interconnectivity and complexity of leadership (Denyer & James, 2016).

How can you develop 21st century leadership as practice development?

According to Denyer and James (2016), follow the four LaPD principles below.

1 Review and discuss how workers perceive leadership in their organisation.
2 Surface how leadership practices and interactions emerge at work.
3 Work in the learners' contexts on their specific adaptive challenges.
4 Work with the emotional and political dynamics of leadership.

Denyer and James (2016) argue that collaborative leadership learning groups are particularly beneficial to help leadership learners practise the four aforementioned LaPD principles. This is because collaborative learning groups focus not only on supporting individual learning, but also on developing learning about collaborative or shared leadership practices per se. In other words, the real-world challenges that such collaborative leadership learning groups often work through are the by-product of generating capacity to engage effectively with others in a complex system of collective leadership in action.

Box 4.2 Case study – Exploring Leadership

Between 2015 and 2016, Cranfield University's School of Management developed and delivered the LaPD intervention 'Exploring Leadership' to BG Group, a multinational oil and gas company with 5000 employees operating in 20 countries.

BG Group approached Cranfield University because of its need for adaptive leadership performance due to the sector's deepest downturn since the 1990s. The organisation expressed a specific need to become 'comfortable in ambiguity'.

The six-month programme that emerged was designed to engage people by combining group and individual activities, short, focused lectures, coaching, outdoor learning, and personal development activities.

Denyer and James' (2016) four principles of LaPD were translated into concrete learning outcomes for the 'Exploring Leadership' programme in the following ways:

1 Review and discuss how workers perceive leadership in their organisation.

Having reviewed BG Group's wants and needs for the programme through an extended diagnostic process, the what, how and why of the programme was distilled into three principles for engagement. Each programme participant was invited to be present, be curious, and suspend judgement.

2 Surface how leadership practices and interactions emerge at work.

The programme included a 'Looking up and out' activity for each participant; an experience outside of BG Group which provided them with an opportunity to explore how learning and leadership challenges are dealt with in a different context. Participants needed to arrange these activities by themselves with limited guidance from the learning facilitators.

3 Work in the learners' contexts on their specific adaptive challenges.

During the virtual module between residential learning activities with Cranfield University's learning facilitators, participants engaged in a 'Leadership exchange'. This involved participants pairing up with another cohort member and taking turns to visit each other at work, observing and exchanging feedback on what they noticed about each other's leadership challenges and behaviour patterns.

4 Work with the emotional and political dynamics of leadership.

During the first module of the programme, all participants took part in 'The Solo', a six-hour period of reflection alone in nature. Participants were invited to reflect on three questions during this quiet time: (1) Who am I? (2) Where am I going? (3) Why am I going there?
  The programme design included an impact assessment that measured learning outcomes at individual and group level over the course of six months following the programme. Besides several personal-level benefits including increased self-awareness and awareness of the leaders' impact on others, group-level outcomes of the programme included improved networked relationships with colleagues at BG Group and greater collective motivation to join forces to overcome leadership challenges together.

Future directions in the field

As the world becomes increasingly interconnected, the need for a more 'global' definition of leadership is growing. Global leadership refers to 'the process of influencing the thinking, attitudes, and behaviours of a global community to work together synergistically toward a common vision and common goal' (Bird et al., 2010, p. 811). Notably, this definition does not only apply to individual leaders who hold formal leadership positions but to anyone who is willing or able to engage in global leadership practices.

Organisations such as McKinsey and Company have called for a greater understanding of the what and how to generate global leadership expertise, arguing that a lack of global leadership expertise is a major issue for organisations worldwide (Ghemawat, 2012).

Global leadership is typically subdivided into six core dimensions, grouped into global business competencies (global business expertise, global organising expertise, and strategic vision) on the one hand, and intercultural competencies on the other (Bird & Osland, 2004). Intercultural competence for global leaders is relevant for organisational psychology, and this is where much scientist and practitioner effort is being generated currently.

Intercultural competence consists of three dimensions: perception management, relationship management, and self-management. Perception management is about managing uncertainty, pattern recognition, and improvisation; relationship management consists of cross-cultural and interpersonal skills, teaming skills, and the capacity to empower others; while self-management is about mindset: curiosity, resilience, and flexibility (Bird et al., 2010).

As global leadership competence becomes more important, so does an increased focus on global leadership development competencies. Osland and Bird (2018) suggest that individuals and teams intent on developing global leadership competency need to be willing and able to transform themselves; they need to extract and absorb tacit knowledge; they need to be open to experiential learning and reflection; and they need to be prepared to practise global leadership competencies extensively. The authors argue that formal classroom learning in global leadership competency may in future only represent 10% of learning activities while structured group learning and social exchange activities will form 20% of learning opportunities, and 70% of global leadership learning will derive from specific, planned work experience and reflection.

What does this mean for the field of leadership and its development?

Grasping the specific context of leadership, developing self- and situational awareness to thrive in different situations and contexts, collaborating with a diverse set of co-workers in interdependent settings, and developing a psychologically flexible and mindful outlook will become ever more critical. This is good news for organisational psychologists, because our expertise in these domains can make a useful contribution to leadership today and in future.

Conclusion

Leadership theory and practice have changed dramatically since social scientists started to map the characteristics of great leaders in the early 20th century. In this chapter, I have offered a brief history of how our scientific understanding of leaders, and leadership, and how to develop it in workplaces has evolved. Leadership in the 21st century is complex and multifaceted, and you can observe – and engage in – leadership at all levels of an organisation. Leadership today isn't only found in the traits of people at the helm of organisations, but also in shared team qualities, in leadership networks, and in the complex and dynamic routines, structures, and processes that people at work engage in. This matters not only for scientists, but also for organisations intent on developing effective leaders in the 21st century. The future of leadership and its development involves a global mindset and the recognition that leadership in organisations is a multi-level endeavour. This means there are many opportunities for organisational psychology scientist-practitioners to help people at work address the complexities that today's leadership challenges present to individuals, teams, and communities in our global society.

Explore further

Here are relevant media resources to stimulate further exploration of this topic:

Center for Creative Leadership: This is a prominent scientist-practitioner network offering research summaries, practical insights, and other resources on leadership.

Cranfield University's Gender, Leadership and Inclusion Centre: A respected research centre, famous for producing The Female FTSE Board Report (examining female representation on FTSE 100 and FTSE 250 boards) since 1999, offering free research reports and Women to Watch.

Cambridge Institute for Sustainability Leadership: A global research institute dedicated to developing leadership and solutions for a sustainable economy.

Ethical Leadership with Professor Donna Ladkin: A 60-second video on what ethical leadership is (Ladkin, 2010).

Diverse City Unexpected Leaders: A performing arts company showcasing innovative leadership development programmes in communities around the UK to build equality and social justice.

The books below offer a comprehensive overview of where leadership theory and practice is today, as well as insights into future research and practice in the field.

Pendleton, D., Furnham, A.F. & Cowell, J. (2021). Leadership: No more heroes (3rd 2021. ed.). Springer International Publishing.

Northouse, P.G. (2019). Leadership: Theory and practice (8th, International student ed.). SAGE.

References

Ali, A., Wang, H. & Johnson, R.E. (2020). Empirical analysis of shared leadership promotion and team creativity: An adaptive leadership perspective. *Journal of Organizational Behavior, 41*(5), 405–443.

Arena, M.J. & Uhl-Bien, M. (2016). Complexity Leadership Theory: Shifting from human capital to social capital. *People & Strategy: Journal of the Human Resource Planning Society., 39*(2), 22–27. https://doi.org/info:doi/

Avolio, B.J. & Gardner, W.L. (2005). Authentic leadership development: Getting to the root of positive forms of leadership. *The Leadership Quarterly, 16*, 315–338.

Bakker, A.B., Demerouti, E. (2017). Job Demands-Resources Theory: Taking stock and looking forward. *Journal of Occupational Health Psychology, 22* (3), 273–285.

Bass, B.M. (1999). Two decades of research and development in transformational leadership. *European Journal of Work and Organizational Psychology, 8*, 9–32.

Bass, B.M. & Avolio, B.J. (1990) Developing trans-formational leadership: 1992 and beyond. *Journal of European Industrial Training, 14*, 21–27.

Bell, B.S., McAlpine, K.L. & Hill, N.S. (2023). Leading virtually. *Annual Review of Organizational Psychology and Organizational Behavior, 10*.

Bennis, W.G. (2007). The challenges of leadership in the modern world: An introduction to the special issue. *American Psychologist, 62*(1), 2–5.

Bennis, W. & Nanus, B. (1985). *Leaders: The strategies for taking charge*. New York: Harper Collins.

Bird, A., Mendenhall, M., Stevens, M.J. & Oddou, G. (2010), Defining the content domain of intercultural competence for global leaders, *Journal of Managerial Psychology*, 25(8), 810–828.

Bird, A. & Osland, J. (2004), Global competencies: an introduction, in H. Lane, M. Maznevski, M. Mendenhall & J. McNett (Eds), *Handbook of Global Management* (pp. 57–80). Oxford: Blackwell.

Blau, P.M. (1964) Justice in Social Exchange. *Sociological Inquiry, 34*, 193–206.

Boal, K.B. & Hooijberg, R. (2000). Strategic leadership research: Moving on. *The Leadership Quarterly, 11*(4), 515–549. https://doi.org/10.1016/S1048-9843(00)00057-6

Brech, E.F.L. (1957). *Organisation: The framework of management*. London: Longmans, Green and Co.

Burgoyne, P.J. (2010). An overview and history of leadership and leadership development. [Online] [Accessed 15/01/2023]. Available from: https://hstalks.com/t/1777/an-overview-and-history-of-leadership-and-leadersh/

Burns, J.M. (1978). *Leadership*. New York: Harper & Row.

Buytendijk, F. (2008). *Performance leadership*. New York: McGraw-Hill.

Cappelli, P. & Sherer, P.D. (1991). The missing role of context in OB: The need for a meso-level approach. *Research in Organizational Behavior, 13*(April), 55–110.

Chia, R. & Holt, R. (2006). Strategy as practical coping: A Heideggerian perspective. *Organization Studies, 27*(5): 635–655.

Crevani, L., Lindgren, M. & Packendorff, J. (2010). Leadership, not leaders: On the study of leadership as practices and interaction. *Scandinavian Journal of Management, 26*, 77–86.

Dalai Lama, T.G. & van den Muyzenberg, L. (2009). *The leader's way: Business, Buddhism and happiness in an interconnected world*. London: Nicholas Brealey Publishing.

Dansereau, F.J., Graen, G. & Haga, W.J. (1975) A Vertical Dyad Linkage Approach to Leadership within Formal Organizations: A Longitudinal Investigation of the Role-Making Process. *Organizational Behavior and Human Performance, 13*, 46–78.

Day, D.V. (2001). Leadership development: A review in context. *The Leadership Quarterly, 11*, 581–613.

Deci, E.L. & Ryan, R.M. (2000). The what and why of goal pursuits: Human needs and self-determination of behavior. *Psychological Inquiry, 11*, 227–268

Demerouti, E. & Cropanzano, R. (2010). From thought to action: Employee work engagement and job performance. In A.B. Bakker & M.P. Leiter (Eds.), *Work engagement: A handbook of essential theory and research* (pp. 147–163). Psychology Press.

Denis, J.-L., Lamothe, L. & Langley, A. (2001). The dynamics of collective leadership and strategic change in pluralistic organizations. *Academy of Management Journal, 44*, 809–837.

Denyer, D. & James, K.T. (2016). Doing leadership-as-practice development. In J.A. Raelin (Ed.), *Leadership-as-practice: Theory and application* (pp. 262–283). Routledge/Taylor & Francis Group.

Dinh, J.E., Lord, R.G., Gardner, W.L., Meuser, J.D., Liden, R.C. & Hu, J. (2014). Leadership theory and research in the new millennium: Current theoretical trends and changing perspectives. *Leadership Quarterly, 25*(1), 36–62.

Drath, W.H., McCauley, C.J., Palus, C.J., Van Velsor, E., O'Connor, M.G. & McGuire, J.B. (2008). Direction, alignment, commitment: Toward a more integrative ontology of leadership. *Leadership Quarterly, 19*, 635–653.

Dunoon, D. & Langer, E.J. (2011). Mindfulness and leadership: Opening up to possibilities. *Integral Leadership Review, 11*(5).

Edmondson, A.C. & Lei, Z. (2014) Psychological safety: The history, renaissance, and future of an inter-personal construct. *Annual Review of Organizational Psychology and Organizational Behavior, 1*, 23–43.

Fernandez-Duque, D., Baird, J.A. & Posner, M.I. 2000. Executive attention and metacognitive regulation. *Consciousness and Cognition*, 9: 288–307.

Fiedler, F.E. (1967). *Theory of Leadership Effectiveness*. New York: McGraw-Hill Inc.

Gerstner, Charlotte R. & Day, David V. (1997). Meta-Analytic review of leader–member exchange theory: Correlates and construct issues. *Journal of Applied Psychology. American Psychological Association.* 82 (6): 827–844. doi:10.1037/0021-9010.82.6.827

Ghemawat, P. (2012). Developing global leaders. *McKinsey Quarterly*, 3(1), 100–109.

Graen, George B. & Uhl-Bien, Mary (1995). Relationship-based approach to leadership: Development of leader-member exchange (LMX) theory of leadership over 25 years: Applying a multi-level multi-domain perspective. *The Leadership Quarterly.* 6 (2): 219–247. doi:10.1016/1048-9843(95)90036-5

Grint, K. (2005). Problems, problems, problems: The social construction of 'leadership'. *Human Relations*, 58(11), 1467–1494.

Grint, K. (2010). Wicked problems and clumsy solutions: The role of leadership. In: S. Brookes & K. Grint (Eds.) *The new public leadership challenge*. London: Palgrave Macmillan.

Hersey, P. & Blanchard, K.H. (1969). Life cycle theory of leadership. *Training and Development Journal*, 23 (5): 26–34.

Hersey, P. & Blanchard, K.H. (1974) So you want to know your leadership style? *Training and Development Journal*, 28, 22–37.

Hieker, C. & Pringle, J. (2021). *The future of leadership development: Disruption and the impact of megatrends* (First 2021. ed.). Springer International Publishing.

Hogg, M.A. (2001). A social identity theory of leadership. *Personality and Social Psychology Review*, 5(3), 184–200. https://doi.org/10.1207/S15327957PSPR0503_1

House, R. (1976). A 1976 theory of charismatic leadership. *University of Toronto, Faculty of Management Studies*, 77, 1–34.

House, R.J. & Aditya, R.N. (1997). The social scientific study of leadership: Quo vadis? *Journal of Management*, 23, 409–473.

Jones, G. & George, J.M. (2018). *Contemporary management / (10th ed.)*. New York: McGraw-Hill.

Kacmar, K.M., Bachrach, D.G., Harris, K.J. & Zivnuska, S. (2011). Fostering good citizenship through ethical leadership: exploring the moderating role of gender and organizational politics. *J. Appl. Psycho.* 96, 633. doi: 10.1037/a0021872.

Kahn, W.A. (1990). Psychological conditions of personal engagement and disengagement at work. *Academy of Management Journal*, 33, 692–724.

Kanat-Maymon, Y., Elimelech, M. & Roth, G. (2020). Work motivations as antecedents and outcomes of leadership: Integrating self-determination theory and the full range leadership theory. *European Management Journal*, 38(4), 555–564. https://doi.org/10.1016/j.emj.2020.01.003

Kleiner, A., Schwartz, J. & Thomson, J. (2019). *The wise advocate: The inner voice of strategic leadership*. Columbia University. Press. https://doi.org/10.7312/klei17804

Kouzes, J. & Posner, B. (1991). Credible leaders. *Executive Excellence* 8.4: 9–10.

Kouzes, J. & Posner, B. (2002) *The leadership challenge. How to get extraordinary things done in organizations*. San Francisco, CA: Jossey-Bass.

Ladkin, D. (2010). *Re-thinking leadership: A new look at old questions*. Cheltenham: Edward Elgar.

Lechner, A. & Tobias Mortlock, J. (2021). How to create psychological safety in virtual teams. *Organizational Dynamics*, 100849–100849. doi:10.1016/j.orgdyn.2021.100849

Lemoine, G.J., Hartnell, C.A. & Leroy, H. (2019). Taking stock of moral approaches to leadership: An integrative review of ethical, authentic, and servant leadership. *The Academy of Management Annals*, 13(1), 148–187. https://doi.org/10.5465/annals.2016.0121

Lewin K. (1943). Defining the 'Field at a Given Time.' *Psychological Review.* 50: 292–310.

Lewin, K. (1947). Frontiers in group dynamics: II. *Channels of Group Life; Social Planning & Action Research. Human Relations*, 1(1), 143–153.

Lewin, K., Lippitt, R. & White, R. (1939). Patterns of aggressive behavior in experimentally created social climates. *Journal of Social Psychology*, 271–301.

Lichtenstein, B., Uhl-Bien, M., Marion, R., Seers, A., Orton, J.D. & Schreiber, C. (2006). Complexity leadership theory: An interactive perspective on leading in complex adaptive systems. *E:CO Emergence: Complexity and Organization*, 8(4), 2–12.

Liden, R.C., Sparrowe, R.T. & Wayne, S.J. (1997). *Leader-member exchange theory: The past and potential for the future*. In G.R. Ferris (Ed.), *Research in personnel and human resources management*, Vol. 15, (pp. 47–119). Oxford: Elsevier Science/JAI Press..

Maier, N.R.F. (1955). *Psychology in Industry*, 2nd. Ed. Boston: Houghton-Mifflin.

Maskor, M., Steffens, N.K. & Haslam, S.A. (2020). The psychology of leadership destabilization: An analysis of the 2016 US Presidential debates. *Political Psychology*, 42, 465–489. https://doi.org/10.1111/pops.12698

McCauley, C.D., Moxley, R.S. & Van Velsor, E. (1998). *The Center for Creative Leadership handbook of leadership development*. San Francisco: Jossey-Bass.

Mehra, A., Smith, B.R., Dixon, A.L. & Robertson, B. (2006). Distributed leadership in teams: The network of leadership perceptions and team performance. *The Leadership Quarterly*, 17, 232–245.

Mumford, M.D., Antes, A.L., Caughron, J.J. & Friedrich, T.L. (2008). Charismatic, ideological, and pragmatic leadership: Multi-level influences on emergence and performance. *The Leadership Quarterly*, 19, 144–160.

Osland, J.S. (2008), Overview of the global leadership literature, in M. Mendenhall, J.S. Osland, A. Bird, G. Oddou & M. Maznevski (Eds.), *Global leadership: research, practice and development* (pp. 34–63). London: Routledge.

Osland, J.S. & Bird, A. (2018). Process Models of Global Leadership Development. In M. Mendenhall, J.S. Osland, A. Bird, G. Oddou & M. Maznevski (Eds), *Global leadership: research, practice and development*, London: Routledge.

Pearce, C.L. & Conger, J.A. (2003). *Shared leadership: Reframing the hows and whys of leadership*. Thousand Oaks, CA: Sage.

Pentland, A. (2012). The new science of building great teams. *Harvard Business Review*, 90, 60–69.

Purvanova, R.K., Charlier, S.D., Reeves, C.J. & Greco, L.M. (2021). Who emerges into virtual team leadership roles? The role of achievement and ascription antecedents for leadership emergence across the virtuality spectrum. *Journal of Business and Psychology*, 36(4), 713–733. https://doi.org/10.1007/s10869-020-09698-0

Raelin, J.A. (2018). What are you afraid of: Collective leadership and its learning implications. *Management Learning*, 49(1), 59–66.

Rahmani, M., Roels, G. & Karmarkar, U.S. (2018). Team leadership and performance: Combining the roles of direction and contribution. *Management Science*, 64(11), 5234–5249. https://doi.org/10.1287/mnsc.2017.2911

Reijseger, G., Peeters, M.C.W., Taris, T.W. & Schaufeli, W.B. (2017). From motivation to activation: Why engaged workers are better performers. *Journal of Business and Psychology*, 32(2), 117–130. https://doi.org/10.1007/s10869-016-9435-z

Schaufeli, W.B. & Bakker, A.B. (2004). Job demands, job resources, and their relationship with burnout and engagement: A multi-sample study. *Journal of Organisational Behaviour*, 25, 293–315.

Schein, V.E. (1973). The relationship between sex role stereotypes and requisite management characteristics. *Journal of Applied Psychology*, 57, 95–100.

Senge, P., Kleiner, A., Roberts, C., Ross, R., Roth, G., Smith, B. & Guman, E.C. (1999). *The dance of change: The challenges to sustaining momentum in learning organizations*. New York, NY: Doubleday Currency.

Stogdill, R.M. (1948). Personal factors associated with leadership: a survey of the literature. *Journal of Psychology*, 25, 35–71.

Subašić, E., Mohamed, S., Reynolds, K.J., Rushton, C. & Haslam, S.A. (2022). Collective mobilisation as a contest for influence: Leading for change or against the status quo? *European Journal of Social Psychology, 52*(7), 1111–1127. https://doi.org/10.1002/ejsp.2891

Tannenbaum, R. & Schmidt, W.H. (1973). How to choose a leadership pattern. *Harvard Business Review, 51*, 162–180.

Tobias Mortlock, J. & Robinson, J. (2019). Mindful leadership. In I. Ivtzan, (Ed.), *Handbook of mindfulness-based programmes: Mindfulness interventions from education to health and therapy*. London: Routledge. ISBN 978-1-138-24094-0.

Uhl-Bien, M., Marion, R. & McKelvey, B. (2007). Complexity leadership theory: Shifting leadership from the industrial age to the knowledge era. *Leadership Quarterly, 18*(4), 298–318.

University of Cambridge Institute for Sustainability Leadership (2017). *Global definitions of leadership and theories of leadership development: literature review*. Cambridge, UK: Cambridge Institute for Sustainability Leadership, available at www.cisl.cam.ac.uk/resources/sustainability-leadership/global-definitions-of-leadership

Vroom, V.H. 1964. *Work and motivation*. New York: Wiley.

Vroom, V. & Yetton, P. (1973). *Leadership and decision-making*. Pittsburgh, PA: University of Pittsburgh Press.

Chapter 5

Well-being and work

Lara Zibarras, Julia Yates, Shannon Horan and Lucie Zernerova

Overview

This chapter focuses on psychological health in the workplace and considers the role of the employee in the stress and coping process. First, we outline the important role of psychological well-being in work life and consider some of the most relevant theories. We explore the relationship between stress and well-being and highlight some of the causes and consequences of workplace stress and examine the impact of technology on stress. We then turn to employee-focused interventions that are designed to improve psychological well-being, giving an introduction to resilience training, cognitive behavioural therapy, and acceptance and commitment therapy.

Learning outcomes

By the end of this chapter, you will:

- understand what well-being is and why it is important to organisations;
- recognise the causes and consequences of workplace stress;
- know about a range of evidence-based interventions for reducing stress and promoting workplace well-being.

Introduction

If you were asked: how did you feel this past week, what would you say? Perhaps you would say that you felt 'good' or 'really well'. What if I also asked you *why*? *Why did you feel good, or really well*? In this instance you might think about some fun activities you did, perhaps you enjoyed time with friends, or you had a particularly successful day at work.

Now let's imagine we changed the question and asked you 'do you have a sense of purpose in your life?' How might you respond to this question? Perhaps you do because your values fit your work and you have a general sense of going somewhere in life. Or perhaps you feel a little lost, wondering what your life's purpose is?

DOI: 10.4324/9781003302087-6

These two questions highlight two different perspectives on well-being (Ryff et al., 2021). Well-being is generally thought to be a multidimensional construct including both *hedonic* and *eudaimonic well-being*. Hedonic well-being (illustrated by the first question) includes pursuing pleasurable experiences, having high levels of positive feelings and low levels of negative feelings. Eudaimonic well-being (illustrated by the second question) relates to a pursuit of meaning, having a sense of purpose in your life, personal growth, focus on values and generally having a direction in life.

There are in fact several different ways to consider well-being, with different theories and frameworks found in the literature, some of which are explored in more detail below.

Well-being and stress

Daily tasks, the monetary pressures of employment and interpersonal relationships within the office can all leave employees feeling stressed. But what exactly is stress? Stress is often conceptualised as the opposite of well-being and in organisational psychology, 'stress' is considered alongside well-being both within academic research and practice. 'Stress' is an ambiguous term and typically used to describe a variety of different physical and emotional phenomena. Selye's original definition explained stress as a non-specific bodily response to any demand for change (Selye, 1936) but definitions have since become a bit more complicated, and it has been used to refer to both the experience of internal stress (stress-induced thoughts and behaviours) and external causes of stress (such as certain life-events or circumstances that are outside of one's control). More recently, in an attempt to bring together various diverse conceptualisations of stress and its underlying processes, Epel and her colleagues proposed a view of stress as 'an emergent process that involves interactions between individual and environmental factors, historical and current events, allostatic states, and psychological and physiological reactivity' (Epel et al., 2018, p. 146).

You might also come across the word 'stressor' in the literature. A 'stressor' refers to a *cause* of stress, and 'strain' is the *reaction* to or outcome of a stressor. For example, if a manager asks an employee to give a presentation to a key stakeholder and this makes the employee feel uneasy, the stressor is the presentation, and the strain reaction is what follows. This may involve feeling uneasy and anxious, worrying thoughts, physical sensations of tightness on the chest, wobbly tummy or a headache and tendencies to behave in certain ways, such as procrastination or eating too much chocolate.

Within the context of a job, there are many stressors which may impact employees' psychological and physical well-being. Work-related stressors include workload and work overload, conflict between different roles, pressures or tension with managers or senior leadership, job uncertainty or instability, a lack of job control (or autonomy at work), organisational change, restructuring, or merging, approaching project deadlines, the adoption of new tools or technologies, and much more (Johnson et al., 2018).

Why should organisations care about staff well-being?

There is currently considerable interest in workplace well-being both in organisations and within the research community. This focus is clearly justified. Evidence suggests that organisations are well advised to focus both on managing and reducing stress and on creating environments where workers can flourish.

The consequences of workplace stress

There is a significant and measurable cost associated with poor psychological well-being. According to Health and Safety Executive's (2021) annual statistics, work-related stress, anxiety or depression accounted for 51% of all work-related ill health cases and 55% of all working days lost due to ill health in the UK. The Chartered Institute of Personnel and Development (CIPD, 2022) has similarly reported that stress and employee mental ill health were among the top three causes of long-term absence. A total of 17 million working days were lost in 2021/22 due to work-related stress, anxiety and depression; with higher rates of stress found in professional occupations.

The growing interdependence of work, health and well-being has been recognised in almost all industrialised societies globally. In the UK, there have been many studies that have found work-related stressors to be responsible for a myriad of ill-health effects of employees in many difficult jobs, organisations and industries (Cooper, 2001). Work, in broad terms, is beneficial for people's well-being but Terkel, a social anthropologist, interviewed hundreds of American workers, and concluded that work comes with risks for all employees, from those in top leadership positions through to frontline workers (Terkel, 1977). Besides having a direct impact on mental and physical health, stress can also diminish creativity and prevent personal development, which then negatively impacts motivation and pleasure associated with one's work. Stress can also impact the quality of social interactions and relationships, which can lead to relationship conflicts or isolation. Overall, it is globally recognised that work-related stress can lead to all kinds of psychological and physical complaints and illnesses for individuals and groups of employees (Cooper & Quick, 2017; Schabracq et al., 2003).

Extreme and prolonged work-related stress can also lead to employees experiencing burnout. The term 'burnout' was first used to describe the psychological difficulties faced by workers in healthcare and social service. As research continued, it was found that burnout could be experienced in any occupation or role. The definition of burnout includes three separate dimensions: emotional exhaustion, cynicism and reduced personal accomplishment. Emotional exhaustion refers to the individualised stress dimension of burnout and is characterised by feelings of being depleted of one's emotional and/or physical energy and resources. The cynicism component, also known as depersonalisation, can emerge when employees attempt to cope with exhaustion. It represents the interpersonal context or social dimension of burnout, and is characterised by feeling pessimistic about one's role and experiencing a hardened or detached attitude toward the recipients of one's work. Finally, reduced personal accomplishment, or reduced professional efficacy, represents the self-evaluation dimension of burnout and is characterised by a lack of motivation, productivity and achievement at work.

Research on burnout began in the 1970s by researchers Herbert Freudenberger and Christina Maslach, and expanded rapidly over the following decades. There are now thousands of research articles published each year on the topic (Aronsson et al., 2017). The World Health Organisation's diagnostic handbook, the International Classification of Diseases (ICD-11), officially classified burnout as 'a syndrome resulting from chronic workplace stress that has not been successfully managed' (World Health Organisation, 2018). There is substantial evidence for the link between burnout and illness, and research has shown that it can have a devastating impact on employees' mental and physical health (Maslach & Leiter, 2017).

The damage that high levels of stress cause individuals and the knock-on detrimental impact on organisational performance are clearly compelling reasons for organisations to focus on well-being. But what about the converse of this? Do happy workers bring benefits to organisations?

The Happy Productive Worker Thesis

Organisational psychologists and business leaders are inevitably interested in research that could help to increase the productivity of the workforce. The Happy Productive Worker Thesis (HPWT) offers a popularised approach to this. It is grounded in the assumption that happy workers are more productive and suggests that anything that organisations can do to increase staff morale will have a positive knock-on impact on organisational outcomes. This explanation feels intuitively satisfying: of course happy workers are more likely to do their best at work, and by contrast, unhappy workers must surely be unlikely to do more than the bare minimum. But obvious though it sounds, the evidence supporting the HPWT is surprisingly unconvincing (Wright & Cropanzano, 2004). In general, most studies do seem to suggest that there is a positive link between job satisfaction and productivity, but the link is generally shown to be quite small, and the findings are also inconsistent, with some showing a reasonable link between the two, others showing something more marginal, and some studies actually finding a negative correlation, suggesting that sometimes higher job satisfaction actually makes workers *less* productive (Zelenski et al., 2008).

One explanation for the inconsistent results in the research is the wide variety of definitions of 'happiness' that have been used. Happiness has been interpreted as job satisfaction, positive emotions, a lack of negative emotions, or subjective or psychological well-being. These different conceptualisations of happiness all sound reasonable, but each one is slightly different and that could explain why different studies have ended up with different messages (Wright & Cropanzano, 2004). When conceptualised as general psychological well-being, happiness has been associated with lower levels of absenteeism and turnover, and higher levels of job performance.

A review by Peiro and colleagues (2021) has tried to make some sense of the conflicting data. They explain two different well-established types of happiness: hedonism and eudaimonia, as stated earlier. Hedonistic well-being comes from pure pleasure and feeling happy; eudaimonic well-being is a more complex concept, but is generally described as meaning and fulfilment, and involves being engaged with activities that allow you to be the best version of yourself – sometimes described as self-actualisation. It seems that the link between eudaimonic well-being and productivity is reasonably strong, particularly when you look at work engagement – workers who are highly engaged with work tend to be more productive (Peiro et al., 2021). The message to employers is that a potential route to higher productivity is to focus on the opportunities for employees to find meaning and fulfilment in their work and working relationships.

One question that remains regards the direction of influence between happiness and productivity. Most of the research has assumed that the relationship is a straightforward one: happiness leads to productivity, and therefore increasing happiness will lead to higher productivity. But more recent research has begun to question this, suggesting that we should start to explore whether the influence works the other way round arguing that productivity could lead to greater happiness. Also, performance is often measured via supervisory ratings, and supervisors may like (and hence give higher ratings to) colleagues who display higher levels of happiness at work (regardless of whether they are the best performers). It is also possible that there is what the academics call a *bi-directional influence* – where happiness and productivity both lead to each other, resulting in a virtuous circle in which greater happiness leads to greater productivity which in turn leads to greater happiness, and so on.

We have established that workplace well-being is important to individuals and to organisations. Clearly stress has a significant impact on employees, and organisations are well advised to put policies and practices in place to improve worker well-being. But in order to do this, we need to make sure that we understand what exactly well-being is; and it turns out that it is quite complicated. Let us move on now to an overview of the features and factors that constitute and create workplace well-being.

What are the antecedents of workplace well-being?

We mentioned earlier the difference between eudaimonic and hedonic well-being, but there are also a number of other ways to conceptualise the different facets of well-being. In 1989 Carol Ryff offered one of the most well-supported models of positive functioning. It comprises six elements:

1 self-acceptance
2 positive relationships with others
3 autonomy
4 environmental mastery
5 purpose in life
6 personal growth.

According to this model, individuals have psychological well-being or optimal mental health when they 'like most parts of themselves, have warm and trusting relationships, see themselves developing into better people, have a direction in life, are able to shape their environments and have a degree of self-determination' (Keyes, 2002, pp. 208–209).

A more recent, well-evidenced well-being model comes from Martin Seligman (2011). Seligman was one of the founders of the positive psychology movement – a sub-discipline of psychology that focuses on generating research and developing interventions that allow people to flourish. His model is known as the PERMA model and identifies five components of well-being:

* Positive emotions, including joy, hope and gratitude;
* Engagement, defined as vitality, absorption and vigour;
* Relationships, positive relationships with a range of people in work and outside work;
* Meaning, feeling that your life has some purpose and that you are working towards something beyond yourself;
* Achievement, working towards and achieving goals.

The PERMA model is widely supported by empirical research which indicates that each of these five components is linked to physical health, vitality, job satisfaction, life satisfaction and organisational commitment (Kern et al., 2014)

In terms of understanding healthy and unhealthy features of the work itself, a number of work design theories help to capture job characteristics that can be linked to stress or well-being outcomes. For example, the Job Demand Control (or 'job strain') model, and more recently the Job Demands-Resources (JD-R) model, offer explanations for job stress, burnout, work engagement and motivation.

In 1979 Karasek published a theory to explain job stress, which explored the link between job demands such as heavy workload, role conflict and time pressure, and negative outcomes such as strain, burnout and physical ill health. Karasek proposed that job demands will lead to negative outcomes only when workers are subject to the *combination* of high levels of job demands *and* low levels of control. He suggested that giving workers high levels of job decision latitude (i.e., job control) would result in more motivated workers who would be able to convert potential stress into work-orientated action. Karasek's model can be illustrated with a simple 2x2 diagram, shown in Figure 5.1 (Karasek, 1979). In the bottom left quadrant are jobs which have low jobdemands and low control – these workers are told exactly what to do and how to do it. The jobs are not onerous but are also not very appealing – workers are not highly engaged with the work but still find themselves under a certain amount of stress simply because they have no autonomy. In the top left quadrant, the jobs are low in demands, but here the employees have some control over what they do and how and when they do it. Workers in this quadrant likely have lower levels of stress because they are in a position to make some decisions of their own, and as a consequence, have a little more motivation. In the top right quadrant, there are what Karasek calls active jobs: this is an employee's dream. In this quadrant, workers have high job demands – high workloads and challenging tasks – but because they have high levels of control, they do not find this too stressful. Instead these workers can end up highly motivated; they find themselves learning new skills and developing their own knowledge, and they are better able to perform well. Finally, in the bottom right corner we find the worst of all worlds – workers who have highly

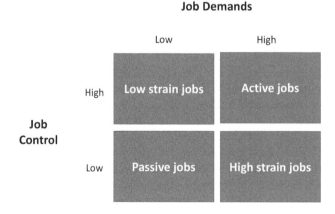

Figure 5.1 Karasek's Job Demand Control Model.
Adapted from Karasek, 1979.

demanding jobs but lack autonomy. These workers are likely to be highly stressed both physically and mentally, and may be at risk of burnout.

Karasek's conclusion then was that it is not necessarily those who have the most demanding jobs who have the highest levels of strain, but those who have the least control and influence over their work: perhaps it's not the over-burdened chief executives we should worry about, but the highly micro-managed call-centre operators. Empirical findings have broadly supported some aspects of this theory (for example, Podsakoff et al., 2007): people in high-demand, low-control positions are generally most susceptible to job strain. However, the buffering effects of having more control is not borne out in the literature: the research suggests that even very high levels of autonomy don't always seem to compensate for an unreasonably demanding job (Guthier et al., 2020).

A recent and more compelling extension of this theory has emerged from Demerouti and her colleagues (2001) in the form of their job demands-resources (JD-R) model. This builds on the core ideas from the JDC model, and can incorporate a greater range of work and individual characteristics. As with the JDC model, the JD-R model focuses on job demands but broadens Karasek's category beyond *job control* to include *job resources*, such as social support, feedback and rewards; and, more recently, personal resources, such as self-efficacy, resilience, hope or optimism. Empirical evidence supporting this model seems robust, with meta-analyses (e.g., Lessener et al., 2019) showing that a broad range of job resources can mitigate against the risks of a highly demanding job, and can lead to less burnout and higher levels of work engagement. The key message here for employers is that workers need to be supported by the work environment to do the jobs they are being asked to do, both in terms of physical resources such as time and equipment, effective supervisory behaviour (e.g., provision of feedback), and other job resources such as autonomy.

Other causes of workplace stress

Of course, not all employees are the same and pre-existing differences can make certain employees more prone to workplace stress than others. Within the last few decades, research has explored different individual factors that could play a role in employees' work-related health and well-being (Lazarus, 1995).

Some stressors may be self-created or self-enhanced. Some people are prone to overthinking and over-preparing, and others may be more confrontational and often end up creating a hostile work environment. Employees also differ in how they deal or cope with work-related stress in the form of adaptive and maladaptive coping strategies, which in turn can affect their well-being (Brown et al., 2005). These differences typically occur within individuals themselves, and *also* amongst multiple individuals and even between different groups of employees within the workplace (Schabracq et al., 2003).

Research in this area has allowed for a greater understanding of the environmental factors that contribute to individual well-being and to some degree, a worker's levels of stress will be determined by their specific job. Certain professions, for example, may be intrinsically more stressful (for example surgeons or secondary school teachers), and different positions may lead to different levels of stress – those in senior positions may be shielded from some of the pressures facing frontline workers. Other influential factors are linked to the leadership choices made within the specific organisation. Employment relations research suggests that individual well-being can be enhanced through engaging work, organisational support, employee voice and a good work environment, specifically an environment that includes equal opportunities as a core value. Additionally, well-being research has often focused on employees' lack of control or voice within their workplace. Having a voice in or control over decisions being made about well-being policies or practices will alter how employees view them and also whether they will participate or adopt them (Guest, 2017).

Technology and workplace well-being

With the increased use of technology in the workplace and in our lives more broadly, the new field of *cyberpsychology* has emerged. This sub-discipline, examining human inter-action with digital technology, is still in its infancy, but has generated some interesting findings that we would be well advised to keep an eye on.

Some interesting research has examined the impact of work-related social media, and in particular, the use of the professional networking site LinkedIn. LinkedIn seems to be the go-to place for building your professional brand, bringing recruiting employers and job seekers together and allowing us to keep up to date with the latest news and oppor-tunities in our fields. But whilst LinkedIn clearly has benefits, the overall picture emerging from the research is mixed. One of the risks associated with all social media sites is social comparison: we can't help but compare our messy, insecure, vulnerable, real insides with the beautifully curated lifestyles we see others post on social media. This phenomenon has been observed in users of a range of social media sites, but, perhaps curiously, LinkedIn seems to be one of the worst offenders, apparently leading to stronger social comparison than Instagram, blogs or Twitter (Chae, 2018). More engagement with LinkedIn seems to lead to increased depression and anxiety (Jones et al., 2016) and using LinkedIn for job searching has also been shown to have negative consequences, with time spent on LinkedIn leading to lowered self-efficacy (Johnson & Leo, 2020). The overall message seems to be that whilst LinkedIn can be very useful professionally, it is perhaps best to limit the time you spend on it.

One technology-enabled trend that we touch on from different angles throughout the book is working from home. It is clearly having a significant impact on many aspects of organisations and work life. In terms of employee well-being, the impact of working from home seems to be somewhat mixed: whilst it seems to improve job satisfaction and performance, it also appears to increase isolation, reduce work commitment, and con-tribute to 'over-availability syndrome' where individuals feel obliged to work beyond normal working hours (Bailey & Kurland, 2002; Harpaz, 2002). Video conferencing technology such as Zoom and Microsoft Teams seems to increase productivity (meetings tend to be much shorter and more to the point than in-person meetings) but worsen both well-being (Tan et al., 2022) and work–family conflict (Jia & Li, 2022). Organisations need to be aware of the potential well-being risks associated with this new trend, and consider how to mitigate them.

A section on the impact of technology on well-being at work would not be complete without an acknowledgement of the impact of smartphones. Smartphones have revo-lutionised our lives, and have become so useful and convenient that many of us feel that we couldn't be without them. But with our entire work lives in our pockets at all times, our work / home boundaries have become increasingly blurred. Smartphones have led to more after-hours working, and a sense of increased pressure to respond to emails whenever we receive them. Some people appreciate being able to keep on top of their work, but boundaries are very important for well-being, ensuring that there is sufficient time and mental space to recover from work in preparation for the following day (Mellner, 2016).

The message overall seems to be that whilst technology at work is allowing us to be more productive and better informed, it can come at a cost to our well-being. But more research is needed, and fast. Technology is evolving rapidly and the ways in which it is used at work are changing all the time – research really needs to keep up to make sure that organisations are able to capitalise on the benefits technology brings without creating damaging environments.

In the chapter so far, we have looked at what is meant by workplace well-being, and at its causes and consequences for organisations. The evidence is clear that stress can be highly problematic, even dangerous for employers and employees, and organisations are rightly interested in what they can do to boost well-being and alleviate stress. In the next part of the chapter we will move on to some practical interventions that have been shown to help.

Coping with stress and enhancing well-being

We have established that workplace well-being, whilst being a complex construct, is important for organisations. But who should be responsible for individual well-being? Some may argue that organisations have a social responsibility to take care of their employees' health and well-being, at least while they are in the workplace (see Box 5.1 for an example of this).

Box 5.1   UK Management Standards

It's probably clear by now that it's important to consider employees' well-being within the workplace, but how are organisations and practitioners meant to approach promoting well-being at work? In the UK, the Health and Safety Executive (HSE) developed the Management Standards approach to standardise how to develop interventions to address work-related stress and its consequences.

The UK Management Standards highlighted that a bottom-up approach is key, meaning that employees who will participate within interventions should be involved in their design and creation. The overall aim of accessing the current state or problem and developing a solution should always be focused on creating an action plan or intervention for improving the employees' well-being.

Before designing a solution, it is important to consider three main factors, (1) what type of intervention will be created, (2) what level of the organisation will the intervention be focused on, and (3) what is the overall time period of the intervention?

1 The type of intervention: **primary**, preventative interventions which focus on addressing the source of issues; **secondary**, which focus on helping employees deal with the current situation or problem; and **tertiary**, which are aimed at improving the well-being of employees who have become ill by their work.

2 The levels of the organisation can include: the organisational or strategic level, where the current issue is affecting employees throughout the organisation; team, group or macro level, where the issue is central to only a current group of employees; and the individual or micro level, which would focus on a small, affected number of individuals.

3 Lastly, the time period of interventions is typically seen as either: short, which are considered quick wins and should see positive results almost immediately; medium, which are expected to be delivered over a few months; and long, where the intervention is not planning to see a positive outcome for several months or even years.

It is also important to consider evaluating the interventions to ensure that they are having the desired positive impact as intended (Health and Safety Executive, 2019).

However, organisations should not and cannot be left to bear the responsibility on their own. An organisation may have many different programmes, policies or development opportunities in place to help their employees, but it is down to the employees to take advantage of these. Making use of organisational resources requires employees to develop their own attitudes and practices to make well-being a core personal value. But it has been shown that individuals are much more likely to focus on their own well-being when it is also a core organisational value (Cooper & Leiter, 2017).

Let us look now at four approaches than can enhance workplace well-being: resilience, cognitive behavioural therapy, acceptance and commitment therapy, and recovery time.

Resilience

Resilience has been broadly defined as an individual's ability to achieve a positive outcome despite serious threats to adaptation or development (e.g. Masten, 2001; Pangallo et al., 2015). Positive outcomes associated with resilience may include healthy psychological functioning in different life domains (e.g., work, family, social) and emotional, behavioural and biological responses to acute stressors (Schetter & Dolbier, 2011). Bonanno and Mancini (2012) conceptualise resilience in terms of outcome patterns following potentially traumatic events. Other researchers (e.g. Tedeschi & Calhoun, 2004) use the term *thriving* to refer to resilient outcomes suggesting an improved level of functioning after an adverse event.

Despite the substantial amount of research on resilience to date, there are many varied conceptualisations of resilience in the literature. One definition offered by Windle (2011) is particularly useful and comprehensive:

...the process of effectively negotiating, adapting to, or managing significant sources of stress or trauma. Assets and resources within the individual, their life and environment facilitate this capacity for adaptation and 'bouncing back' in the face of adversity. Across the life course, the experience of resilience will vary.

(Windle, 2011, p. 152)

Woven through the literature there are four key conceptual features of resilience:

- Resilience occurs in response to exposure to adversity and results in positive outcomes or adaptation that may change over an individual's life (Windle, 2011).
- There is some disparity in the way researchers have conceptualised adversity, yet it is reasonable to suggest that a precursor to resilience must be significant enough to carry the threat of a negative outcome.
- Irrespective of the threat, as exposure to risk increases, the likelihood of resilient outcomes decreases significantly.
- Resilient functioning is not defined by one specific criterion, instead there are many resilience pathways.

In Box 5.2, we offer a case study on how resilience training could be used as an employee-focused intervention to improve psychological well-being. This case study was set in the context of palliative care workers.

Box 5.2   Case study: measuring resilience in palliative care setting

Context

Palliative care workers face additional workplace stressors compared with those working in typical hospital environments because of the burdens associated with making life-changing decisions for patients, the strains of providing bereavement support for family members, and the feeling of loss relating to the inevitable death of patients.

Relatively little research has focused on assessing resilience in the palliative care context. Given the stressors associated with providing the level of care required, this explored a way to assess resilience in palliative care workers.

Methodology

A situational judgement test was developed in order to measure the specific behaviours associated with resilience in the palliative care context. Participants (N=284) were acute ward, hospice and palliative care workers.

Findings suggested that resilience was negatively related to self-reported sickness absence and positively related to well-being and employee attitudes (turnover intention, job satisfaction and organisational commitment). In two-wave longitudinal research, resilience (as measured by the SJT) predicted well-being and employee attitudes at two time points (this was over and above other variables such as personality, education and experience).

Conclusions

The findings suggested that, not only was the SJT a valid assessment of resilience in at-risk workers, but also that it could be used in either summative or formative assessment. It was put forward as a formative tool to support palliative care workers in developing their resilience (Pangallo et al., 2016).

Resilience training in organisations continues to be widely offered to workers to help them to develop techniques to cope with pressures at work, and it has been shown to be very effective. But this approach is not without its critics. The assumption underpinning resilience training is that when workers can't cope it is their fault, and the solution is to fix them: it's all about the individual worker. But as we have established, workplace stress is generally down to a combination of the worker and the workplace, and any individual will experience stress if the pressures put on them at work are too great. Some see the focus on enhancing individual workers' resilience as an excuse that employers can use to continue to impose heavy workloads or make unreasonable demands on their workforce. Workplace well-being is everyone's responsibility, and whilst resilience training can offer employees valuable techniques, it should not come at the expense of a fair, reasonable and well-designed system (Card, 2018).

Cognitive behavioural therapy

Some of the most promising workplace behavioural well-being interventions that have been developed over recent decades are derived from behavioural analysis and focus on behavioural outcomes and on cognitive therapies, acknowledging the link between thoughts, feelings and behaviour.

Cognitive behavioural therapy (CBT) is perhaps the most well-known. It was developed in the 1960s by Ellis and Beck, drawing together their respective work on rational emotive behaviour and cognitive therapy. At the heart of CBT is the belief that it is not events that cause us distress, but our response to those events. Our response to a difficult event may be complex, involving negative thoughts and feelings which lead to certain behaviours, all designed to protect us and make sure that we don't have to face such distress again.

Sometimes these kinds of defence mechanisms can help to protect us from harm. But often the negative thoughts and feelings are disproportionate or are based on faulty thinking and not grounded in reality. In these cases, these defence mechanisms can be detrimental, preventing us from doing our jobs to our best ability, or living our lives the way we want to.

CBT acknowledges that behaviour is hard to change on its own but that with conscious effort, we can develop new thinking habits. CBT interventions encourage people to identify persistent and invasive negative or unhelpful thoughts and then try to change them, replacing them with more helpful, realistic or positive thoughts. CBT offers techniques to help people to re-frame their experiences, to keep their response to them proportionate, and to help people to develop new, more positive and helpful habits or patterns of thought.

CBT is solidly evidence-based, with studies, reviews and meta-analyses that demonstrate its value with different types of positive outcomes in a wide range of organisational contexts (Nigatu et al., 2019; Vega-Escano et al., 2020). But it is not a quick-fix or an easy answer. CBT works through developing new habits, and therefore requires both engagement and time.

Acceptance and commitment therapy

Along with mindfulness-based approaches, acceptance and commitment therapy (ACT – pronounced as a single word) represents a different type of CBT approach. ACT understands that we all have negative and unhelpful thoughts and feelings and that sometimes these get in the way and prevent us from doing the things we want to do or living the lives we want to live. ACT too acknowledges the links between behaviour, thoughts and feelings, but where CBT tries to change the thoughts, ACT focuses more on modifying the behavioural *function* or impact of those inner experiences. That is, ACT interventions focus on the relationship between the thoughts or feelings and the action – aiming to change the nature of the impact that the thoughts and feelings have, rather than to change the form, frequency or intensity of the thoughts and feelings themselves.

The goal of ACT is to equip people with psychological flexibility – the ability to engage in personally valued behaviour even while experiencing difficult or unhelpful inner states. In this way, ACT helps people let go of the struggle with undesirable thoughts and feelings, and learn how to pursue a meaningful life while making room for those inner experiences.

ACT works towards psychological flexibility by encouraging people to be aware, to open up and to do what matters. We become *aware* by noticing what is going on inside us – noticing the negative and unhelpful thoughts and feelings and observing the impact that they have on us both inside and outside. When we *open up*, we can become more willing to experience negative or unhelpful thoughts and feelings, without them necessarily controlling our behavioural choices. *Doing what matters* entails clarifying our personal values (the qualities we most want to express in our actions), and then building patterns of action guided by these values.

ACT has several exercises that can help people to develop psychological flexibility. Mindfulness (which we explore in more depth in Chapter 10), can help people to become more aware as they focus on the present moment. An exercise that helps people disentangle themselves from negative thoughts and become more open is the *Passengers on the Bus* metaphor which reinforces the idea the people can make choices about their actions, even while experiencing a range of unwanted or unhelpful thoughts. The metaphor runs along these lines:

> Imagine that you are driving a bus. This bus represents your life, or your career, and as the bus driver, you are generally in charge of the direction, the route, and the speed. On the bus are some disruptive, unruly passengers. These represent your unhelpful or negative thoughts and feelings. The passengers might be hurling abuse at you, trying to force you to slow down, or speed up, or turn left, or stop altogether. But as the driver you have choice. Your hands are on the steering wheel and your feet on the pedals, and you can choose what you do. You can't easily stop the passengers from shouting; or change what they are saying. But you can decide how to respond. You can listen to the passengers and do what they say, if that helps you to be the person you want to be: slow down or speed up or turn left or stop. Or you can continue on your journey regardless of what they say if what they say is not very helpful to you. You don't have to spend time and energy trying to keep the passengers quiet or trying to get them off the bus – instead you can practise welcoming them along for this journey.

An approach to support doing what matters is The Retirement Party exercise, which helps people to identify their values. In this, people are invited to think ahead into the future and to imagine their own retirement party. They are asked to write the speech that they would like their boss to give in their honour – highlighting the kinds of achievements they might have made throughout their working lives, the strengths they could have shown and the impact that they might have made during their career. This exercise helps people to identify their values and work out what a values-driven career could look like for them.

ACT is a popular approach with organisational psychologists because it is academically robust. It is based on relational frame theory (Hayes et al., 2001) which explores the link between experiences, language and behaviour, and it has a robust and growing evidence base, with studies and meta-analyses that demonstrate its value in organisations, showing how it can contribute to employees' mental health (Flaxman et al., 2022; Prudenzi et al., 2021; Towey-Swift et al., 2022; Unruh et al., 2022; Waters et al., 2018).

In addition to workplace well-being training programmes that have emerged from the CBT movement, many workplace interventions have emerged from the positive psychology movement. (Donaldson et al., 2019). These programmes include strength-based training (i.e. identifying and using one's key strengths at work), job crafting and gratitude interventions for employees.

Recovery time and psychological detachment from work

'Work-life balance' is a concept that explains the interactive relationship between working and non-working environments and how they contribute to overall well-being. The term 'work-life balance' is defined as the relationship between the working lives and non-working lives of individuals, and how they can balance the two. Achieving a satisfactory balance is normally seen as reducing one side to have more time for the other (typically reducing the work side). The benefits of understanding what work-life balance is, how one can achieve it, and what the possible consequences of a 'good' or 'bad' balance might be, has been crucial to understand how organisations might be able to develop policies to encourage it. There has arisen a debate about what constitutes 'balance'. Some believe balance to be an equal distribution of commitment, time and energy to both work and non-work lives. Whereas others believe balance should be approached more subjectively, each person's individual situation and circumstances would equate to a different view of what balance is for them (Kelliher et al., 2019).

Detaching or disconnecting from one's work can be an important aspect of work-life balance. By segmenting work time and non-work time within each person's life, you can detach from work physically and psychologically. Physical detachment could include not checking or answering emails outside of your workplace or work hours. Psychological detachment could involve not ruminating on past events and not worrying about the future (Brosschot et al., 2005). The detachment or separation between work and non-work is important for employees to recover from work-related demands and stressors. Non-working periods offer that time away from work to take a break and can include both *internal* or *external* recovery. Internal recovery refers to shorter breaks during the workday, such as a shift or lunch break. External recovery refers to longer breaks outside of the workday, such as the evening after the working day, sleeping periods in the evening, days off or the weekend, and longer holiday periods. Recovering from workplace demands during external and longer periods has been widely accepted as an important factor for maintaining employees' health. Research specifically into vacation periods has become a topic of interest because it offers an ideal opportunity to recover from work-related stress. The importance of holidays was highlighted in the findings of a longitudinal study by Gump and Matthews (2000), which revealed that not taking annual holidays was associated with illness and even premature death. It is crucial to detach from work, recover from work-related stress and take longer breaks to reduce and even prevent ailments associated with being over-exposed to job stress (Kühnel & Sonnentag, 2011; Sonnentag, 2018).

Box 5.3   Effort-Recovery model

One of the core theories that helps to explain the critical role of recovering from work-related stress is the Effort-Recovery theory (E-R theory, Meijman & Mulder, 1998). The main assumption of this theory is that the exertion, energy or effort one expends at their job is unavoidable. Each working day brings different tasks and responsibilities, both mental or/and physical, that need to be completed by each employee within their role. It does not matter if this is a small task or a very large task, or whether this is a very critical task or more of a mundane task; all require some amount of effort from the employee. This effort being exerted is associated with physical reactions, such as elevated blood pressure and accelerated heart rate, as well as feelings of being tired or fatigued. These 'load reactions' are generally considered adaptive, because they are the functioning way our bodies cope with external stress from the environment. However, recovering from this reaction is crucial to return to baseline and maintain health and well-being. Without adequate recovery, these reactions begin to accumulate which can be damaging both mentally and physically. For example, if someone exerts effort during one work day and returns to baseline in the evening after work before the following work day, then there is little risk for ill health. However, if they fail to recover during the evening, they may return to work the following day with residual stress reactions and have less effort to give. This will require the employee to exert even more energy to complete tasks when already starting in a suboptimal condition. This begins a vicious cycle which would require more recovery to maintain well-being (Demerouti et al., 2009; Geurts & Sonnentag, 2006).

Conclusion

There is considerable emphasis currently on workplace well-being, both within organisations and in the research community. And rightly so. As we have seen in this chapter, low levels of well-being can lead to significant loss in productivity, not to mention the human cost of an unhappy or stressed workforce. Yet despite this focus on resilience and well-being at work, and our understanding of both what causes stress and how to boost workplace well-being, employee stress and strain is still widespread. Well-being is an area where organisational psychologists can really take advantage of their scientist practitioner philosophy (which we describe in more detail in Chapter 13), using evidence-based approaches that have been shown to work. Organisational psychologists can help organisations understand and implement a combination of primary (e.g., participatory work redesign), secondary (e.g., personal resilience or gratitude training) and tertiary (e.g., psychotherapeutic) level intervention approaches. There are plenty of different approaches that we can use to support organisations and individuals, and help to ensure that work design, policies, training, culture and practices facilitate worker well-being, allowing every worker, whatever their position and whatever their industry, to flourish.

References

Aronsson, G., Theorell, T., Grape, T., Hammarström. A., Hogstedt, C., Marteinsdottir, I., Skoog, I., Traskman-Bendz, L. & Hall, C. (2017). A systematic review including meta-analysis of work environment and burnout symptoms. *BMC Public Health*, 17, 264. https://doi.org/10.1186/s12 889-017-4153-7

Bailey, D.E. & Kurland, N.B. (2002). A review of telework research: Findings, new directions, and lessons for the study of modern work. *Journal of Organizational Behavior: The International Journal of Industrial, Occupational and Organizational Psychology and Behavior*, 23(4), 383–400.

Bonanno, G.A. & Mancini, A.D. (2012). Beyond resilience and PTSD: Mapping the heterogeneity of responses to potential trauma. *Psychological Trauma: Theory, Research, Practice, and Policy*, 4(1), 74.

Brosschot, J.F., Pieper, S. & Thayer, J.F. (2005). Expanding stress theory: Prolonged activation and perseverative cognition. *Psychoneuroendocrinology*, 30(10), 1043–1049. https://doi.org/10.1016/ j.psyneuen.2005.04.008

Brown, S.P., Westbrook, R.A. & Challagalla, G. (2005). Good cope, bad cope: adaptive and maladaptive coping strategies following a critical negative work event. *Journal of Applied Psychology*, 90(4), 792. DOI: 10.1037/0021-9010.90.4.792

Card, A.J. (2018). Physician burnout: resilience training is only part of the solution. *The Annals of Family Medicine*, 16(3), 267–270.

Chae, J. (2018). Re-examining the relationship between social media and happiness: The effects of various social media platforms on reconceptualized happiness. *Telematics and Informatics*, 35(6), 1656–1664

CIPD (2022, April). Health and Wellbeing at Work 2022. *Survey report April 2022*. Date accessed 1st May 2023. www.cipd.org/globalassets/media/comms/news/ahealth-wellbeing-work-report-2022_tcm18-108440.pdf

Cooper, C.L. (2001). *Managerial, occupational and organizational stress research*. Hampshire: Ashgate Publishers.

Cooper, C.L. & Leiter, M.P. (Eds.) (2017). *The Routledge companion to well-being at work*. Taylor & Francis.

Cooper, C.L. & Quick, J.C. (2017). *The handbook of stress and health: A guide to research and practice*. John Wiley and sons.

Demerouti, E., Bakker, A.B., Geurts, S.A. & Taris, T.W. (2009). Daily recovery from work-related effort during non-work time. In S. Sonnentag, P.L. Perrewé & D.C. Ganster (Eds.), *Research in occupational stress and well-being: Vol. 7. Current perspectives on job-stress recovery* (pp. 85–123). JAI Press/Emerald Group Publishing.

Demerouti, E., Bakker, A.B., Nachreiner, F. & Schaufeli, W.B. (2001). The job demands-resources model of burnout. *Journal of Applied Psychology*, 86(3), 499–512.

Donaldson, S.I., Lee, J.Y. & Donaldson, S.I. (2019) Evaluating positive psychology interventions at work: a Systematic review and meta-analysis. *International Journal of Applied Positive Psychology* 4, 113–134. https://doi.org/10.1007/s41042-019-00021-8

Epel, Elissa S., Crosswell, Alexandra D., Mayer, Stefanie E., Prather, Aric A., Slavich, George M., Puterman, Eli & Mendes, Wendy Berry. (2018). 'More than a feeling: A unified view of stress measurement for population science.' *Frontiers in neuroendocrinology* 49, 146–169. https://doi.org/10.1016/j.yfrne.2018.03.001

Flaxman, P., Prudenzi, A. & Zernerova, L. (2022). Acceptance and commitment training in the workplace. In: M.P. Twohig, M.E. Levin, & J.M. Petersen, (Eds.), *The Oxford handbook of acceptance and commitment therapy*. Oxford, UK: Oxford University Press.

Geurts, S.A. & Sonnentag, S. (2006). Recovery as an explanatory mechanism in the relation between acute stress reactions and chronic health impairment. *Scandinavian Journal of Work, Environment & Health*, 32(6), 482–492. DOI: 10.5271/sjweh.1053

Guest, D.E. (2017). Human resource management and employee well-being: towards a new analytic framework. *Human Resource Management Journal*, 27(10): 22–38. Doi 10.1111/1748-8583.12139

Gump, B.B. & Matthews, K.A. (2000). Are vacations good for your health? The 9-year mortality experience after the multiple risk factor intervention trial. *Psychosomatic Medicine*, 62(5), 608–612. doi:10.1097/00006842-200009000-00003

Guthier, C., Dormann, C. & Voelkle, M.C. (2020). Reciprocal effects between job stressors and burnout: A continuous time meta-analysis of longitudinal studies. *Psychological Bulletin*, 146(12), 1146–1173.

Harpaz, I. (2002). Advantages and disadvantages of telecommuting for the individual, organization and society. *Work Study*, 51(2), 74–80.

Hayes, S.C., Barnes-Holmes, D. & Roche, B. (Eds.). (2001). *Relational Frame Theory: A Post-Skinnerian account of human language and cognition*. New York: Plenum Press.

Health and Safety Executive. (2019). *Tackling work-related stress using the Management Standards approach: A step-by-step workbook*. Accessed 1st May 2023. www.hse.gov.uk/pubns/wbk01.pdf.

Health and Safety Executive. (2021). *How to develop solutions*. Work related stress–How to develop solutions. Retrieved June 2022, from www.hse.gov.uk/stress/standards/step3/developsolutions.html

Jia, C.X. & Li, J.C.M. (2022). Work-family conflict, burnout, and turnover intention among Chinese social workers: The moderating role of work support. *Journal of Social Service Research*, 48(1).

Johnson, M.A. & Leo, C. (2020). The inefficacy of LinkedIn? A latent change model and experimental test of using LinkedIn for job search. *Journal of Applied Psychology*, 105(11), 1262–1280.

Johnson, S., Robertson, I. & Cooper, C.L. (2018). Well-being and employee engagement. In S. Johnson, I. Robertson & C.L. Cooper (Eds.), *Well-Being: Productivity and happiness at work*. Cham: Palgrave Macmillan. https://doi.org/10.1007/978-3-319-62548-5_3

Jones, J. R., Colditz, J.B., Shensa, A., Sidani, J.E., Lin, L.Y., Terry, M.A. & Primack, B.A. (2016). Associations between internet-based professional social networking and emotional distress. *Cyberpsychology, Behavior, and Social Networking*, 19(10), 601–608.

Karasek, R. (1979). Job demands, job decision latitude and mental strain: Implications for job redesign. *Administrative Science Quarterly*, 24, 285–306.

Kelliher, C., Richardson, J. & Boiarintseva, G. (2019). All of work? All of life? Reconceptualising work-life balance for the 21st century. *Human Resource Management Journal*, 29(2), 97–112. https://doi.org/10.1111/1748-8583.12215

Kern, M. L., Waters, L., Adler, A. & White, M. (2014). Assessing employee wellbeing in schools using a multifaceted approach: Associations with physical health, life satisfaction, and professional thriving. *Psychology*, 5, 500–513. http://dx.doi.org/10.4236/psych.2014.56060

Keyes, C.L. (2002). The mental health continuum: From languishing to flourishing in life. *Journal of Health and Social Behavior*, 207–222.

Kühnel, J. & Sonnentag, S. (2011). How long do you benefit from vacation? *Journal of Organizational Behavior, 32*(1), 125–143. doi:10.1002/job.699

Lazarus, R.S. (1995). Psychological stress in the workplace. In R. Crandall & P. L. Perrewé (Eds.), *Series in health psychology and behavioral medicine. Occupational stress: A handbook* (pp. 3–14). Taylor & Francis.

Lessener, T., Gusy, B. & Wolter, C. (2019). The job demands-resources model: A meta-analytic review of longitudinal studies. *Work Stress, 33*, 76–103. doi: 10.1080/02678373.2018.1529065.

Maslach, C. & Leiter, M.P. (2017). Understanding burnout: New models. In C.L. Cooper & J.C. Quick (Eds.), *The handbook of stress and health: A guide to research and practice* (pp. 36–56). Wiley Blackwell. https://doi.org/10.1002/9781118993811.ch3

Masten, A.S. (2001). Ordinary magic: Resilience processes in development. *American Psychologist, 56*(3), 227.

Meijman, T.F. & Mulder, G. (1998). Psychological aspects of workload. In P.J.D Drenth & H. Thierry (Eds.), *Handbook of work and organizational psychology: Work psychology* (pp. 5–33). Hove, UK: Psychology Press.

Mellner, C. (2016). After-hours availability expectations, work-related smartphone use during leisure, and psychological detachment: The moderating role of boundary control. *International Journal of Workplace Health Management, 9*(2), 146–164.

Nigatu, Y.T., Huang, J., Rao, S., Gillis, K., Merali, Z. & Wang, J. (2019). Indicated prevention interventions in the workplace for depressive symptoms: A systematic review and meta-analysis. *American Journal of Preventive Medicine, 56*(1), e23–e33.

Pangallo, A., Zibarras, L., Lewis, R. & Flaxman, P. (2015). Resilience through the lens of interactionism: A systematic review. *Psychological Assessment, 27*(1), 1.

Pangallo, A., Zibarras, L. & Patterson, F. (2016). Measuring resilience in palliative care workers using the situational judgement test methodology. *Medical Education, 50*(11), 1131–1142.

Peiro, J.M., Montesa, D., Soriano, A., Kozusznik, M.W., Villajos, E., Magdaleno, J., ... & Ayala, Y. (2021). Revisiting the happy-productive worker thesis from a Eudaimonic perspective: A systematic review. *Sustainability, 13*(6), 3174.

Podsakoff, N.P., LePine, J.A. & LePine, M.A. (2007). Differential challenge stressor-hindrance stressor relationships with job attitudes, turnover intentions, turnover, and withdrawal behavior: a meta-analysis. *Journal of Applied Psychology, 92*(2), 438.

Prudenzi, A., Graham, C.D., Clancy, F., Hill, D., O'Driscoll, R., Day, F. & O'Connor, D.B. (2021). Group-based acceptance and commitment therapy interventions for improving general distress and work-related distress in healthcare professionals: A systematic review and meta-analysis. *Journal of Affective Disorders, 295*, 192–202. https://10.1016/j.jad.2021.07.084

Ryff, C.D. (1989). Happiness is everything, or is it? Explorations on the meaning of psychological well-being. *Journal of Personality and Social Psychology, 57*(6), 1069.

Ryff, C.D., Boylan, J.M. & Kirsch, J.A. (2021). Eudaimonic and hedonic well-being. *Measuring Well-Being, 92–15.*

Schabracq, M.J., Winnubst, J.A. & Cooper, C. (Eds.). (2003). *The handbook of work and health psychology.* John Wiley & Sons.

Schetter, C.D. & Dolbier, C. (2011). Resilience in the context of chronic stress and health in adults. *Social and Personality Psychology Compass, 5*(9), 634–652.

Seligman, M.E. (2011). *Flourish: A visionary new understanding of happiness and well-being.* New York: Simon and Schuster.

Selye, H. (1936). A syndrome produced by diverse nocuous agents. *Nature, 138*(3479), 32–32. https://doi.org/10.1038/138032a0

Sonnentag, S. (2018). The recovery paradox: Portraying the complex interplay between job stressors, lack of recovery, and poor well-being. *Research in Organizational Behavior, 38, 169–185.* https://doi.org/10.1016/j.riob.2018.11.002

Tan, N., Yao, J., Lu, Y. & Narayanan, J. (2022). Is 'Zoom fatigue' Real? Video conferencing boosts productivity but worsens well-being. In *Academy of Management Proceedings*, Vol. 2022, No. 1, p. 11198). Briarcliff Manor, NY 10510: Academy of .Management.

Tedeschi, R.G. & Calhoun, L.G. (2004). Posttraumatic growth: conceptual foundations and empirical evidence. *Psychological Inquiry*, *15*(1), 1–8.

Terkel, S. (1977). *Working*. Harmondsworth: Penguin.

Towey-Swift, K.D., Lauvrud, C. & Whittington, R. (2022). Acceptance and commitment therapy (ACT) for professional staff burnout: a systematic review and narrative synthesis of controlled trials. *Journal of Mental Health, 32*(2), 452–464

Unruh, I., Neubert, M., Wilhelm, M. & Euteneuer, F. (2022). ACT in the workplace: A meta-analytic examination of randomized controlled trials. *Journal of Contextual Behavioral Science, 26*, 114–124. https://10.1016/j.jcbs.2022.09.003

Vega-Escaño, J., Porcel-Gálvez, A.M., de Diego-Cordero, R., Romero-Sánchez, J.M., Romero-Saldaña, M. & Barrientos-Trigo, S. (2020). Insomnia interventions in the workplace: a systematic review and meta-analysis. *International Journal of Environmental Research and Public Health, 17*(17), 6401.

Waters, C.S., Frude, N., Flaxman, P.E. & Boyd, J. (2018). Acceptance and commitment therapy (ACT) for clinically distressed health care workers: Waitlist-controlled evaluation of an ACT workshop in a routine practice setting. *British Journal of Clinical Psychology, 57*(1), 82–98.

Windle, G. (2011). What is resilience? A review and concept analysis. *Reviews in Clinical Gerontology, 21*(2), 152–169.

World Health Organization. (2018). International Classification of Diseases, 11th revision, Geneva, Switzerland.

Wright, T.A. & Cropanzano, R. (2004). The role of psychological well-being in job performance: A fresh look at an age-old quest. *Organizational Dynamics*, *33*(4), 338–351.

Zelenski, J.M., Murphy, S.A. & Jenkins, D.A. (2008). The happy-productive worker thesis revisited. *Journal of Happiness Studies, 9*(4), 521–537.

Chapter 6

Work design, organisational change and development

Claire Stone

Overview

This chapter offers an introduction to this field of work, providing insights into the evolution and theoretical underpinnings of both traditional and contemporary organisation development (OD), and describing the relevance of these change approaches to different organisational structures, cultures and needs. The chapter then turns to practical applications, describing two popular contemporary approaches – Appreciative Inquiry and The World Café – before highlighting some important considerations for practitioners on how to approach OD interventions. The chapter ends by highlighting some core practitioner skills and providing insights about working as a practitioner; including the types of roles which are commonly available and how they fit alongside other professional activities, given the wider context for occupational psychology in organisations today.

Learning outcomes

By the end of this chapter you will:

- understand the ways in which organisations evolve through organisational interventions;
- appreciate the differences between traditional and contemporary approaches, and their relevance to different organisational structures, cultures and needs;
- know more about the theoretical underpinnings of this field of work and understand the current developments in relevant research;
- learn about some practical contemporary 'dialogic' organisational development techniques;
- have some ideas for incorporating these skills and approaches in your work.

What is organisational change and development?

A whistle stop tour of four industrial revolutions serves to illustrate how far the nature of work has evolved over the last few centuries (see Figure 6.1 and Chapter 11 for more detail). Different shaped organisations have supported the introduction of water and

DOI: 10.4324/9781003302087-7

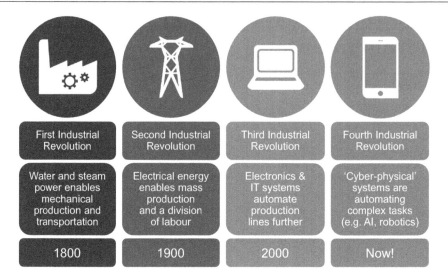

Figure 6.1 The changing focus of work.

steam power; the first assembly line powered by electrical energy; the use of electronics, IT and automation, and the 'cyber-physical' systems in operation today. Just as the purpose and characteristics of organisations have changed radically over time, so has the relevance of different approaches to organisational change and development.

The field of organisation development (OD) emerged around the late 1950s from 'insights from group dynamics and from the theory and practice of planned change' (French & Bell, 1999, p. 1).

As such, traditional organisation development is focused on measuring progress towards a pre-set goal and adopting a problem-solving focus. An early definition is:

> A system-wide application and transfer of behavioural science knowledge to the planned development, improvement, and reinforcement of the strategies, structures and processes that lead to organisation effectiveness.
>
> (Cummings & Worley, 2005, p. 1)

The field has continued to evolve, in line with the 'increasingly turbulent' context of work (French & Bell, 1999), leading up to the VUCA (Volatility, Uncertainty, Complexity and Ambiguity) description of the environment used today (discussed in more depth in Chapter 4). From the 1980s, contemporary organisation development approaches have become more prominent. These more recent additions to our change toolkit are focused on organic, emergent change and adopting a solutions focus. A wider, more recent definition of OD is:

> ... the interdisciplinary field of scholars and practitioners who work collaboratively with organizations and communities to develop their system-wide capacity for effectiveness and vitality ... grounded in the organization and social sciences.
>
> (OD Network, 2022)

In practical terms, a whole spectrum of approaches continues to be used in organisations today. However, the best results are achieved when the adopted change paradigm matches well with an organisation's structure and its culture – 'the way we do things around here' – and when an appropriate consulting stance is used. We will take a look at these important elements in turn.

Traditional organisational development

Traditional organisation development views change as a scientific, logical, rational process and was influenced greatly by the work of Kurt Lewin, Rensis Likert, Douglas McGregor and their colleagues after the Second World War. Lewin's three-stage model describing episodic change – a process of *unfreezing* the old situation, *moving* to a new situation, and *refreezing* changes that have been made – still underlies many change interventions today (French & Bell, 1999). Likert's work on introducing attitude surveys and feedback cycles, to share and improve results, also continues to be used as a 'powerful process for change' (Cummings & Worley, 2005, p. 8). The foundational premises of OD were first influenced by the mechanical sciences (from the 1900s) and biological sciences (from the 1960s). In this paradigm, the focus is on diagnosing the problem that an organisation is facing and working to fix it – or identify changing aspects of the environment in order to adapt internal practices accordingly. Interventions may focus on (a) organising arrangements, such as goals or structure; (b) social factors, such as culture or management style; (c) technology and job design; and / or (d) the physical working environment (Porras & Silvers, 1991). Themes from this era of change include efficiency, local plans, structure and productivity; and strategic plans, alignment and congruence with them (Marshak, 2010).

'Diagnostic' OD

Relatively recently, Bushe and Marshak introduced the term 'Diagnostic OD' to better encapsulate the Traditional OD mindset (Bushe & Marshak, 2009). Diagnostic approaches are based on the paradigm of positivism; meaning that an objective, data-driven analysis takes place to assess the situation, before a step-by-step intervention is planned (Marshak, 2010). Research may involve small groups of employees, including a representative 'diagonal slice' of the organisation. The facilitator, who is external to the system, may take the stance of 'the content expert' – providing information that the client decides that they need, or 'the doctor' – diagnosing what is wrong and prescribing action to remedy the situation. We will return to this idea in more detail later. Consulting methodologies from this era, which share similar problem-solving roots, include Business Process Re-Engineering, Total Quality Management, Continuous Improvement and Six Sigma.

Structure, culture and Diagnostic OD

Organisational structures are described using the following characteristics (Robbins & Judge, 2019):

- Work specialisation – the degree to which activities are subdivided into separate jobs.
- Departmentalisation – the degree to which common tasks are grouped together.

- Chain of command – the line of authority explaining who reports to whom.
- Span of control – the number of individuals a manager can efficiently and effectively manage.
- (De)Centralisation – the location in the structure where decision-making authority lies.
- Formalisation – the degree to which rules and regulations for job behaviours are standardised.
- Boundary spanning – the degree of interaction across set departments.

'The Mechanistic Model' (Burns & Stalker, 1961) – which describes one extreme of organisational structure (see Figure 6.2) – can help to bring to mind the type of culture where Diagnostic OD will fit especially well. Built on Frederick Taylor's *Principles of Scientific Management*, these types of organisation are renowned for bureaucracy and control; have a hierarchical structure with defined departments; have a clear chain of command with decision-making taking place 'at the top'; and have formalised rules and regulations about how people are expected to carry out their roles (Robbins & Judge, 2019). Because their structures are 'functional' and traditionally focused, mature organisations which have been around for three or four decades (Stanford, 2007) are likely to be a good home for Diagnostic OD interventions. These are implemented in a 'top-down', step-by-step manner, enabling leaders in the hierarchy to continue to monitor progress – and to maintain an all-important sense of control.

Work redesign interventions

Work design is an enormously important area of focus for organisational psychologists. Improving the design of work and work environments ('what' we focus on) is frequently the objective of organisational development and change interventions ('how' we go

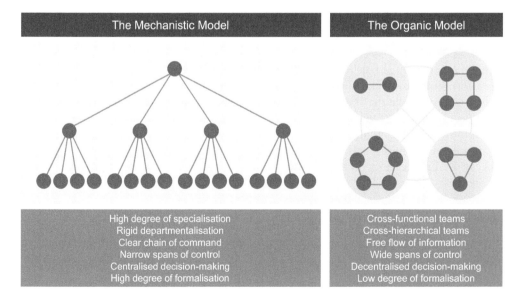

Figure 6.2 Mechanistic vs organic models (adapted from Robbins & Judge, 2019, p. 522).

about it), which will be illustrated when we look at stress risk management interventions. According to the UK Health and Safety Executive (HSE), 17.9 million working days were lost to stress, anxiety or depression in 2019/20 (*IOSH*, 2020) – even before the start of the Covid-19 pandemic. As such, researchers have long sought to understand how to counter workplace stress and improve employee well-being (discussed in more depth in Chapter 5) – and to positively impact individual and organisational performance through their interventions.

Stress risk management interventions

An example of work design at a national level comes from the UK's health and safety regulator, the Health and Safety Executive (HSE), which introduced a set of Management Standards in the early 2000s aimed firmly at the reduction of workplace stress. The standards themselves were informed by 'landmark studies', such as Karasek's (1979) demands-control model (focusing on psychological demands and decision latitude) and subsequent discoveries around the importance of social support at work (Mackay et al., 2004). This stress risk management approach encourages employers to assess risks related to the following areas and to take preventative action:

- Demands – including areas such as workload, work patterns and the working environment.
- Control – how much control (or say) people have in the way they do their work.
- Support – i.e. encouragement, sponsorship and resources provided by managers and colleagues.
- Relationships – i.e. promoting positive working environments, addressing unacceptable behaviour.
- Role – how clear people are on their role and ensuring that they do not have conflicting roles.
- Change – how change (large or small) is managed and communicated in the organisation.

The approach is designed to be introduced within organisations using Diagnostic OD and change methods – and commonly involves a cross-section of employees as part of a 'participative' approach, which we will return to later. Evidence from recent reviews indicates that successful outcomes of such interventions are associated with employee involvement, strong management commitment, and wider integration and alignment with established organisational systems (Daniels et al., 2017; Knight & Parker, 2021).

Contemporary organisational development

Contemporary organisation development techniques are a more recent addition to the OD toolkit, viewing change as an organic process, in direct contrast to Diagnostic OD (see Table 6.1). The contemporary body of knowledge has grown through the work of academics and practitioners alike, and includes widely used techniques such as Appreciative Inquiry (Cooperrider & Srivastva, 1987), Future Search (Weisbord & Janoff, 2000), Open Space Technology (Owen, 1997) and The World Café (Brown & Isaacs, 1995).

Table 6.1 Contrasting assumptions for OD practice (adapted from Marshak 2015, p. 48)

	Diagnostic OD	Dialogic OD
Influence organisation action via:	Objective diagnosis and analysis of existing facts and forces before intervening.	Social inquiry processes that themselves create new awareness, knowledge and possibilities.
Change happens when:	Application of known expertise is used to identify, plan and manage the implementation of episodic change: unfreeze-movement-refreeze.	Engagement of stakeholders in ways that create disruptions and shifts in the on-going patterns of communication and stability lead to the emergence of new possibilities.
Consultant orientation:	Neutral facilitator who stands apart from and acts on the system.	Involved facilitator (or host / convener) who becomes part of and acts with the system.

Illustrations of two of these approaches appear later in this chapter. Bunker and Alban (1997) document this exciting period of evolution, as champions of this school of thought.

The foundational premises of Contemporary OD were influenced by the interpretive sciences (from the 1980s) and the complexity sciences (from the 1990s). In this paradigm, the focus is on solutions or strengths-based inquiry, as opposed to the more traditional problem-focused approach. Bunker and Alban (2006) provide compelling evidence of dialogic interventions being used to facilitate change within and between a whole host of organisations, sectors and communities, and across a range of national cultures. Themes from this era of change include discourse, meaning-making, culture and consciousness; chaos, self-organisation and emergent design (Marshak, 2010).

'Dialogic' OD

At the same time as introducing the term Diagnostic OD, Bushe and Marshak introduced the term 'Dialogic OD' to better encapsulate the Contemporary OD mindset (Bushe & Marshak, 2009). Dialogic approaches are based on the paradigm of social constructionism; meaning that participants each bring along a perspective which is true for them and – when they share their collective knowledge and views – they create new meaning and possibilities (Marshak, 2010). Dialogic techniques use 'Large Group Methods' (Bunker & Alban, 2006) which take place at large events. The target is 'getting the whole system in the room' (Weisbord & Janoff, 2000) as far as possible, and gathering together whole teams and organisations, with a view to creating a compelling future.

But how does change actually occur? In his 'Theory of Change', Bushe describes how a generative image at the heart of the intervention – which may take the form of a picture, a question, a story or an idea – is used to introduce 'disruption' to a system. The generative image is used to evoke a shift in conversations: changing the way people think, influencing the decisions they make, influencing shared attitudes and assumptions, and further shaping their culture. This opens up new ways of thinking and allows new possibilities to emerge (Bushe, 2013). The facilitator, who may be known as a 'host' or 'convener', is considered to be integral to the system; their role is to create a psychologically safe space for these all-important conversations to occur (Bushe, 2010; Marshak, 2015).

Box 6.1   Appreciative Inquiry

Appreciative Inquiry (AI) was developed by David Cooperrider in the 1980s. It is built on the premise that organisations 'move in the direction of what they study' and he describes AI as a 'radical departure from traditional deficit-based change to a positive, strengths-based change approach' (Cooperrider, 2022). In their exploration of positive psychology and work, Linley et al. (2010, p. 6) welcome this 'uplifting' and 'celebratory' approach.

- The methodology involves the 4-D Cycle (see Figure 6.3) which guides an organisation and its members through four stages of exploration of an 'affirmative topic' – an area that they want to discover more about. Large group methods like Appreciative Inquiry take place in the form of large workshops, events or summits, which may last for a few hours or a number of days. The greater the number of people from the system who can be involved in conversation the better.
- During the *Discovery* stage, positive questions are used to identify the unique factors in place when things are going really well. In the *Dream* stage, the focus moves to the vision of the future and 'what might be?' – building on real and positive examples from the past. In the *Design* stage, participants bridge discussions from the preceding stages ('the best of what is' and 'what might be') by generating idealistic propositions on 'what should be'. In the *Destiny* stage, participants are invited to turn the new collective vision into reality by working to align their own activities, interactions and associated processes, with this renewed sense of purpose.

In practical terms, Appreciative Inquiry has been used as a catalyst for positive change in a wide variety of organisations and communities. Well-documented examples include work by the BBC, focusing on culture change, involving 27,000 employees (Cheung-Judge & Powley, 2006) and work by World Vision, focusing on global strategic planning, involving 150 leaders in person and 4,500 individuals by remote, on-line means (Kaplan & Fry, 2006).

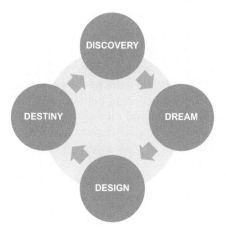

Figure 6.3 Appreciative Inquiry '4-D Cycle' (Adapted from Cooperrider, 2022).

Structure, culture and Dialogic OD

'The Organic Model' (Burns & Stalker, 1961) describes another extreme of organisation structure and can help to bring to mind the type of culture where Dialogic OD will resonate especially well. Renowned for flexibility and innovation, organic organisations have flatter structures – decentralised decision-making (and multiple decision makers) – and operate more loosely, with fewer formal rules, regulations and procedures, and more informal networks (Robbins & Judge, 2019). Stanford (2007) describes modern structures which are nearer to the organic end of the design continuum, including innovative and faster-moving matrix, network and cluster structures. Dialogic techniques are best suited to adaptable cultures where ideas are valued wherever they come from in the organisational structure, and where leaders are comfortable with ambiguity, as Marshak describes:

> While offering new insights and approaches to organisational change, they also suggest a less controllable, more ambiguous world of work calling again for letting go of long established and culturally reinforced notions of command and control leadership.
>
> (Marshak, 2016, p. 14)

A summary of the contrasting assumptions between traditional Diagnostic OD and contemporary Dialogic OD that have been discussed appear in Table 6.1.

Box 6.2   Case study: welcome to the World Café

Following significant changes in working practices during the Covid-19 pandemic, the Chief Executive of Uttlesford Citizens Advice – consisting of 13 members of staff, 61 volunteers and 10 trustees – decided to bring together her team to better define what they stand for and to continue to improve the way they work together. A facilitator was appointed to design a series of 2-hour interactive workshops to enable the team to build connections between existing and new staff, volunteers and trustees. Discussions centred on Citizens Advice national role in society, and their mission and collective values, as well as the special skills and qualities the team use locally on a day-to-day basis, and their accompanying everyday behaviours. The workshop sessions used a World Café approach to explore behaviours that participants see, hear and experience on a daily basis and how well they align with the organisation's mission and values. This promoted discussions about behaviours they all want to continue to see – or see 'more of' – and behaviours which are less congruent with what the organisation stands for, and they all want to see 'less of'.

During the three rounds of World Café activity, participants were invited to 'step into the shoes' of staff, volunteers and clients to look at the service they provide from different perspectives.

In Round 1, each group started with a blank sheet of flipchart paper and red, green or blue marker pens and were asked to explore one of three perspectives. After intense discussion and note making, they were asked to move clockwise to explore a new viewpoint, taking the pens with them.

In Round 2, their task was to read carefully what the preceding group had written and to build on their thoughts.

In Round 3, they moved to the remaining perspective and their task was to build on the other two groups' work. They then moved 'home' to their original flipchart to discover how other groups (who had written in other colours) had built on their work – and to explore the themes that were emerging across the group as a whole.

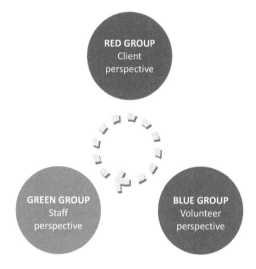

Figure 6.4 'Trying on' different perspectives as part of World Café activity.

Whilst engaging in lively and passionate discussions during these sessions, participants identified significant areas for positive organisational change and development. Event outputs were used to develop a 'Charter for Volunteers' and a 'Charter for Clients', setting expectations for everyone involved in the service, and helping them to provide an even better experience for their clients.

How to approach OD interventions

In this chapter so far we have explored two contrasting types of intervention – traditional Diagnostic OD and contemporary Dialogic OD. But how do practitioners go about introducing these approaches and working with their clients? A number of consulting stances are offered that can be adopted, as appropriate, depending on the situation and the client's needs.

Participative action research

Lewin's well-cited phrase 'no action without research, and no research without action' neatly summarises the action-research process which he and others developed. With its focus on working with objective data, action research is described as a 'cornerstone' of traditional organisation development by French and Bell, who define it as:

... the process of systematically collecting research data about an on-going system relative to some objective, goal, or need of that system; feeding these data back into the
system; taking actions by altering selected variables within the system based both on the
data and on hypotheses; and evaluating the results of actions by collecting more data.

(French and Bell, 1999, p. 130)

Cummings and Worley (2005) bring this definition to life by outlining eight main steps
of the process:

- Problem identification – which occurs when a sponsor in an organisation identifies a
  problem and decides to seek the help of an OD practitioner to help to solve it.
- Consultation with a behavioural science expert – which involves an initial discussion
  between the client sponsor and practitioner, who exchange perspectives, and begin a
  process of collaboration.
- Data gathering and preliminary diagnosis – which is undertaken by the practitioner,
  working with organisation members, using interviews, observation, questionnaires
  and performance data.
- Feedback to a key client or group – which involves a presentation of initial findings to all of the involved stakeholders in a meeting format, enabling discussion and
  collaboration.
- Joint diagnosis of the problem – where involved parties discuss and validate the data,
  deciding which problem(s) they want to work on and agreeing the future direction of
  the work.
- Joint action planning – where involved parties work together to jointly agree a specific
  course of action (marking the beginning of the moving phase of Lewin's three-stage
  model).
- Action – which involves the organisation moving from the present state to a desired
  state, through a process of transition.
- Data gathering after action – which marks the beginning of a new cyclical process; this
  data is fed back to the key client or group and the iterative process continues.

The process is undertaken as a partnership between the client and the practitioner. It
brings value to everyone involved, solving a practical problem for the client, adding
knowledge of theory and practice in the given area for the practitioner, and facilitating
a sharing of skills between all of the parties involved – thus making the client more
self-sufficient in future. Participative Action Research works particularly well as part of
a Diagnostic OD intervention – and this type of cycle is advocated as part of the HSE
Management Standards process, which was explored earlier. In this variation of the
approach, the groups who will ultimately be involved in taking action are involved in the
process from the outset. This garners engagement from the group; enhances the accuracy
and relevance of data gathered; ensures that recommendations are grounded in practical
reality; and increases the likelihood that actions from the agenda for change will be car-
ried out (French & Bell, 1999).

Process Consultation and the helping relationship

Edgar Schein's body of work, which has greatly advanced theory in the areas of culture,
leadership and working in organisations, spans six decades. His early work on Process

Consultation has been revisited over a number of years (Schein, 1969; 1999) and focuses on developing an authentic helping relationship between the practitioner and the client – driven by the client's needs. Cummings and Worley describe this stance below:

> Process consultation is as much a philosophy as a set of techniques aimed at performing this helping relationship. The philosophy ensures that those who are receiving the help own their problems, gains the skills and expertise to diagnose them and solve them themselves. Process consultation is an approach to helping people and groups help themselves.
>
> (Cummings & Worley, 2005, p. 220)

Schein initially proposed ten principles to guide practitioners in their helping actions (Schein, 1999). These included 'always try to be helpful'; 'always stay in touch with the current reality' (being mindful of the client's and your own reactions); 'access your ignorance' (think about what is known, assumed, or remains unknown); and – role modelling openness – 'when in doubt, share the problem'. Practitioners were reminded that even an *initial* conversation is part of the intervention.

Whilst Participative Action Research involves working jointly with the client from the outset, Schein argues that 'it would also be understood tacitly that the OD practitioner's knowledge and experience would influence how the client thinks and what solution might be developed' – i.e. the intervention will always be biased by the research agenda (Schein, 2016a, p. 239). Working instead to match the client's agenda, Schein explains how he uses his 'agility' to move between three fundamentally different helping roles during the course of their relationship. These roles are:

- the expert – whose role is directly providing information that the client decides that they need;
- the doctor – whose role is making a diagnosis of what is wrong and prescribing a remedy; and
- the process consultant – whose role is staying in the role of 'helping the client to solve a problem or achieve whatever it is that the client aspires to' (Schein, 2016a, p. 239).

In recent work – such as Humble Inquiry (Schein, 2013, 2021), Humble Consulting (Schein, 2016b), and Humble Leadership (Schein, 2018) – Schein's starting position is always now as 'the process consultant'; operating with an attitude of curiosity, commitment and caring, and fuelled by the 'spirit of inquiry'. This enables him to begin to build a trusting relationship, to best understand where the client is coming from, and to determine which of the three helping roles he should adopt next. In his own words:

> This process must start by intervening in a Dialogic OD manner using Humble Inquiry to build a relationship with the client that enables us to determine how best to help. We can then decide whether to continue in a dialogic manner or shift to being an expert or doctor in the more Diagnostic OD process. That, in turn, will be determined by our joint assessment with the client of whether we are dealing with a technical or adaptive type of problem.
>
> (Schein, 2016a, p. 258)

In the final section, we will explore the new knowledge and skills needed by OD practitioners today, as well as looking at an array of settings where practitioners can put these skills into practice.

Box 6.3   Knowledge and skills for a new era

Recommended skills for future practitioners include (Warrick, 2016, p. 433):

- knowledge of OD – including its history and its values, and past and present practices;
- consulting skills – such as contracting; communicating ideas; traditional data collection, analysis and feedback; and learning from practice;
- conceptual skills – including an ability to take a 'big picture' perspective, to design interventions to fit with the client's culture and needs;
- interpersonal skills – such as self-awareness, an ability to build trusting relationships, a willingness to grow and learn, and a desire to promote the value and success of others;
- communication skills – such as listening, coaching, facilitating, and providing helpful feedback;
- training and development skills – such as 'educating people on the importance of OD, change, and transformation'; and
- sound ethical and business awareness.

As we enter a new era, where Dialogic OD becomes a more prominent practice, Bushe and Marshak argue for an increasing focus on the knowledge and skills which underpin contemporary activities. This is especially important, as many Dialogic OD practitioners enter the field because of specialist involvement in a specific method, such as Appreciative Inquiry or Future Search, rather than adopting a more general view (Bushe, 2013). They encourage a further focus on:

- knowledge areas – such as appreciation of Diagnostic and Dialogic philosophical standpoints;
- dialogic skills – including an ability to work with generative images and facilitate 'generativity';
- strategic process design skills – including an ability to amplify new ideas across the organisation;
- event facilitation skills – such as creating a 'safe space' which enables conversations to occur;
- ethical considerations – including encouraging the practitioner to develop awareness of their own impact on the system, through self-reflexive learning (Bushe & Marshak, 2015, p. 411).

Working as a practitioner

Organisational development practitioners work in a variety of settings, including in-house roles and external consultancies, as well as working as independent consultants. In large organisations, specialist organisational development roles may sit within human resources, employee engagement or change teams (or other strategic roles which have a remit to work right across the company); whilst in smaller organisations, these activities may be part of a role which has a wider array of OD responsibilities. The naming of roles varies from sector to sector. In the NHS, where there are 1.2 million employees working in England alone, there is a great focus on building a skilled OD community through the efforts of NHS Employers and the NHS Leadership Academy:

> OD practitioners make a real difference to the lives of staff and patients ... They lead and contribute to work that improves patient safety, reduces waiting times, improves the experiences of staff and creates conditions for transformation ... CEOs want OD practitioners to co-create the processes for exploration of deep-rooted problems, cor-relating theory and practice as well as holding up a mirror to the organisation.
>
> (Taylor-Pitt & Dumain, 2022)

If you are interested in becoming an OD practitioner, the CIPD (Chartered Institute of Personnel and Development) consider Organisation Development and Design to be an area of specialist knowledge of their Profession Map. They provide learning resources and 'thought pieces' to help practitioners – and would-be practitioners – to develop their knowledge and skills and to become accredited members of the CIPD, as a professional body. Alternatively, the Organisation Development Network has developed a Global OD Competency Framework™ and provides a wide range of learning and development resources, including webinars and virtual access to their annual conference. The Association for Business Psychology (ABP), championing work in employee, marketing and consumer psychology, and behavioural economics, also provides multi-media news, learning resources and case studies which provide useful insights into working in these types of roles.

Conclusion

The skills of organisational development practitioners can be used in a wide range of settings – from small informal team meetings to large-scale organisation-wide interventions – and can help to act as a catalyst for change across whole communities. In this chapter, we have looked at different types of organisational development; a helpful delineation is 'Diagnostic OD is all about solving technical problems and Dialogic OD is all about helping clients to adapt to their complex, ever-changing environment' (Schein, 2016a, p. 238). We have also looked at the structures and cultures in which approaches best fit, alongside different consulting stances that practitioners may choose to adopt, according to their client's needs. Further resources and links are provided below, in case you would like to find out more about this complex and intriguing area of work.

Explore further

More information on methods described in this chapter can be accessed via the following
    weblinks:

Appreciative Inquiry – www.davidcooperrider.com/ai-process
The World Café – http://theworldcafe.com
Future Search – https://futuresearch.net
Open Space Technology – https://openspaceworld.org
Practical advice and insights are offered by the following practitioner bodies:
Chartered Institute of Personnel and Development (CIPD) – www.cipd.co.uk
Organization Development Network (ODN) – www.odnetwork.org
The Association for Business Psychology (ABP) – https://theabp.org.uk
NHS 'Do OD' – www.leadershipacademy.nhs.uk/resources/organisational-development/
HSE www.hse.gov.uk/stress)

The following books provide invaluable insights on helping people to navigate through
    change:
Bridges, W. (2009). Managing Transitions: Making the Most of Change (3rd Edition).
    London: Nicholas Brealey Publishing. For information on the Transition Model see
    https://wmbridges.com/
Kübler-Ross, E. (1969). On Death and Dying. New York: Simon & Schuster. For informa-
    tion on the Change Curve see www.ekrfoundation.org/5-stages-of-grief/change-curve/

References

Brown, J. & Isaacs, D. (1995). Building corporations as communities: Merging the best of two
    worlds. In K. Gozdz (Ed.) *Community building: Renewing spirit and learning in business* (pp.
    69–83). San Francisco: New Leaders Press.
Bunker, B.B. & Alban, B.T. (1997). *Large group interventions: engaging the whole system for rapid
    change.* San Francisco: Jossey-Bass.
Bunker, B.B. & Alban, B.T. (2006). *The handbook of large group methods: Creating systemic
    change in organizations and communities.* San Francisco: Jossey-Bass Business & Management.
Burns, T. & Stalker, G.M. (1961). *The management of innovation.* [On-line]. Oxford. Available
    from: www.doi.org/10.1093/acprof:oso/9780198288787.001.0001 [Accessed November 2022].
Bushe, G.R. (2010). Being the container in Dialogic OD. *Practising Social Change.* Issue 2, 10–15.
Bushe, G.R. (2013). Dialogic OD: A theory of practice. *OD Practitioner.* 45(1), 11–17.
Bushe, G.R. & Marshak, R.J. (2009). Revisioning organization development: Diagnostic and
    dialogic premises and patterns of practice. *The Journal of Applied Behavioral Science.* 45(3),
    348–368.
Bushe, G.R. & Marshak, R.J. (Eds.) (2015). *Dialogic organization development: The theory and
    practice of transformational change.* Oakland, CA: Berrett-Koehler Publishers.
Cheung-Judge, M. & Powley, E.H. (2006). Innovation at the BBC: Engaging an entire organization.
    In Bunker, B.B. & Alban, B.T. (Eds.). *The handbook of large group methods: Creating systemic
    change in organizations and communities* (pp. 45–61). Jossey-Bass Business & Management.
Cooperrider, D. (2022). What is Appreciative Inquiry? [On-line]. Cleveland, Ohio. Available from
    www.davidcooperrider.com/ai-process/ [Accessed November 2022].
Cooperrider, D.L. & Srivastva, S. (1987). Appreciative Inquiry in organizational life. *Research in
    Organizational Change and Development.* 1, 129–169.

Cummings, T.G. & Worley, C.G. (2005). *Organisation Development & Change* (Eighth Edition). Thomson South-Western.

Daniels, K., Gedikli, C., Watson, D., Semkina, A. & Vaughn, O. (2017). Job design, employment practices and well-being: A systematic review of intervention studies. *Ergonomics*. 60(9), 1177–1196. https://doi.org/10.1080/00140139.2017.1303085

French, W.L. & Bell, C.H. (1999). *Organisation Development* (Sixth Edition). New Jersey: Prentice Hall.

IOSH (2020) 17.9 million working days lost due to mental ill-health. *IOSH Magazine*, 5 November. www.ioshmagazine.com/2020/11/05/179-million-working-days-lost-due-mental-ill-health

Kaplan, S. & Fry, R. (2006). Whole system engagement through collaborative technology at World Vision. In B.B. Bunker & B.T. Alban (Eds.). *The handbook of large group methods: Creating systemic change in organizations and communities* (pp. 62–77). Jossey-Bass Business & Management.

Karasek, R.A. (1979). Job demands, job decision latitude, and mental strain: Implications for job redesign. *Administrative Science Quarterly*, 24(2), 285–308. https://doi.org/10.2307/2392498

Knight, C. & Parker, S.K. (2021). How work redesign interventions affect performance: An evidence-based model from a systematic review. *Human Relations*. 74(1), 69–104. https://doi.org/10.1177/0018726719865604

Linley, P.A., Harrington, S. & Garcea, N. (2010). *Oxford handbook of positive psychology and work*. New York, USA: Oxford University Press.

Mackay, C.J., Cousins, R., Kelly, P.J., Lee, S. & McCaig, R.H. (2004). 'Management Standards' and work-related stress in the UK: Policy background and science. *Work and Stress*. 18(2), 91–112. www.doi.org/10.1080/02678370410001727474

Marshak, R.J. (2010). OD morphogenesis: The emerging dialogic platform of premises. *Practising Social Change*. 2, 4–9.

Marshak, R.J. (2015). My journey into dialogic organization development. *OD Practitioner*. 47(2) 47–52.

Marshak, R.J. (2016). Anxiety and Change in contemporary organization development. *OD Practitioner*. 48(1).

OD Network (2022). *What is Organization Development?* [On-line]. Minnesota, USA. Available from www.odnetwork.org/page/what-is-od [Accessed November 2022].

Owen, H.H. (1997). *Open space technology: A user's guide* (Second Edition). San Francisco: Berrett-Koehler.

Porras, J.I. & Silvers, R.C. (1991). Organization development and transformation. *Annual Review of Psychology*. 42, 51–78. https://doi.org/10.1146/annurev.ps.42.020191.000411

Robbins, S. & Judge, T. (2019) *Organisational behaviour* (Eighteenth Edition). Harlow, UK: Pearson Education Limited.

Schein, E.H. (1969). *Process consultation: Its role in organization development*. Reading, MA: Addison-Wesley.

Schein, E.H. (1999). *Process consultation revisited: Building the helping relationship*. Englewood Cliffs, NJ: Prentice-Hall.

Schein, E.H. (2013). *Humble Inquiry: The gentle art of asking instead of telling*. San Francisco, CA: Berrett-Koehler Publishers.

Schein, E.H. (2016a). Taking culture seriously in organization development. In W.J. Rothwell, J.M. Stavros & R.L. Sullivan (Eds.) *Practicing organization development: Leading transformation and change* (Fourth Edition) (pp. 233–244). New York: John Wiley and Sons, Inc.

Schein, E.H. (2016b). *Humble consulting: How to provide real help faster*. San Francisco, CA: Berrett-Koehler Publishers.

Schein, E.H. & Schein, P.A. (2018). *Humble leadership: The power of relationships, openness, and trust*. San Francisco, CA: Berrett-Koehler Publishers.

Schein, E.H. & Schein, P.A. (2021). *Humble Inquiry: The gentle art of asking instead of telling* (Second Edition, Revised and Expanded). San Francisco, CA: Berrett-Koehler Publishers.

Stanford, N. (2007). *Guide to organisational design: Creating high-performing and adaptable enterprises.* New York, USA: Economist Intelligence Unit.

Taylor-Pitt, P. & Dumain, K. (2022). *Building a career within organisation development.* [Online]. London: CIPD. Available from: www.cipd.co.uk/knowledge/strategy/organisational-development/thought-pieces/professional-development [Accessed November 2022].

Warrick, D.D. (2016). Authors' insights on important organization development issues. In W.J. Rothwell, J.M. Stavros & R.L. Sullivan (Eds.) *Practicing organization development: Leading transformation and change* (Fourth Edition, pp. 429–437). New York: John Wiley and Sons, Inc..

Weisbord, M.R. & Janoff, S. (2000). *Future search: An action guide to finding common ground in organizations and communities* (Second *Edition).* San Francisco: Berrett Koehler.

Part II

The core areas in focus

Chapter 7

Psychological assessment in focus
Psychometrics

Suchi Pathak

Overview

This chapter offers an overview of the field of psychometrics, past and present. It discusses the different types of psychometric assessments that are commonly used, and provides a brief history of how they have evolved over time. It then focuses on the use and benefits of psychometrics in the workplace, the different types of assessments, the theories behind them and different formats of assessments. The chapter covers how psychometric assessments are constructed to help you understand the science and rigour behind a credible assessment. A case study shows the tangible outcomes and Return on Investment (ROI) of using psychometrics for decision support in recruitment and retention and the chapter ends with a brief glance at how the field of psychometrics is evolving using technology, big data and social media.

Learning outcomes

By the end of this chapter, you will:

- have learnt the definition of psychometrics and the benefits of using them in the workplace;
- understand the differences between types of tests, including examples of test items, and the history behind them;
- know how psychometrics are constructed, scored and evaluated
- realise the value of demonstrating the return on investment (ROI) for using psychometrics for selection;
- understand the role that technology plays in psychometrics, and how it has advanced the field, including some areas that require further research.

What are psychometrics?

Psychometric tests and assessments are tools used to measure psychological characteristics (e.g., people's motivation, personality traits and general intelligence). This area of

DOI: 10.4324/9781003302087-9

psychology is concerned with designing and evaluating assessments that measure and quantify psychological attributes such as behaviour, cognitive function and performance.

With regards to terminology, psychometric assessments are often referred to as 'tests' – but some of these assessments are not 'tests' with right or wrong answers, so other terms can be *tool, survey, inventory, assessment* or *instrument*.

Why use psychometrics?

Psychometrics are a way of gathering information about a person's characteristics and behaviour. An alternative to psychometrics would be observation. However, gathering the kind of information that you could deduce from a psychometric assessment through observation could take months, or years, of watching people in different situations. Imagine trying to uncover what motivates someone, how they react emotionally to a variety of situations, and how open they are to learning new things by observation alone? This is practically impossible at work, and you may find yourself served with a restraining order by the person you are observing!

Therefore, a psychometric assessment is a much faster way to understand how someone is likely to behave in a variety of different situations. Psychometric tests tend to be accurate – in fact, a study found that personality predictions from psychometric data were more accurate than those made by participants' friends and family members (Youyou et al., 2015).

Another benefit of psychometrics is that everyone's results are compared to a benchmark, so psychometrics are considered less biased and more objective than people's opinion. Relying on people's opinions can be problematic, because many times they are distorted by unconscious bias. Unconscious biases are omnipresent in life and the workplace and can negatively shape the culture of an organisation and affect who is hired, promoted and developed (McCormick, 2015).

Why use psychometrics in the workplace?

Well-researched and credible psychometric assessments are:

- objective because they compare people in a standardised way and therefore are not influenced by personal opinions or biases;
- reliable and provide consistent results – everyone who takes the assessment benefits from the same experience and are assessed in controlled conditions, regardless of their gender, age, ethnicity or job role;
- valid and therefore accurately measure what they are aiming to measure.

The information deduced by psychometrics can predict individuals' motivation, performance, advancement and attitudes (Barrick et al., 2001; Judge et al., 2002; Ones et al., 2007).

How can psychometrics be used in the workplace?

Psychometrics can be used for many purposes in organisations. The most prominent uses are:

- **Recruitment, selection and promotion** – psychometrics can help to identify and select applicants with the potential to fit the role's demands and become high-performing employees. This can reduce the time and cost of recruitment and succession planning.
- **Retention** – psychometrics can identify who is more suited for a role and therefore likely to stay in the organisation for a longer period of time.
- **Training and development** – psychometrics help to identify individual and group training needs, for more motivated, engaged and productive teams.
- **Career development and progression** – psychometrics can help to gauge if someone is suited to another role and identify training and development areas to help them to transition into that role.
- **Coaching** – psychometric assessments can assist people being coached to increase their awareness of their preferences, work style and aspects about themselves that they would like to develop. It can help the coach and the coachee to identify goals to work towards.
- **Team building** – Team cooperation and cohesion can be improved by using psychometrics to help each team member better understand their colleagues' communication style, what motivates them, their preferred way to receive information and their learning preferences.

What type of psychometric tests are there?

Psychometric assessments fall into two broad categories: assessments of maximum performance, and assessments of typical performance.

Measures of maximum performance

These include attainment (e.g., testing knowledge of skills or a curriculum) and ability (e.g., testing your potential to learn). These tests usually include questions that have correct and incorrect answers or measure how well someone can perform a task.

Attainment tests assess people's knowledge or assess what they can do (e.g., fixing a motor or rectifying a programming bug).

Ability tests assess what people are capable of learning or doing. For example, how quickly someone is likely to understand written passages or handle and interpret numerical data.

Early measures of intelligence were authored by Sir Francis Galton (Galton, 1892) and Alfred Binet (Binet & Simon, 1948). Since then, there have been many theories of intelligence (and many debates about what intelligence is!), but the main types of tests seen in the workplace tend to support a theory called 'General Intelligence', also known as 'G' (Carroll, 1993). General Intelligence assumes that people's general mental ability is what underlies their ability to perform more specific mental skills.

An example of how G works is by looking at athleticism – if someone is a very good swimmer, that doesn't necessarily mean that they will be a great cyclist. However, because the swimmer is athletic, they will probably perform much better on other physical activities than people who have less stamina or are less coordinated.

So if someone has high General Intelligence, or G, they are more likely to be skilled at tasks such as working with numbers (numerical ability), spatial ability, reasoning or deducing from written information (verbal reasoning), and spotting similarities and differences quickly (perceptual speed).

Different formats of maximum performance tests: speed tests versus power tests

Measures of maximum performance can be further classified by their format. Some tests have questions that are relatively easy to complete but are scored on how many questions are completed correctly within a strict time limit. Scoring tends to reflect the speed and accuracy with which someone answers questions. These are called **Speed Tests.**

Other tests have items that are more difficult to complete and are designed to see how many questions someone can answer correctly. Although these tests usually have a time limit, they are designed so that most people can answer all the questions within it. These are called **Power Tests.**

Measures of typical performance

Examples of typical performance include:

- attitudes
- emotional intelligence
- integrity
- interests
- motivation values
- personality.

These tests do not have 'right' or 'wrong' answers, nor do they tend to have time limits, as they are measuring how someone typically behaves in a work or team setting. Measures of typical performance assume that by measuring someone's typical behaviour, you can gauge how they would react to most situations.

Personality questionnaires

Like ability tests, personality questionnaires are underpinned by a specific theory of personality. There are many theories of personality, such as psychoanalytic (Freud, 1900), Humanistic (Rogers, 1959), Type (Jung, 1921) and Trait (Cattell, 1965, McCrae & Costa, 1987).

However, many personality measures used in occupational settings are based on 'Trait' personality theory, which assumes that people have habitual patterns driven by their underlying personality traits. These traits are deeply embedded and are relatively consistent over situations and influence how someone behaves (McCrae & Costa, 1984).

Trait theory also assumes that traits fall on a spectrum, from being exhibited rarely at one end of the spectrum to being exhibited frequently at the other end. For example, some people are very talkative and social, and some people are quiet and prefer to spend time on their own. Others are in the middle and can be talkative, social, *and* like to spend periods of time on their own.

The Five Factor Theory of personality (McCrae & Costa, 1987), also referred to as the 'Big 5' theory, is an example of a trait theory, and assumes that people differ on five main factors of personality

- Openness to Experience (how curious and creative people are);
- Conscientiousness (how organised, productive and responsible people are);
- Extraversion (how sociable and talkative people are);
- Agreeableness (how cooperative and supportive people are); and
- Neuroticism (how emotionally stable people are).

Box 7.1   Different assessment formats

There are many types of questions with psychometrics assessments, all serving a different purpose with their own pros and cons. For more information on rating scales, please see the book *Modern Psychometrics* (Rust et al., 2020):

Multiple-choice questions – test takers are given a few responses to choose from and must select a single response. For example:

17 rounded to the nearest 10 is:

a 10
b 17
c 20

Forced Choice Scale – test takers must choose between options. For example, they might be presented with four statements or words from which they choose one statement that is most like them and one statement that is least like them:

Please choose which statement is 'most' like you and 'least' like you:

a I enjoy socialising with people at work
b I plan out all of my tasks for the week
c I enjoy debating with people
d I prefer working in environments with variety

Rating Scale – test takers are asked to rate the degree of agreement or disagreement to a certain statement by choosing a response on a continuum:

I enjoy socialising with people at work:

Strongly Disagree   Strongly Agree

1	2	3	4	5	6	7	8	9	10

How are psychometric tests constructed?

Psychometric tests are created by an individual or a group of Test Authors. The process for constructing a psychometric test is outlined below – please note this is a high-level overview of constructing an assessment. For more detail, please refer to *Modern Psychometrics* by Rust et al. (2020) (see Figure 7.1).

Step 1 – What is the purpose or idea? What are you trying to achieve?

If you were designing a psychometric assessment, first you would need to decide why you are developing the assessment – what do you want to measure and why?

Do you want the assessment to understand what motivates people so that you can use it for job coaching? Do you want to measure people's interests to see which career they are well-suited for? Or do you want to measure personality to understand which personality traits are related to high performance in job roles?

The reason for creating the test will help you decide which psychological theory you choose to base your assessment on.

For example, imagine you want to understand which elements of personality are related to job performance.

• **Choosing a theory** – first, you need to choose a theory of personality that you believe will help you to achieve your purpose. For example, if you intend to measure the trait of extraversion, you might choose a well-known and well-researched theory such as

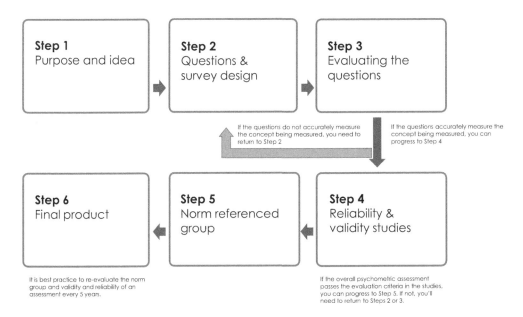

Figure 7.1 The process of designing psychometrics.

the Five Factor Theory of personality (McCrae & Costa, 1987). It is important to ensure the foundation of your assessment is credible.

Step 2 – Designing the questionnaire and writing questions/items

Once you have a theory of personality that you would like to measure, you need to write questions for each of the elements you want to measure (this process is called item writing) and the format of the questionnaire (this is often called questionnaire design).

- **Questionnaire design** – Before you write your items, you'll need to decide the type of response scale you would like to use – i.e., multiple choice, forced choice or a rating scale (see Box 7.1). Each response format has its benefits. But importantly, the format of your questions will influence how you write your questions. There are lots of studies showing the benefits and issues with different formats, and as a test author myself, I can say that this is not an easy decision to make!
- **Item writing** – Next you will need to write the questions in the questionnaire. Let's take conscientiousness as a factor of personality as an example – if you want to measure how conscientiousness people are, you need to write questions that address all the ways that conscientiousness manifests itself in the workplace. For example, *how much someone tends to plan and organise their work*; or *how much someone strives to complete high-quality work*. It is important to phrase these questions carefully to elicit the right traits. Therefore, you often write the same question in a few different ways, with many items/questions for each personality factor. The reason for this is outlined below in 'item evaluation'.

Step 3 – Item evaluation

To evaluate the questions, you would give them to a sample of respondents that reflect the types of people you are going to use the test for. So, if you are creating an assessment aimed at people at work, you will need a representative group of the working population to test your questions on.

Once the sample of people have completed the assessment, a series of checks need to be performed to see which questions are working (there will always be some questions that don't work out, so be prepared!).

Writing questions and evaluating them is a process in itself – you analyse items, some of them don't work, so you re-write them or write different questions. You then run a series of analyses to evaluate the new questions, and the cycle goes on until you have your final set of questions, and a final assessment.

Some examples of item analysis are mentioned below, but for a comprehensive guide to item analysis, please see the book *Modern Psychometrics* by Rust et al., 2020.

- **Item discrimination** – in this case, the word 'discrimination' is a good thing. It ensures that test items can distinguish between people who are high scoring on a trait (e.g. high or low IQ).
- **Item distribution** – This evaluates how 'spread out' people's responses are for each item. The item would not be particularly useful if everyone had the same response, and therefore such an item would be discarded.

Step 4 – Reliability and validity studies

Once you have your final items, a series of analyses need to be conducted on the assessment as a whole to prove it is accurate (reliability) and serves its purpose (validity). Below are some of the main ways to analyse reliability and validity:

Reliability

Internal consistency

This determines whether the questions that measure specific cognitive or personality factors correlate with each other – this is also called Cronbach's Alpha (Cronbach, 1951). This analysis can be conducted by utilising software such as Statistical Package for Social Sciences (SPSS), R-Studio or Python.

   Another way to measure internal consistency is to conduct a 'split-half test'. This can also be conducted using software and involves randomly splitting a test into two halves to see how consistent people's responses are.

Test-retest reliability

If you are measuring a stable construct such as personality or cognitive ability, people's scores are unlikely to change in a relatively short period of time, so you need to test the reliability of your assessment results. This involves administering the assessment to people for the first time (test) and then again later (retest) to see if their responses are consistent. If they are not consistent, someone might score high on conscientiousness the first time they take the assessment and low on conscientiousness the second time they take the assessment – this means your questionnaire has low test-retest reliability. If this is the case, some of your questions may need to be rewritten and trialled again.

Parallel forms

You can also determine the reliability of your assessment by creating 'parallel forms' where you have two similar versions of the same test. Each version is given to the same group of people to see how consistent their overall scores are.

Validity

Content validity

This measures whether your assessment fully covers the content that you designed it to measure. When a test has content validity, the questions on the test represent the entire range of questions the test should cover. Content validity is usually judged by subject matter experts.

Construct validity

This might seem obvious, but you do need to check that your psychometrics assessment measures what you want it to measure(!). The best way to do this is to administer a separate assessment that purports to measure what you are trying to measure (and has already been under the rigorous checks of reliability and validity) to the same group of people you are testing your assessment on. For example, if your assessment measures extraversion, you can also ask respondents to take a well-researched assessment that measures sociability. Once you have the results of the two assessments, you can correlate them to see if you are accurately measuring the construct you intended. In other words, people who score high on extraversion in your assessment should score high on sociability in the other assessment (and vice versa).

Criterion-related validity

Criterion-related validity is also referred to as 'Predictive Validity' and measures whether your assessment relates to a certain outcome (criterion). A test has criterion-related validity when it is effective at predicting certain criteria. If we take job performance as an example of a criterion, your assessment will have demonstrated criterion-related validity if people's assessment scores are related to job performance.

See Chapter 2 for further detail on reliability and validity in the context of selection more broadly.

Test equivalence and adverse impact testing

It is important that your test is fair and free from bias. This means that a test should not inadvertently disadvantage people based on their age, gender, ethnicity etc. For example, some studies have shown that tests of general cognitive ability demonstrate adverse impact against minorities (Campbell, 1996).

Adverse impact is demonstrated when cognitive ability tests are used in selection decisions and group differences between people in majority and minority group lead to lower job selection rates for minority groups because they score lower (on average) than the majority group (Schmidt, 1988). Therefore, it is important to check that your assessment does not have significant group differences that may lead to adverse impact. If your assessment does show group differences, you will have to analyse the assessment questions/items (referred to as Differential Item Functioning, or DIF), as this will indicate the extent to which specific items might be measuring different abilities for different subgroups. (For more information see Holland & Wainer, 2012).

Step 5 – Creating a norm referenced group

Psychometric assessments results are standardised. This often means that a person's score is compared to a 'norm group', which is a large group of people who have completed the same test or questionnaire.

The reasons for comparing a person's score to a norm group is to give context to the score. For example, if you receive a score of '115' on a test, what does this mean? It's impossible to tell until you compare it to a group of other people who have completed the same test. You can then say whether your score of 115 is below average, average or above average.

It's important that a norm group is representative of the people you intend to use the assessment for. To ensure a fair assessment, if you are using the assessment for people in jobs, you need to ensure that the norm group contains a representative sample of people from the working population (including a variety of roles, industries, ages, genders and ethnicities).

Step 6 – Final assessment and making sure your assessment stays up to date

Once you have your final assessment and norm group, it is important to ensure that the assessment stays current for the purpose for which you are using it. Therefore, updating the norm group periodically is important (Evers et al., 2013). For example, there have been significant changes in the demographic makeup in the workplace. One example is there are now 185% more over-65s in the workforce than in 1992 (Boys, 2019). It is important to ensure your norm group is updated to reflect these changes.

The process that is described above is a basic overview of designing and validating an assessment. There are more advanced methodologies that are beyond the scope of this chapter that you may want to explore further. Please refer to the 'Explore Further' section.

Box 7.2   Case study: using psychometrics in practice

Overview

The client's sales organisation struggled with low performance and a high rate of turnover in their sales team. By understanding the personality traits that differentiated high performers and low performers, the client understood why some people performed better than others. By using this information, the client saw significant improvements in their business.

The problem

The client was hiring new people into the role who were not fulfilling their sales targets until they had been in the role for at least 18 months. The organisation also suffered from high turnover as 30% of people were leaving after six months in the role. Both of these issues meant that the organisation was over-spending in the areas of recruitment and training.

The solution

The client worked with a psychometrician to understand why some people were performing better than others, by identifying the key behavioural style that differentiated high performing salespeople from low performing salespeople. To find these behavioural differences, the psychometrician administered a personality assessment to the current sales team and used performance and tenure data to perform statistical analyses to find which personality traits were related to high performance and time spent in the role.

Once a 'high performer trait profile' was established, the client used the personality assessment as part of their recruitment process to understand how each candidate aligned with the high performer traits.

Eighteen months later, the client and the psychometrician conducted a criterion-related validity study to assess whether using the personality assessment had improved performance and lowered turnover.

They found that new hires who were aligned to the personality traits in the high performer trait profile sold 2.7 times more than new hires that did not align with the high performer traits. They also found that by hiring people who were aligned to the high performer traits, their attrition rates dropped, and more people were staying in the role.

The role of technology in psychometrics and future directions

The field of psychometrics has changed in recent years. It has incorporated technology and emerging principles from other fields, some of which are listed below:

Gauging personality and ability via digital footprints

The traditional way to capture psychometric information has been via questionnaires, surveys and tests administered to the test taker. Recently, researchers have started to use technology and people's digital footprints to *predict* their behaviour, skills or cognitive ability instead. One example is using someone's Facebook profile information to predict personality (more information in the box below). Others include using people's Facebook profile pictures to predict how extraverted, agreeable and conscientious they are (Hall et al., 2014). Words from people's Twitter 'Tweets' (Lima & de Castro, 2014) and Smartphone data has also been used to predict personality; for example, Chittaranjan et al. (2013) found that extraverts were more likely to receive calls and spend more time on calls.

There could even be benefits from collecting data via digital footprints – imagine not having to complete an actual assessment. Organisations could save time and money; and individuals may prefer to avoid completing tests.

Think, for example, how convenient it is when a website or app knows your location automatically instead of manually inputting it, or you don't know your location (if you are lost or in a new area and need a navigation app to help you get somewhere). Or receiving suggestions based on other people's interests with your personality or cognitive traits (for example, things you might want to buy, tickets for music events, songs or podcasts). Within the context of work, what if you could be sent suggestions for jobs that you would naturally enjoy and be good at without you having to apply for the role? What if you were sent suggestions for roles that you hadn't even heard of?

When organisations are recruiting people, they often find candidates may not want to complete a survey, or take too much time to complete the survey, which delays their recruitment process, so from an organisation's point of view, predicting someone's traits from their digital footprint could make the recruitment process a lot quicker and more accurate (see Box 7.1).

A further benefit of using digital footprints to predict what people are like, is that the amount of data from people's digital footprint can result in relatively accurate predictions (Azucar et al., 2018). Think about all the information points you can get if you track which apps people use (whether they are social, creative or educational apps), *how* people use their apps (do they check their apps only when they receive a notification, do they spend hours on the same app, do they change apps frequently?). Do they take part in online conversations or just observe other people's posts?

However, there are downsides of using digital footprints to predict personality that should be noted. For example, data privacy issues and whether the information is going to be used ethically. Another issue is that social media data may not be as accurate as you might think. It is prone to impression management, or 'self-promoting' (Buffardi & Campbell, 2008) which might reduce the accuracy of predicting what someone is like, rather than what they are portraying online.

Game-based assessments

Data from games are now being used to measure personality and cognitive ability – in other words, people are asked to play game-based assessments instead of answering questions or agreeing or disagreeing with statements like in traditional assessments. For some people, game-based assessment might be more enjoyable. Some studies have shown applicants that play game-based assessments are more likely to accept job offers (Collmus et al., 2016), and that faking and cheating game-based assessments might be harder than traditional assessments (Armstrong et al., 2016).

However, game-based assessments might not be well received by all candidates and employees, especially people who are unfamiliar with games or have not had access to games. More research on the adverse impact of game-based assessments for people in certain demographic groups is still required (for example people of different ages, genders, ethnicities, nationalities, cultures and socio-economic status).

The nature of game-based assessments makes it more difficult to prove their validity and reliability in the way that traditional psychometrics are assessed, so there is a need for more research in this area.

Box 7.3   Using social media to predict someone's personality

Facebook had 2.9 billion monthly active users in January 2022 (Meta Platforms, Inc., 2022). As people utilise social media platforms such as Facebook, they are leaving a digital footprint behind based on their 'likes', what they post and how much they post.

Researchers at the Psychometrics Centre at the University of Cambridge launched a personality assessment on Facebook called 'myPersonality' and it quickly went viral, attracting over six million participants in four years. They then measured how well people's Facebook activity could predict their personality. In one study (Youyou et al., 2015) the authors used Facebook users' likes to predict their self-reported personality traits and found that the correlation between likes and personality was 0.56.

To put that in perspective, if you ask someone's work colleague to predict their personality the accuracy is 0.27, friends can predict at 0.45, family at 0.50 and even someone's spouse can only predict at 0.58. In other words, the computer knows you almost as well as your husband or wife – and better than almost everyone else.

(Stillwell, 2016)

What could the role of technology mean for the future of selection and assessment?

Potentially, companies could surmise applicants' personality without the applicant even completing a psychometrics assessment. There are various 'pros' and 'cons' of this approach:

Pros

Improve hiring efficiency – in the era of the 'great resignation' where 4.4 million Americans resigned from their jobs in March 2021(U.S. Bureau of Labour Statistics, 2022), there are many open vacancies in organisations. If organisations could capture people's personality using social media and utilise this information to assess suitability for the role, this could (a) reduce the time to hire (as applicants would not need to take a personality assessment in the recruitment process), (b) increase the number of applicants per role (as organisations could reach out to people who were suitable for the role, without having to wait for the person to actively apply for the role).

Cons

Potentially perpetuating bias – there are some ethical issues with using people's social media for recruitment (discussed in the 'Psychological Assessment' chapter). Information such as race/ethnicity, gender, religion, marital status, pregnancy status or political affiliation are also available through social media channels (Kluemper & Rosen, 2009; Slovensky & Ross, 2012) and many of these are unrelated to the requirements of the role, and in some cases may result in biasing the views of the recruiter.

Conclusion

In this chapter, we explored the origins and rationale behind psychometric assessments–to objectively measure people's individual differences. We looked at different types of assessments and what they measure. We discussed how psychometric assessments are constructed and the rigorous testing that takes place to prove the effectiveness of the assessment. We discussed how psychometric assessments are currently used to improve various organisational processes, including a case study demonstrating the effectiveness of using psychometrics for hiring. Based on the latest developments in of the field, we speculated about future directions. Throughout the chapter, we discussed the importance of ethical usage of assessments, to ensure they increase the fairness and accuracy of workplace decisions. In the next few years, ethics is likely to become more important than ever, as we are likely to see a rise in the use of digital footprint data, Artificial Intelligence (AI) and Machine Learning (ML) within the field. It is therefore important for psychometricians and psychometric users to stay up to date with the latest technology, to ensure the field of psychometrics is used responsibly.

Explore further

This chapter served as an introduction to the field of psychometrics. If you would like to explore certain elements of this chapter in more detail, below are some useful citations, books and links:

- The British Psychological Society's Psychological Testing Centre has published guides for both test authors and test users. Please see a catalogue of their resources on www.bps.org.uk/about-psychological-testing-centre
- A more detailed exploration of the field of psychometrics, past, present and future can be found in Rust, J., Kosinski, M, Stillwell, D. (2020). *Modern psychometrics: The science of psychological assessment* (Rust et al., 2020).
- Item Response Theory (IRT) is described in an article by Brown and Maydeu-Olivares (2012)
- For information on how psychometrics can be used in effective coaching conversations, please see *Using Psychometrics in Coaching: A Practical Guide* (Florance, 2022).
- Computer Adaptive Testing (CAT) is described in books such as Rust et al. (2020) and Wainer et al. (2000).
- For more information on game-based assessments, please see *Technology and testing: Improving educational and psychological measurement* (Drasgow, 2016).

References

Armstrong, M.B., Landers, R N. & Collmus, A. B. (2016). Gamifying recruitment, selection, training, and performance management: Game-thinking in human resource management. In Harsha Gangadharbatla, Donna Z. Davis (Eds.), *Emerging research and trends in gamification* (pp. 140–165). IGI Global.

Azucar, D., Marengo, D. & Settanni, M. (2018). Predicting the Big 5 personality traits from digital footprints on social media: A meta-analysis. *Personality and Individual Differences, 124,* 150–159.

Barrick, M.R., Mount, M.K. & Judge, T.A. (2001). Personality and performance at the beginning of the new millennium: What do we know and where do we go next? *International Journal of Selection and Assessment, 9,* 9–30.

Binet, A. & Simon, T. (1948). The development of the Binet-Simon Scale, 1905–1908. In W. Dennis (Ed.), *Readings in the history of psychology* (pp. 412–424). Appleton-Century-Crofts. https://doi.org/10.1037/11304-047

Brown, A. & Maydeu-Olivares, A. (2012). Fitting a Thurstonian IRT model to forced-choice data using Mplus. *Behavior Research Methods, 44,* 1135–1147.

Boys, J. (2019). *Megatrends: ageing gracefully: The opportunities of an older workforce.* London, England: CIPD.

Buffardi, L.E. & Campbell, W.K. (2008). Narcissism and social networking web sites. *Personality and Social Psychology Bulletin, 34*(10), 1303–1314.

Campbell, J.P. (1996). Group differences and personnel decisions: Validity, fairness and affirmative action. *Journal of Vocational Behaviour, 49,* 122–158.

Carroll, J.B. (1993). *Human cognitive abilities: A survey of factor-analytic studies* (No. 1). Cambridge University Press.

Cattell, R.B. (1965). *The scientific analysis of Personality.* Baltimore: Penguin Books.

Chittaranjan, G., Blom, J. & Gatica-Perez, D. (2013). Mining large-scale smartphone data for personality studies. *Personal and Ubiquitous Computing, 17,* 433–450. http://dx.doi.org/10.1007/s00779-011-0490-1

Collmus, A.B., Armstrong, M.B. & Landers, R.N. (2016). Game-thinking within social media to recruit and select job candidates. In R.N. Landers & G.B. Schmidt (Eds.) *Social media in employee selection and recruitment* (pp. 103–124). Cham: Springer.

Cronbach L (1951) Coefficient alpha and the internal structure of tests. *Psychometrika* 16: 297–334.

Drasgow, F. (2016). *Technology and testing: Improving educational and psychological measurement* (p. 376). Taylor & Francis.

Evers, A., Muñiz, J., Hagemeister, C., Høstmælingen, A., Lindley, P., Sjöberg, A. & Bartram, D. (2013). Assessing the quality of tests: Revision of the EFPA review model. *Psicothema, 25*(3), 283–291.

Florance, I. (2022). *Using psychometrics in coaching: A practical guide.* Open University Press.

Freud, S. (1900). *The interpretation of dreams.* Leipzig & Vienna: Franz Deuticke.

Galton, F. (1892). *Hereditary genius: An inquiry into its laws and consequences* (Second Edition). London: Macmillan.

Hall, J.A., Pennington, N. & Lueders, A. (2014). Impression management and formation on Facebook: A lens model approach. *New Media & Society, 16*(6), 958–982.

Holland, P.W. & Wainer, H. (2012). *Differential item functioning.* Routledge.

Judge, T.A., Heller, D. & Mount, M.K. (2002). Five-factor model of personality and job satisfaction: A meta-analysis. *Journal of Applied Psychology, 87,* 530–541.

Jung, C.G. (1921, 1971). *Psychological types,* a revision by R.F.C. Hull, trans. by H.G. Baynes. Princeton, NJ: Princeton University Press.

Kemp, S. (2022, February). *Facebook Statistics and Trends.* https://datareportal.com/essential-facebook-stats

Kluemper, D.H. & Rosen, P.A. (2009). Future employment selection methods: evaluating social networking web sites. *Journal of Managerial Psychology, 24*(6), 567–580.

Lima, A.C.E. & De Castro, L.N. (2014). A multi-label, semi-supervised classification approach applied to personality prediction in social media. *Neural Networks, 58,* 122–130.

McCormick, H. (2015). *The real effects of unconscious bias in the workplace.* UNC Executive Development, Kenan-Flagler Business School.

McCrae, R.R. & Costa, P.T. (1984). *Emerging lives, enduring dispositions*. Little, Brown and Co.

McCrae, R.R. & Costa, P.T. (1987). Validation of the five-factor model of personality across instruments and observers. *Journal of Personality and Social Psychology, 52*(1), 81.

Meta Platforms, Inc. (2022) *Meta Reports First Quarter Results 2022*. Menlo Park: Meta Platforms, Inc. https://s21.q4cdn.com/399680738/files/doc_financials/2022/q1/Meta-03.31.2022-Exhibit-99.1_Final.pdf

Ones, D.S., Dilchert, S., Viswesvaran, C. & Judge, T.A. (2007). In support of personality assessment in organizational settings. *Personnel Psychology, 60*, 995–1027.

Rogers, C. (1959). A theory of therapy, personality and interpersonal relationships as developed in the client-centered framework. In S. Koch (ed.), *Psychology: A study of a science. Vol. 3: Formulations of the person and the social context*. New York: McGraw Hill.

Rust, J., Kosinski, M. & Stillwell, D. (2020). *Modern psychometrics: The science of psychological assessment*. Routledge.

Schmidt, F. (1988). The problem of group differences in ability test scores in employment selection. *Journal of Vocational Behaviour, 33*, 272–292.

Slovensky, R. & Ross, W.H. (2012). Should human resource managers use social media to screen job applicants? *Managerial and Legal Issues in the USA, 14*(1), 55–69.

Stillwell, D. (November 2016) There really is a link between your Facebook posts and your personality. www.jbs.cam.ac.uk/insight/2016/link-facebook-posts-your-personality/

U.S. Bureau of Labour Statistics. (2022, May 7) Job Openings and Labour Turnover Summary. Retrieved May 3, 2021) www.bls.gov/news.release/jolts.nr0.htm

Wainer, H., Dorans, N.J., Flaugher, R., Green, B.F. & Mislevy, R.J. (2000). *Computerized adaptive testing: A primer*. Routledge.

Youyou, W., Kosinski, M. & Stillwell, D.J. (2015). Computer-based personality judgements are more accurate than those made by humans. *Proceedings of the National Academy of Sciences (PNAS), 112*(4), 1036–1040

Chapter 8

Learning, training and development in focus
Coaching psychology

Julia Yates

Overview

This chapter offers an introduction to the academic field of coaching psychology, offering some definitions and an overview of the theoretical underpinnings of coaching and the current state of research. The chapter then turns to the practical application, describing one of the most popular models for structuring a coaching conversation, the GROW model, and highlighting some core coaching skills. The chapter will end with a few words about working as a coach – what types of coaching roles are commonly available and what factors an aspiring coach might need to think about if they are considering taking coaching further.

> **Learning outcomes**
>
> By the end of this chapter you will:
>
> * understand the ways in which individuals in organisations learn and develop through coaching;
> * appreciate the differences between coaching, mentoring and counselling;
> * know about the theoretical underpinnings and have an understanding of the current developments in relevant research;
> * appreciate the practical application of coaching;
> * have some ideas for incorporating coaching in your work.

What is coaching?

The conceptual roots of coaching psychology can be traced right back to Homer's *Odyssey* and the character Telemachus who had meaningful one-to-one conversations with his trusted wise old friend Mentor. This, of course, gave us the word 'mentor' and established the idea of a one-to-one conversation that focuses on the development of one of the parties. We can see the origins of modern-day coaching in the work of Maslow and Rogers in the 1960s, who pioneered humanistic psychology (Maslow, 1968; Rogers, 1961) and the behavioural scientists of the early 20th century who were concerned with

DOI: 10.4324/9781003302087-10

behavioural change. There are occasional references in the psychological academic literature to workplace coaching from the 1920s onwards (such as Griffith, 1926), but arguably the game-changing publication was Gallwey's 1974 book *The Inner Game of Tennis*. In this, Gallwey proposed that the inner, psychological game of a tennis player was as important as their external game, suggesting that training needed to focus on a player's mental state as much as their technical skills. This idea was soon adopted by the business community and the field of workplace coaching became increasingly established through the latter part of the 20th century (van Nieuwerburgh, 2021).

The most famous definition of coaching comes from Sir John Whitmore – one of the founders of developmental coaching. He suggests that

> Coaching is unlocking a person's potential to maximise their own performance. It is helping them to learn rather than teaching them.
>
> (Whitmore, 1992, p. 8)

This quote reflects one of coaching's key tenets, highlighting that coaching is not about telling people what to do, or advising them, or giving them answers; it's an approach that empowers people to make their own choices and solve their own problems. A more process orientated definition comes from Bachkirova, who explains:

> Coaching is a human development process that involves structured, focused interaction and the use of appropriate strategies, tools, and techniques to promote desirable and sustained change for the benefit of the client and potentially for other stakeholders.
>
> (Bachkirova et al., 2018, p.1)

Her definition highlights that coaching conversations need to have a structure and a goal and will often make use of a range of coaching-specific techniques. She also stresses one of the key ethical principles underpinning coaching, that it is client-led: the topic discussed in a coaching session must be of interest and of value to the client themselves. The 'other stakeholders' she mentions will usually be the client's organisation or line manager, who may well be funding the coaching and might have a vested interest in the outcome. This tension between the goals of the client and the goals of the organisation can sometimes need to be managed carefully, and a three-way contract, negotiated collaboratively between the coach, the client and the organisation, is often a valuable starting point.

Coaching usually takes place in a one-to-one conversation, although it is possible to use coaching approaches and principles within a group setting. It is usually goal-directed and person-focused, meaning that it is the client who sets their own goals, and the coach supports the client to identify their own solutions. But coaching can take many forms. De Haan's blended model of coaching, (Figure 8.1), illustrates the range of approaches.

Coaches mostly position themselves in the bottom right-hand quadrant of de Haan's model, encouraging and supporting their clients. However, they might move into any of the other three quadrants, sometimes even within a single coaching session, depending on the demands of the context, the client and the particular issue under discussion.

Coaching is in some ways similar to other developmental approaches, most notably mentoring and counselling. The difference between coaching and mentoring is straightforward: good-quality mentoring makes use of coaching skills, and can use coaching

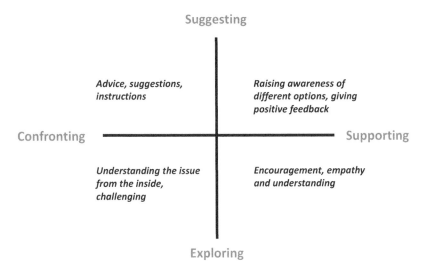

Suggesting

Advice, suggestions, instructions

Raising awareness of different options, giving positive feedback

Confronting ⎯⎯⎯⎯⎯⎯⎯⎯⎯⎯⎯⎯⎯⎯ Supporting

Understanding the issue from the inside, challenging

Encouragement, empathy and understanding

Exploring

Figure 8.1 De Haan's blended model of coaching.
Adapted from de Haan, (2008).

models, but a mentor tends to be someone who has specific existing expertise in the client's field or industry. As well as giving the mentee the chance to explore and reflect on their own thoughts and feelings (as you would in coaching), a mentor can offer advice or access to specific opportunities (Clutterbuck, 2008).

The difference between coaching and counselling is a little more nuanced. Some would suggest that the key difference is whether the process aims to unpick the past to understand the origins of any blocks or patterns of unhelpful behaviour (counselling) or it is focused on identifying solutions and plans for the future (coaching) (Grant, 2006). But this isn't wholly convincing. Although there are some therapeutic approaches that are, more or less, exclusive to either coaching or counselling, there are others such as cognitive-behavioural or humanistic approaches which are described in almost identical terms in the counselling and the coaching literature (Bluckert, 2005). An alternative explanation for the differences between coaching and counselling lies in the attitudes or expectations of the clients. The coaching 'brand' is goal-orientated and future-focused, and so it may be that clients who are looking for a goal-orientated, future-focused conversation opt for coaching, and those who are interested in unpicking patterns of past behaviour opt for counselling. Thus, it is the attitude of the client, rather than the nature of the therapeutic approach, that leads to a difference between coaching and counselling (Yates, 2011).

Coaching psychology

The field of coaching is unregulated. Anyone can decide to call themselves a coach and set themselves up in business, charging vast sums, using any kind of untested techniques and adhering to no ethical codes; and no-one could stop them. To try to impose some standards, rigour and professionalism on the field, the sub-discipline of Coaching Psychology was developed in the 1990s by, amongst others, Tony Grant in Australia and Stephen Palmer in the UK. Coaching psychology aimed to distinguish itself from coaching by identifying coaching practices that have a solid evidence base, grounded in psychological theories, and by conducting academic research that develops and evaluates tools and techniques that are valid and reliable. This approach is summed up by Grant (2006, p. 15) who describes coaching psychology as 'the systematic application of behavioural science to the enhancement of life experience, work performance and well-being for individuals, groups and organisations'. The efforts to apply rigorous scientific methods to this field have led to significant robust research data (as we will see in the next section), and have been recognised by the profession, in the establishment of a new Division of Coaching Psychology within the British Psychological Society in 2021.

Coaching psychology is grounded in psychological theories. The earliest theoretical underpinning to coaching was behaviourism. Behaviourism focuses exclusively on observable behaviour, and early incarnations of coaching were all about changing and improving performance. The GROW model (Whitmore, 1992) – explained later in this chapter – is a behavioural model, focused clearly on developing plans to change behaviour that also draws on our understanding of cognitive processes, making use of goal setting (Locke & Latham, 1990), problem solving (Palmer, 2011) and decision-making techniques (Kahnemann, 2011).

These days, coaching draws on a wide range of psychological approaches, including behaviourism, humanism, existentialism, learning theory and social psychology. One of the most popular recent approaches builds on the research conducted within the Positive Psychology movement, described in more detail in Box 8.1. Practical coaching approaches are also adapted from other fields of applied psychology including health psychology, counselling psychology and family therapy.

Coaching psychology has set itself up as a scientifically robust field of applied psychology, but let us now have a look at the evidence for its effectiveness in practice.

Box 8.1   Positive coaching psychology

In 2000 Seligman and Csikszentmihalyi wrote a seminal paper (2000) that launched a new field within psychology, which they called 'positive psychology'. The traditional model of psychology, they explained, was a deficit model, one in which researchers and practitioners sought to improve the lives of those who were struggling. Seligman and Csikszentmihalyi (2000) argued that whilst that was an important endeavour, psychology had the potential to reach more people. They proposed their new branch of psychology as one that would run alongside the traditional approach, but would be directed towards those whose lives were already reasonably good and aimed to offer them techniques and approaches to help them to flourish.

The field of positive psychology has become closely linked to coaching psychology (Lomas, 2020). Coaching has been described as a 'natural home' for positive psychology (Grant & Cavanagh, 2007) and the synergies are not hard to find. Positive psychology and coaching both strive to inspire growth and change by focusing on the positive aspects of human nature, and both aim to support optimal functioning in individuals, groups and society. This shared philosophy has led to the description of coaching as 'an ideal vehicle through which the science of positive psychology can be applied' (Kauffman et al., 2010, p. 159).

In practical terms, positive psychology has contributed numerous interventions which can be used in coaching. One set of exercises capitalises on the value that gratitude can have. Gratitude exercises can be used in coaching as a way to boost positive emotions or help difficult relationships (Passmore & Oades, 2016; Trom & Burke, 2021). Strengths (defined in positive psychology as things that you are naturally good at and enjoy doing) offer another group of exercises which have been shown to be effective in coaching, particularly valuable in the workplace, raising self-awareness and boosting confidence (McQuaid et al., 2018).

Does coaching work?

The evidence base for workplace coaching is growing in scale and is becoming increasingly academically rigorous, but the effectiveness of coaching is not a straightforward thing to measure (Tooth et al., 2013). Many studies focus on the client's view of whether the coaching was effective. This is, without doubt, important, but is of course quite subjective. Other studies use the opinion of the coach as a measure, which is even less robust – even the most reflective and objective of coaches is likely to be biased towards a favourable assessment of their own practice. A more rigorous measure is to link the outcome measure with the goal that the client set during the coaching: if a client wanted to improve their time keeping, you could measure how many times they have arrived late to work before and after the coaching; if they wanted help with motivating their staff, you could assess whether their team's productivity has increased since the coaching. But not only do these then make for complicated research projects, there can be all sorts of other confounding factors which make it very difficult to know whether a positive change observed is actually the result of the coaching itself: perhaps the better time keeping coincided with the purchase of a new alarm clock, or the increased productivity was actually down to the motivating power of a pay rise.

Notwithstanding these challenges, the evidence base is growing in size and quality. The first set of studies focused on the effectiveness of coaching tended to be small scale, and outcomes were often measured by self-report surveys (Grant, 2009). Although not the gold standard of academic research, these kinds of studies do offer some useful data suggesting that coaching has a positive impact on goal accomplishment (Fischer & Beimer, 2009), professional growth (McGuffin & Obonya, 2010), professional relationships (Kombarakaran et al., 2008, managerial flexibility (Jones et al., 2006), productivity (Olivero et al., 1997) and resilience and workplace well-being (Grant, 2010).

More recently, several meta-analyses have been published. Theeboom et al. (2014) looked at different kinds of coaching (executive, life and health) and examined the impact of the coaching on the individual. They found that coaching overall had a significant positive impact on clients, and specifically helped with skill development, well-being, their ability to cope and attitudes to work. Interestingly, they found no link between outcomes and number of sessions (a single session was shown to be as effective as a series of six), although offered the plausible explanation that people facing more complex challenges were more likely to end up having longer coaching relationships.

Jones et al. (2016) conducted another meta-analysis, looking at studies which had been conducted into executive, or workplace training. They found that coaching had a positive impact overall on organisational outcomes, and at the individual level, people benefited from coaching in terms of their skill development, their attitude towards work and their performance. They also found that internal coaches (i.e. coaches employed by the same organisation) were a little more effective than those brought in from outside, but there was no discernible difference between face-to-face and blended coaching (i.e. face-to-face plus online).

Finally, in 2017, Burt and Talati (2017) conducted a meta-analysis of randomised controlled trials (highly rigorous studies) for executive coaching and found positive benefits for performance, well-being, coping, work attitudes and goal-directed self-regulation.

The evidence seems to be fairly compelling: coaching does work. The next step then is to try and understand how it works: what is it that happens within a coaching conversation that makes a difference?

How does coaching work?

Recent reviews have identified several specific factors which are consistently shown to have an impact on positive coaching outcomes, most frequently the self-efficacy of the client, the range of tools and techniques used by the coach and, most powerful of all, the working alliance between the coach and client (Bozer & Jones, 2018; de Haan et al., 2013; Graßmann & Schermuly, 2021; Molyn et al., 2022. Let us examine each of those in turn.

Self-efficacy of the client

The more confident a client feels about their ability to make a change, the more likely they are to put their plans into action (de Haan et al., 2016). Bandura explains that self-efficacy leads people to set themselves challenging goals, and to expend more effort achieving them (Bandura, 1986). Coaching has been shown to build clients' levels of self-efficacy through, for example, raising self-awareness, encouraging clients to take responsibility and offering opportunities for positive feedback (Whitmore, 2002), so coaching that helps to boost clients' confidence makes clients more likely to put their plans into action.

Range of tools and techniques used by the coach

One intriguing finding in the literature is that no one approach seems to be better than any others (Wampold, 2001). The evidence seems to suggest that person-centred, solution-focused, cognitive-behavioural and positive psychology approaches are all equally likely to produce a positive outcome for a client. This calls into question the value of learning about different coaching approaches – it would certainly save a lot of time if we just picked one approach to study, so why do we bother? There are two other research findings which support the development of expertise in more than one approach (de Haan et al., 2013). The first is that although the specific approach that the coach takes doesn't seem to make much difference, the commitment that the coach has towards their particular approach does: it doesn't matter which technique you use, as long as you are genuinely convinced that the approach works. It therefore makes sense to expose yourself to a wide range of approaches in order to find the one that works best for you. The second relevant finding is that whilst no one approach seems consistently superior to another, having a range of different techniques at your disposal does seem to help. A varied professional toolkit allows you to pick and choose the specific technique that you believe is best going to help your particular client with their particular issue and this seems to have a positive impact.

Working alliance

Beyond anything else, the working alliance seems to be the key to successful coaching. The working alliance consists of the combination of three different factors: a clear and agreed goal for the session; an explicit and shared understanding of the process; a good relationship between the coach and client.

Most coaching models (discussed in the next section) include a goal-setting stage near the start of the conversation, which allows coach and client to spend some time identifying, clarifying and agreeing a goal. A clear and agreed goal for the session is useful because it ensures that the conversation is focused on the matter at hand, and makes sure that both coach and client have a shared understanding of the priorities.

The second important aspect of the working alliance is the shared understanding of the process. To establish an explicit understanding of the process, the coach needs to spend some time before the coaching begins, making sure that the client understands what coaching is and how it works. Then as the coaching itself progresses, the coach should share the process with the client throughout, being explicit about, for example, the models they are using, and explaining the value and purpose of any of tools used.

The third aspect of the working alliance is the client–coach relationship, and two specific aspects of the relationship have been explored in some depth: trust and interpersonal attraction.

Levels of trust have been shown to link with positive coaching outcomes (Boyce et al., 2010), and the value of trust is thought to be explained by the idea of psychological safety (Mayer et al., 1995). The client's trust in the coach allows them to show vulnerability and therefore explore their weaknesses and limitations. Through this, the client builds self-efficacy and can identify solutions to their own problems.

There is some evidence that commonality between the coach and client leads to positive outcomes, in particular same-sex pairings seem to work particularly well, as do coaches and clients who share similar attitudes, beliefs and values (Bozer et al., 2015). This success is explained by the similarity paradigm, or homophily, which is the tendency for humans to identify and attract people similar to themselves (Byrne, 1997): people imagine or anticipate that those who share their own values and worldview are more likely to be trustworthy and therefore are more likely to have open and honest conversations.

Existing research thus shows us that coaching does seem to work, and offers some suggestions of the particular aspects of coaching that seem to make the difference – a good working alliance, a range of techniques at the coach's disposal, and a focus on boosting the client's confidence. Let us now turn to more practical matters, and consider how to coach.

How to coach

Most coaching conversations, certainly most good coaching conversations, follow some kind of process model. A model can help ensure that you make the best use of your time with your client, that you don't get side-lined, and that you see the topic through to a useful conclusion. There are many different models that you can use, and many coaches will have a number of different models that they will rely on, picking and choosing the one that seems most suitable in the moment.

One of the most straightforward and widely used models is a behavioural model, known as the GROW model (Whitmore, 1992). The GROW model offers four distinct stages for each conversation, and the coach should gently steer the client through each stage, making sure to cover all four, in order, within each conversation. In practice, coaching conversations are rarely that neat, but keeping this structure in mind, and returning to it when you feel you have gone off track, can help to make sure that your time together is well spent.

G is for GOAL: in the first stage of the interview, you and your client need to make a decision about what you are going to talk about. The content of the goal should always be determined by your client – it is never the coach's place to suggest something, but as the coach, you might be well placed to decide whether the goal your client has suggested is specific enough to be covered within a single coaching session. You can also play an important part in helping your client to work out what they want to discuss. Clients can often arrive at coaching knowing that something isn't quite right, but needing a bit of help to crystallise that vague sense into something that they can work on; this stage can take some time and you might find that you need to do quite a bit of exploring before the goal feels like the right one. In these situations, your G-R-O-W structure might end up being more of a G-R-G-R-G-R-O-W process, but that's fine.

R is for REALITY: This is when you encourage your client to explore their own thoughts and feelings. During this stage you might find yourself using lots of open questions to really encourage your client to open up. Prompts such as 'tell me more' or 'how did that feel?' can be useful, as can short summaries of your client's story so far. During this stage, you are aiming to get your client to talk about what led them to this point, what they have tried so far. I often start this stage asking clients to 'tell me the story so far', which is a form of words that I find can encourage clients to open up.

O is for OPTIONS: Once you feel that your client has had a chance to tell their story, and has perhaps understood themselves better after talking this through, you can move on to the Options stage. In this stage you need to achieve two things. First, you want to encourage your client to identify as many possible solutions or suggestions as possible, and then second, you want to get your client to evaluate these options, narrowing them down, ending up with just one or two that seem to be most helpful. Coaches often make use of specific techniques in this stage including mind maps, scaling and visualisations.

W is for the WAY FORWARD: In your final stage, you invite your client to draw themselves up an action plan. The action points need to be specific and ideally time bound; for example you might ask 'When do you think you will be able to do that?', and it can be useful to spend a bit of time here talking about any barriers that might get in the way, and how your client could pre-empt or work round them.

All four sections of the model should be covered in each coaching conversation; it can help to share the model explicitly with the client at the start. It's a simple model to explain, and this transparency creates the sense that keeping the conversation on track is a joint responsibility. It also demystifies the process, which can serve to empower the client.

Coaching skills

Alongside making use of coaching models, a coach needs to develop a wide range of coaching skills. Some of these draw on Rogers's work on humanistic counselling (Rogers, 1957). Rogers proposed that for change to occur in a therapeutic context, there were five 'core conditions' which he described as 'necessary and sufficient': *necessary*, in that change cannot take place without them and *sufficient* in that they are all that is needed for the change to take place. This might seem like a somewhat extreme position to take, and a more common contemporary view within coaching is that these core conditions are useful to help change to take place, although perhaps neither necessary nor sufficient (van Nieuwerburgh, 2021).

The core conditions are:

1 Two people (the coach and client) are in psychological contact – they are both psychologically present in the space together and connecting with each other. This can involve effective rapport building and the art of building relationships and establishing trust quickly.
2 The client is 'incongruent' – there is something that the client wants to change, or a problem they want to solve. One challenge that coaches can face is the potential tension that you can face when negotiating a three-way contract between you, the client and the client's employer but even if the employer is paying, and wants the coaching to focus on a particular issue, the coaching is not going to work if the client has no intrinsic interest in that goal.
3 The coach is 'congruent' – the coach is focused on the client and their issues – not distracted or preoccupied by their own issues.
4 The coach feels 'unconditional positive regard' (UPR) for the client. The coach accepts the client for who they are and believes in their potential. A coach might not agree with the choices that they have made, but needs to find a way to value them for themselves, regardless of what they have done. This is not always easy to achieve, and coaches are well advised to arrange regular supervision to help make sure that issues such as this don't jeopardise the quality of the coaching. Supervision offers coaches a chance to talk about their work in a safe, confidential environment to make sure that there aren't any issues that may be getting in the way of the coaching. If you ever find yourself feeling less than unconditionally positive towards your client, this might well be a useful thing to raise in supervision to try and find a positive solution.
5 The coach manages to communicate this UPR to the client to some degree. The coach can communicate their empathy with the client through their active listening, appropriate responses and thoughtful comments.

There are a number of skills needed to achieve these five conditions including rapport building, empathising, self-reflection, and active listening. In addition to these, coaches also need to be skilled in a range of active listening techniques, such as summarising, reflecting and paraphrasing and asking questions to challenge, to probe or to stimulate new thinking.

Box 8.2   Technology in coaching

Traditionally coaching has taken place in person, face to face either in a traditional office, or often in a more neutral space, such as a coffee shop. More recently, coaching has been increasingly conducted online. This trend had been noted before the 2020 pandemic, but the lockdown, as it did in so many spheres, increased the pace of the adoption of technology. Taking the use of technology in coaching a step further, Graßmann and Schermuly (2020) have explored the idea of Artificial Intelligence (AI) Coaching. Although this might sound like a strange idea, the authors argue that AI has already made great inroads to coaching, in the form of self-help apps and websites that support people to make changes in their lives. They also point to the obvious benefits that AI could bring, including anonymity, flexibility and reduced costs. They suggest that AI seems to be capable of guiding clients through a number of steps in the coaching journey, including, rather surprisingly, establishing the all-important working alliance. They point to studies that have shown that clients have managed to bond with virtual therapists (Bickmore et al., 2010) and other studies that indicate that clients feel more comfortable self-disclosing to virtual agents (Gratch et al., 2014). Graßmann and Schermuly also note limitations and question whether AI could help clients to identify their problems effectively, or give personalised feedback. Their conclusion is that in time AI will be incorporated within coaching programmes, but won't take the place of human coaches.

Working as a coach

Coaching has become enormously popular as an approach to workplace learning and development and is now one of the most popular approaches to professional development in organisations (CIPD, 2023). The coaching industry is currently estimated to be worth $15bn per annum worldwide, and the International Coaching Federation estimates that there are around 90,000 coaches across the globe (ICF, 2021).

Coaching empowers others to take responsibility, make their own decisions, use their creativity, solve their own problems and feel more confident about their choices. The skill to help others improve their own performance, leadership or decision making will be useful whatever your role. If you are a manager, a colleague, a trainer, a mentor, and even a friend or a parent, the skills of non-directive, active listening, empathising, asking good questions and suspending judgement can and will be useful for you whatever direction you want your career to go in. But perhaps you are interested in finding out how to make coaching a more central part of your career?

Coaches work in a variety of settings, in-house – usually within a learning and development team, working for an external consultancy, or working freelance. Coaches can choose to specialise, working either with particular topics or particular groups of people. Some of the most common include executive or performance coaching (which I tend to join together and describe as 'workplace coaching'), life coaching, career coaching, retirement coaching, maternity coaching and weight loss coaching. Although it might seem logical to offer a broad range of services early in your coaching career, in order to capitalise on a wide potential client-base, in fact, you are more likely to be successful if you have a particular niche, as it's easier to create the sense of expertise (Van den Born & Van Witteloostuijn, 2013). Many coaches too have a portfolio of expertise, offering facilitation, coach training and consultancy services as well as coaching.

Becoming an accredited coach is worth considering. This will demonstrate your own professional standards to your potential clients, and will encourage you to develop good professional habits. There are some influential professional bodies (listed in the 'Explore Further' section at the end of the chapter) all of whom offer the chance to become accredited. The requirements for accreditation vary from one professional body to another, but generally they include a requirement for some formal training (initial training and CPD), considerable experience, regular supervision and adherence to an ethical code.

Conclusion

The skills that you develop as a coach can add value to whatever strand of organisational psychology you decide to pursue and coaching itself can be a meaningful and fulfilling aspect of your work. We have looked, in this chapter, at definitions, theories, and the empirical basis for coaching psychology, and have focused in on some specific skills that coaches need to develop. I hope this has inspired you to want to find out more!

Box 8.3   Case study: GROW model coaching conversation

Bethan had spent her twenties working in a niche consultancy firm and worked her way up to Director level. She absolutely loved working at the organisation, and really enjoyed the fast pace, the stimulating colleagues and the challenges of the work itself. She worked long hours and socialised almost exclusively with work colleagues and clients, but in her early thirties, she realised that this intensity wasn't great for her physical or mental health and started looking round for a new job. She received some offers, but none of them seemed quite right, and now she had one particular job offer which seemed to tick all the boxes; but still she hesitated. Bethan came to see a coach to try and work out what she should do next.

The coach suggested that they should use the GROW model, and explained the four stages. Establishing the goal took a little time, but eventually Bethan identified that what she wanted was to feel more confident about the decision she thought she had already made.

During the Reality section, the coach asked Bethan to talk about the last six months of job hunting and Bethan spoke about the various jobs she had applied for and the conversations she had had. The coach listened attentively, summarised to help Bethan clarify her thoughts, and then asked if she could offer a reflection. Bethan had been talking a lot about other people's views – what her husband thought, how future recruiters would perceive her, what her current boss would say, but hadn't spoken much about what she herself wanted. 'What about you?' the coach asked. 'When you think about doing this job, how does that make you feel?'. Bethan admitted that she didn't really know, and the coach encouraged Bethan to do a short visualisation exercise, in which she imagined herself in that job. This helped Bethan to feel a little more confident about her own choices, but she was still unsure. The coach suggested that they should try a thought experiment. She asked Bethan to imagine that she had taken the job and that six months down the line, all of Bethan's worst fears were realised: her colleagues were mediocre, the work was repetitive, the promised pay rise had not materialised. The coach asked 'What would you do then?'. This was a light-bulb moment for Bethan, as it dawned on her that if she wasn't happy, she could leave.

Moving on to the Options stage, the coach asked Bethan a direct question 'What do you think you need to do, to help you to decide?'. The question seemed to help Bethan to take a bit more control of the situation and she identified a few concrete suggestions for next steps.

In the final stage of the conversation, the Way Forward, Bethan developed an action plan, and the coach invited her to consider what barriers she might encounter and what support she could put in place. The coach ended with a scaling question, asking Bethan to estimate, on a scale of 1–10, how confident she felt in her decision. Bethan said that she was currently at a seven but felt confident that the steps she had planned would push her up to the eight or nine she needed to make the choice.

Explore further

Professional bodies can provide you with a wealth of information and support if you are interested in finding out more about working in the field. These include The Association for Coaching (www.associationforcoaching.com/), the International Coaching Federation (https://coachingfederation.org/) and the European Mentoring and Coaching Council, (https://emccuk.org/).

Boniwell, I. (2012). *Positive psychology in a nutshell: The science of happiness: The science of happiness*. McGraw-Hill Education (UK).If you are interested in finding out more about Positive Psychology, this is a good place to start
Palmer, S. & Whybrow, A. (Eds.). (2018). *Handbook of coaching psychology: A guide for practitioners*. Hove: Routledge. This one combines practical suggestions with a guide to some key theoretical approaches
Van Nieuwerburgh, C. (2021). *An Introduction to Coaching* London: Sage. This is a great practical guide to help you to develop your own coaching skills
Yates, J. (2022). *An Introduction to Career Coaching* (Second edition) Hove: Routledge. This might be of interest if you like the idea of combining coaching with career support

References

Bachkirova, T., Cox, E. & Clutterbuck, D. (2018). Introduction. In T. Bachkirova, E. Cox & D. Clutterbuck (Eds.), The complete handbook of coaching. London: Sage.

Bandura, A. (1986). *Social foundations of thought and action: A social cognitive theory.* Upper Saddle River, NJ: Prentice-Hall, Inc.

Bickmore, T., Schulman, D. & Yin, L. (2010). Maintaining engagement in long-term interventions with relational agents. *Applied Artificial Intelligence, 24*, 648–666.

Bluckert, P. (2005), The similarities and differences between coaching and therapy. *Industrial and Commercial Training, 37* (2), 91–96.

Boyce, L.A., Jackson, J.R. & Neal, L.J. (2010). Building successful leadership coaching relationships: Examining impact of matching criteria in a leadership coaching program. *Journal of Management Development, 29*(10), 914–931. doi: 10.1108/02621711011084231

Bozer, G. & Jones, R.J. (2018). Understanding the factors that determine workplace coaching effectiveness: A systematic literature review. *European Journal of Work and Organizational Psychology, 27*(3), 342–361.

Bozer, G., Joo, B.-K. & Santora, J.C. (2015). Executive coaching: Does coach-coachee matching based on similarity really matter? *Consulting Psychology: Practice & Research, 67*(3), 218–233. doi: 10.1037/cpb0000044

Burt, D. & Talati, Z. (2017). The unsolved value of executive coaching: A meta-analysis of outcomes using randomised control trial studies. International Journal of Evidence Based Coaching and Mentoring, *15*(2), 17–24.

Byrne, D. (1997). An overview (and underview) of research and theory within the attraction paradigm. *Journal of Social and Personal Relationships, 14*(3), 417–431. doi: 10.1177/0265407597143008

CIPD (2023). *Coaching and mentoring factsheet.* London: CIPD. www.cipd.org/uk/knowledge/factsheets/coaching-mentoring-factsheet/

Clutterbuck, D. (2008). What's happening in coaching and mentoring? And what is the difference between them?. *Development and Learning in Organizations: An International Journal, 22*(4), 8–10.

de Haan, E. (2008). *Relational Coaching.* London: Wiley.

de Haan, E., Duckworth, A., Birch, D. & Jones, C. (2013). Executive coaching outcome research: The predictive value of common factors such as relationship, personality match and self-efficacy. *Consulting Psychology Journal: Practice and Research, 65*(1), 40–57. doi: 10.1037/a0031635

de Haan, E., Grant, A.M., Burger, Y. & Eriksson, P.-O. (2016). A large-scale study of executive and workplace coaching: The relative contributions of relationship, personality match, and self-efficacy. *Consulting Psychology Journal: Practice and Research, 68*(3), 189–207. doi:10.1037/cpb0000058 49

Fischer, R.L. & Beimers, D. (2009). 'Put me in, Coach': A pilot evaluation of executive coaching in the nonprofit sector. Nonprofit Management and Leadership, *19*(4), 507–522.

Gallwey, W.T. (1974). *The inner game of tennis.* London: Jonathan Cape

Grant, A.M. (2006). A personal perspective on professional coaching and the development of coaching psychology. *International Coaching Psychology Review, 1*(1), 12–22.

Grant, A.M. (2009). *Workplace, executive and life coaching: An annotated bibliography from the behavioural science and business literature.* Coaching Psychology Unit, University of Sydney, Australia.

Grant, A.M. (2010). It takes time: A stages of change perspective on the adoption of workplace coaching skills. Journal of Change Management, *10*(1), 61–77.

Grant, A.M. & Cavanagh, M.J. (2007). Evidence-based coaching: Flourishing or languishing?. Australian Psychologist, 42(4), 239–254.

Graßmann, C. & Schermuly, C.C. (2021). Coaching with artificial intelligence: concepts and capabilities. Human Resource Development Review, 20(1), 106–126.

Gratch, J., Lucas, G.M., King, A.A. & Morency, L.P. (2014, May). It's only a computer: The impact of human-agent interaction in clinical interviews. In Proceedings of the 2014 inter-national conference on autonomous agents and multi-agent systems (pp. 85–92).

Griffith, C.R. (1926). Psychology of coaching: A study of coaching methods from the point of view of psychology. C. Scribner's sons.

International Coach Federation. (2016). ICF global coaching study. Retrieved from https://coachfederation.org/files/FileDownloads/2016ICFGlobalCoachingStudy_ExecutiveSu mmary.pdf

ICF (2021). Membership and credentialing fact sheet. Kentucky: ICF. https://coachingfederation.org/app/uploads/2021/02/February2021_FactSheet.pdf.

Jones, R.A., Rafferty, A.E. & Griffin, M.A. (2006). The executive coaching trend: Towards more flexible executives. Leadership & Organization Development Journal, 27(7), 584–596.

Jones, R.J., Woods, S.A. & Guillaume, Y.R.F. (2016). The effectiveness of workplace coaching: A meta-analysis of learning and performance outcomes from coaching. Journal of Occupational and Organizational Psychology, 89(2). doi: 10.1111/joop.12119

Kahneman, D. (2011). Thinking, fast and slow. New York: Macmillan.

Kauffman, C., Boniwell, I. & Silberman, J. (2010) The positive approach to coaching, in E. Cox, T. Bachkirova & D. Clutterbuck (Eds.), The complete handbook of coaching. London: Sage.

Kombarakaran, F.A., Yang, J.A., Baker, M.N. & Fernandes, P.B. (2008). Executive coaching: It works!. Consulting Psychology Journal: Practice and Research, 60(1), 78.

Locke, E.A. & Latham, G.P. (1990). A theory of goal setting & task performance. Prentice-Hall, Inc.

Lomas, T. (2020). Positive coaching psychology: A case study in the hybridization of positive psychology. International Journal of Wellbeing, 10(2).

Maslow, A. (1968). Some educational implications of the humanistic psychologies. Harvard Educational Review, 38(4), 685–696.

Mayer, R.C., Davis, J.H. & Schoorman, F.D. (1995). An integrative model of organizational trust. Academy of Management Review, 20(3), 709–734. doi:10.5465/AMR.1995.9508080335

McGuffin, A.A. & Obonyo, E. (2010). Enhancing performance: A case study of the effects of employee coaching in construction practice. Construction Management and Economics, 28(2), 141–149.

McQuaid, M., Niemiec, R. & Doman, F. (2018). A character strengths-based approach to positive psychology coaching. In S. Green & S. Palmer (Eds.), Positive psychology coaching in practice (pp. 71–79). Abingdon: Routledge.

Molyn, J., de Haan, E., van der Veen, R. & Gray, D.E. (2022). The impact of common factors on coaching outcomes. Coaching: An International Journal of Theory, Research and Practice, 15(2), 214–227.

Olivero, G., Bane, K.D. & Kopelman, R.E. (1997). Executive coaching as a transfer of training tool: Effects on productivity in a public agency. Public Personnel Management, 26(4), 461–469.

Palmer, S. (2011). Revisiting the P in the PRACTICE coaching model. The Coaching Psychologist, 7(2), 156–158.

Passmore, J. & Oades, L.G. (2016). Positive psychology techniques: gratitude. The Coaching Psychologist, 12(1), 34–35.

Rogers, C.R. (1957). The necessary and sufficient conditions of therapeutic personality change. Journal of Consulting Psychology, 21(2), 95–103. https://doi.org/10.1037/h0045357.

Rogers, C.R. (1961). On becoming a person. Boston: Houghton Mifflin.

Seligman, M.E.P. & Csikszentmihalyi, M. (2000). Positive psychology: an introduction. Am. Psychol. 55, 5–14. doi: 10.1037/0003-066X.55.1.5.

Theeboom, T., Beersma, B. & Van Vianen, A.E.M. (2014). Does coaching work? A meta-analysis on the effects of coaching on individual level outcomes in an organizational context. *The Journal of Positive Psychology*, 9(1), 1–18. doi: 10.1080/17439760.2013.837499

Tooth, J.A., Nielsen, S. & Armstrong, H. (2013). Coaching effectiveness survey instruments: Taking stock of measuring the immeasurable. *Coaching: An International Journal of Theory, Research and Practice*, 6(2), 137–151.

Trom, P. & Burke, J. (2021). Positive psychology intervention (PPI) coaching: an experimental application of coaching to improve the effectiveness of a gratitude intervention. *Coaching: An International Journal of Theory, Research and Practice*, 1–12.

Van den Born, A. & Van Witteloostuijn, A. (2013). Drivers of freelance career success. *Journal of Organizational Behavior*, 34(1), 24–46.

Van Nieuwerburgh, C. (2021). An introduction to coaching. London: Sage.

Wampold, B. (2001). *The great psychotherapy debate: Models, methods and findings*. Mahwah, NJ: Erlbaum

Whitmore, J. (1992). *Coaching for performance*. London: Nicholas Brealey

Yates, J. (2011). Can career coaching enhance our profession?. In L. Barham & B. Irving (Eds.), *Constructing the future* (pp. 147–169). Stourbridge: Institute of Career Guidance.

Chapter 9

Leadership, engagement and motivation in focus

Groups and teams

Lynsey Mahmood

Overview

This chapter takes a closer look at how groups and teams influence leadership, engagement, and motivation at work. It draws on social psychology theory and its application to the workplace. Since the development of the Social Identity Theory (SIT) in the 1970s, when Tajfel and colleagues first started investigating the minimal group paradigm, social psychology has been interested in how individuals behave when in groups and teams, versus individually. Since then, a huge amount of research has applied the learnings from broader social psychology to specific sub-disciplines. One area that has shown promise is in organisational behaviour and understanding intragroup and intergroup dynamics within and between organisations. As well as understanding group behaviour, group dynamics also help us to understand the role of leaders within teams and how organisational leaders can harness the power of group identity to influence worker behaviour. This chapter will introduce the broad concept of identity theory and how it relates to organisations, its influence on leadership and followership, and practical applications of the research. The chapter also touches on future directions for dispersed teams or hybrid working patterns.

Learning outcomes

By the end of the chapter you will:

- understand positive and negative aspects in groups and teams at work;
- have an overview of theories and current directions in research relevant to groups and teams at work;
- be aware of the practical applications of groups, teams, and leadership / management;
- recognise how to manage intra – and intergroup processes in the workplace.

DOI: 10.4324/9781003302087-11

Social identification and group dynamics

Under the umbrella of group dynamics, the application of the social identity process can help us to understand how employees interact and behave in work teams, and within an organisation more broadly. Understanding relationships between groups is known as **inter**group relations. Understanding the dynamics that occur between individuals within the same group is known as **intra**group relations. This means that we can explore relationships within work teams and between teams or even whole organisations.

Social Identity Theory (SIT) derived from an interest in how people behave when they are alone versus when they are in groups. At its core SIT relates to the individual and their sense of who they are, or their sense of self, *based* on groups they belong to (Tajfel, 1978; Tajfel & Turner, 1979). Our sense of self is affected cognitively – we know that we are part of a group or not; evaluatively – we understand the social structure and place value in where our group sits within this; and emotionally – we attach how we feel to group memberships, and exclusion from a group can be emotionally detrimental (see Kip Williams' work on the Cyberball experiments for more on the negative impact of group exclusion, Williams & Jarvis, 2006).

Social identity develops through a process of categorisation, identification, and comparison.

Categorisation occurs as we see ourselves belonging to a group of other similar individuals, who are all more similar to each other than to members of other groups. This creates a meta-contrast ratio, where the perceived differences between members of the same group are smaller than the perceived differences between them and other individuals who are members of other groups. A clear example of this is within fans of sports teams. The shared category is the sports team fan base, and distinct categories are further highlighted by things such as team kit. This creates clear, visible categories and shows the similarity within the 'in-group', thus creating the meta-contrast ratio.

After categorising oneself as part of a group, identification with that group begins. Turner (1984) referred to this as a 'psychological group'. That is, those who share a social identification or group category. We then start to attach meaning to our group membership, seeing our sense of self as meaningfully associated with the group and its other members. Among fans of sports teams this is the shared unity for the good of the team. Despite not being involved in wins or losses, psychologically, fans see their own sense of self as part of the team and share in the emotion of a victory or defeat.

Finally, once we establish our membership of, and identification with, a group, we make comparisons with other groups and their members. Our own group becomes the in-group, and those outside of this become the out-group. Psychologically we see our in-group as unique or better than others, a process called positive in-group distinctiveness. This creates in-group homogeneity which refers to the perceived similarity of in-group members. With fans of sports teams, this can create competition and sometimes discrimination between the opposing groups of fans. The visible categorisation (for example, by wearing team colours) creates a clear distinction. A win or loss, or the feeling of one team performing better than the other, provides the grounds for competitive distinction whereby the in-group's reputation is to be protected, often by making negative comparisons to the out-group (fans of the opposing team).

Overall, this can lead to intergroup conflict whereby the differences between in-groups and out-groups are made salient and used as the basis for discrimination. It can also enhance intergroup competition whereby the in-group work together to achieve more than the out-group. This works in both positive and negative ways, in that it can heighten positive relations within the in-group, but can cause tension between the in-group and out-group, especially when there are perceived differences in status between the in-group and out-group (Abrams & Hogg, 2006; Ramiah et al., 2011).

Another factor that influences group dynamics based on identification is inclusiveness. Since people usually belong to several groups, there is an interplay between identities, many of which may cross over or influence each other. However, an important influence on intergroup relations is the breadth of inclusiveness of the group identity. That is, the more people that are perceived as included in the in-group, the more positive are the feelings towards members of the out-group (Brankovic et al., 2015). Continuing the example of sports fans, this can be seen in the fluidity of identification when teams play at different levels, for example, local, national or international. Take the football World Cup as an example – fans support a local league team made up of players from many nationalities, and whilst the league is in season the social identity is at a smaller level, closely linked to that local team. However, as the World Cup comes around, those same players then move back to playing for their national team and come up against teams consisting of players that outside of the World Cup would be their teammates. As a supporter, the social identity shifts up to a much more inclusive level of supporting the national team. The identity is associated with the nation rather than the local support.

At the centre of identity formation is the self and personal identification, around this are wider levels of inclusivity depending on the group category that is currently salient. As depicted in Figure 9.1, this means that depending on the context or situation that a person finds themselves in there may be a greater or lesser degree of inclusivity of others into their identity (see the example of local vs. national football teams above). Figure 9.1 highlights how the level of the salient identity influences how many people are included within that group category, starting with the individual and increasing to capture any human at the highest level of identification. This means that at the most superordinate level, one could identify with 'humans' as broadly as possible, including all other human beings in their sense of self. Although this is less likely and would cognitively be complex, the idea is that there may be more or fewer people included in one's in-group, which in turn influences comparisons and intergroup dynamics.

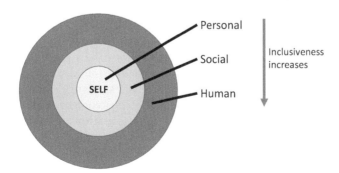

Figure 9.1 Greater numbers of group members included in the identity as the group category is widened.

This overall process, which is described here in the social context, can be applied directly to organisations and work groups / teams.

Organisational identification

The application of SIT to organisations is known as Organisational identification (Ashforth & Mael, 1989). This is where a person identifies with the organisation or work team. Then other organisations or teams become the target of comparison. Organisational leaders may not even realise the impact that identification can have on their employees. Organisations with a clear brand and core values offer a strong identity with which the employee can anchor their sense of self. This can be heightened for organisations that require employees to wear a uniform that clearly displays their role within the organisation (Pratt & Rafaeli, 1997). Uniforms both display to others the employee's identity with the organisation and maintain the saliency of that identity for the employee – they wear a constant reminder of their attachment to the organisation and / or the sub-group within it. Since the organisation becomes the anchor for identification, changes to teams or wider organisational changes can have a great impact on individuals and their sense of self. For a closer look at this see Box 9.1.

Box 9.1   Focus on mergers and acquisitions

As outlined above, applying *identification* to the organisation means that individuals tend to associate their sense of self with their work team, department, or wider organisation. In fact, the wider sector would be an even more inclusive superordinate group. This means that group categories and personal identities are complex and importantly, context dependent. Here we consider the interesting context of mergers (the combining of two organisations) and acquisitions (the absorption of one organisation by another) in relation to organisational identification.

Both mergers and acquisitions can be viewed as the recategorization of two groups into a new group, and thus disrupt employees' existing identification with the pre-merger organisation. For some, their strong sense of identity with the pre-merger organisation may mean that they can't realign their sense of self with the new organisation and don't develop a sense of belonging with the new team, which in turn can lead those employees to leave. On the other hand, some employees can realign their sense of self and develop a new identity with the post-merger organisation, and so remain in post. Later in this chapter the role that leaders play in supporting identity formation and maintenance is explored further, but in a merger or acquisition, the role of leaders and other team members can be crucial to the re-shaping of the group identity and whether employees are all taken along on the journey.

In both mergers and acquisitions there is typically a status differential whereby one organisation will inevitably be bigger or more powerful than the other. This can often mean that the larger or more powerful organisation will maintain more of their existing identity, requiring employees from the smaller or less powerful organisation to realign their identity more than employees in the larger one. More reading on identity management in mergers and acquisitions can be found in the section 'Explore Further' at the end of the chapter.

Early research on the application of SIT to organisations suggested that the strength of identification with organisations can be greater than that with social groups (van Knippenberg & Hogg, 2001). This process has both positive and negative consequences. For example, some research suggests that heightened organisational identity leads to greater job satisfaction and reduced turnover (de Moura et al., 2009), increased work engagement (Karanika-Murray et al., 2015), improved wellbeing (Wietrak et al., 2021), and higher work motivation and task performance (van Knippenberg, 2000).

On the other hand, recent research has begun to explore the possible downsides of strong organisational identification, showing that consequences of particularly high levels of identification include workaholism, which in turn reduces wellbeing (Avanzi et al., 2012), and negatively impacted life satisfaction (Li et al., 2015). Therefore, there is a balance to be achieved when considering identification with the work group. This is something that managers and leaders must consider when managing group dynamics.

Despite Ashforth and Mael's (1989) early work applying the theory to the organisational context, real interest in researching organisational identification did not proliferate until the mid-1990s and has since grown to focus on several areas of interest including leadership, performance, and innovation. In the next section we will take a close look at some of these areas and how identification has influenced research and practice.

Leadership

As we saw in Chapter 4, leadership theory has a long and well-developed history in organisational research, ranging from individualist ideas that leaders are superior beings (Great man theory, charismatic leadership) to more recent conceptualisations of leadership as a contextual process (including transactional and transformational theories). More recently though, thought has turned to the influence of identity processes on leadership in groups.

The identity approach to leadership suggests that leadership is a product of shared social identity (Haslam & Ellemers, 2011) whereby the leader emerges through embodying the group's norms and values (Reicher et al., 2005) and reflecting the group prototype (Hogg, 2001) to the greatest extent (see Box 9.2 for more on leader prototypicality).

Box 9.2 Focus on leadership prototypicality

As outlined earlier in this chapter, members of an in-group create a positive in-group distinctiveness, seeing members of their own group as more similar to each other, and more different to members of out-groups. The similarity between in-group members creates a 'prototype' of how an exemplary group member should behave. That is, a group member who fully embodies the group's norms and values is seen as the most prototypical group member. Since the group's norms and values are linked to the individual's sense of self through the identification process, this means that a prototypical group member is often the favoured group member.

Being seen as the most prototypical group member imbues this person with additional status and credit, so that when the group seeks a new leader, they are typically the most desirable candidate. This means that the more prototypical leaders are given leeway to innovate and even fail, but only to a degree. Field research around the 2012 U.S. presidential election between Obama and Romney showed that when Romney lost the election, those who strongly identified with the political party saw him as less prototypical so he lost his *licence to fail*. This means that he didn't benefit from strong identification embodiment, and rather owing to the strength of identity among followers, he was penalised for the loss.

Non-prototypical leaders can also gain group trust and followership by showing that they are working in the group's best interests. Both prototypical and non-prototypical leaders who aimed for a stretch goal were given more leeway to fail than those aiming for an easier goal (Giessner & van Knippenberg, 2008). Non-prototypical leaders can also benefit from situations of uncertainty, where support for prototypical leaders is reduced (Rast et al., 2012).

There may be a benefit for underrepresented groups to take advantage of their non-prototypical status to gain leadership positions that would otherwise only be held by majority group members. There is a body of research on marginal leadership on this topic. For an overview see Rast et al., 2018.

Judge et al. (2009) suggested that wherever a social structure develops, the defining characteristic of that structure is the emergence of a leader. This is particularly important in organisations where the efficient running of the company relies on effective leadership. However, the leader of an organisation cannot always emerge from the workforce. In such cases leaders can still use the group identity to their advantage by generating a shared sense of 'us' through identity entrepreneurship, or showing they are willing to 'do it for us' through identity advancement (see Steffans et al., 2014 for overview). This can be helpful for organisations making a change or in the context of mergers and acquisitions (see Box 9.1) where the leader may need to shape and re-define the team identity.

Central to the identity approach to leadership is that the group is the core of the leader's effectiveness. That is, without acknowledging the group norms and values, or the cohesion between group members, the leader is likely to have trouble in influencing their workforce. This suggests that the leader must be acutely aware of the dynamics within and between their work teams and the wider organisation. Being able to foster a strong shared sense of 'us', rather than each individual 'I', creates an environment in which team members are encouraged to work towards shared goals and support each other in doing so.

Leaders who are particularly well placed to do this are often people who have been members of the team already, so their leadership emerges as a result of having embodied the teams' values, showing that they are willing to advocate for the group's best interests, showing in-group favouritism and highlighting the meta-contrast ratio between the in-group and the out-group. Those who do this effectively are also given additional 'credit' to drive the team in new directions and propose shifts in the teams' norms. As with the impact of organisational identification on the individual, these credits can be used in both positive and negative ways.

Innovation and transgression

On the positive side, leaders, and to a degree, team members, who foster a strong sense of organisational identification are given idiosyncrasy credit (Hollander, 1985). This means that they are given more leeway to steer the team in new directions and use innovative ideas. The group are more likely to support new ideas that may move the team in a new direction when the leader has shown their commitment to the in-group. However, a leader must balance this with their position within the group. If they move too far from the existing norms or are seen to be putting the in-group reputation at risk, their idiosyncrasy credits can be used up, after which they would be rejected as the leader.

In a similar vein, members of the team who embody the identity most strongly can benefit from innovation credit (Abrams et al., 2008). This allows the most prototypical members to deviate from or define new expected behaviours for the in-group, known as prescriptive norms. This gives them the allowance to innovate how the team works and can be used to shift the team in a new direction. Status within the team has an impact on how much innovation is tolerated. Leaders, and particularly future leaders, are given the most latitude, especially if they are steering the group in a brand-new direction, moving away from existing norms towards a new position. This can therefore be helpful for incoming leaders who could harness their use of the group identity to bring team members with them in a new strategic direction.

On the other hand, prototypical team members, and especially leaders, can be afforded transgression credit, allowing them to get away with poor behaviour (Abrams et al., 2013). This is especially the case when the transgression may work in favour of the in-group, and research suggests that behaviours varying in severity will be forgiven. However, more recent research argues that there is a limit to the transgression credit. One such example is racism. Travaglino et al. (2014) found that although a leader would be given leeway for some transgressive behaviours, displaying racism was seen as a step too far, and could not so easily be overlooked.

The research in this area is, however, primarily focused on samples comprising mainly of students, and using hypothetical scenarios in experimental designs. See Box 9.3 for more on this 'dilemma in the field'.

Box 9.3   Dilemma in the field: access to applied samples

As research on organisational identification is still growing, there are some research areas where samples used in empirical studies rely on the use of students or hypothetical groups and teams. As can be seen by the application of SIT to organisational contexts, findings can be translated into different situations and the outcomes remain similar. However, without additional research in organisational settings we cannot be sure that the same can be said for some of the team dynamics findings. It also means that there isn't yet a consensus on how to apply this particular theory to practice, and the evidence at this stage is still somewhat more theoretical than practical.

For example, the research cited above that investigated innovation and transgression credit relied mostly on student samples. Whilst students are adults, and many may have work experience, there is evidence to suggest that students may be a unique sample and not typically respond in the same way as a working sample. Add to this the fact that in a lot of cases the students are from psychology undergraduate programmes, and therefore may have been exposed to the theory being tested in the study during their course, which could be biasing their responses – this should add to concerns over the validity of these findings for organisational settings.

Furthermore, whilst the use of experimental designs means that the researchers were able to control for other confounding factors, it also means that the findings are based on hypothetical scenarios, rather than relying on real-world problems and experiences. This is a topic explored in greater detail by Bello et al. (2009) who argued that student samples are particularly problematic when the processes being studied are likely to be affected by context and life experiences. In such cases, student samples cannot be generalised to applied contexts. This can then pose a problem for practitioners wanting to apply the research to their organisational issues. It is therefore important that scientist-practitioners in the field of organisational psychology both know how to evaluate the reliability, validity, and generalisability of evidence, and are able where necessary to either conduct or commission research with applied samples to ensure the correct application of theory to practice.

Motivation and engagement

As employees will associate their sense of self with their work team or the organisation as a whole, the work team or organisation becomes the in-group which the employee wants to impress. Therefore, a social identity perspective would suggest that employees will be motivated to work for the benefit of the group and its other members. This phenomenon is seen outside of organisations in friendship groups and sports teams. However, what is also seen in social group contexts is that with the distribution of effort among several individuals there is the opportunity for some to get away with doing less than others, known as social loafing. This suggests that highlighting the shared identity of the team or organisation may help to mitigate some instances of social loafing and may even enhance performance – known as social labouring (Ellemers et al., 2004).

Those with a strong sense of organisational identification self-reported higher work motivation (Wegge et al., 2006). It is also argued that this is seen more when the identity is made salient, and that high performance is seen to be in the team's best interests (van Knippenberg, 2000). Further, employees are more likely to be willing to engage in Organisational Citizenship Behaviours (OCBs) when they are more strongly identified with their team or organisation (Wegge et al., 2006). OCBs are additional tasks that employees take on voluntarily, beyond the work defined in their contract. This means that being strongly identified with the team or organisation is associated with 'going the extra mile' at work. Therefore, organisational leaders could harness the identification among employees to help increase work performance and extra-role behaviours.

As detailed above, this can go too far and lead to a decrease in well-being, so it is important to evaluate such interventions to see what is working and for whom. Additionally, a strong organisational identity can lead to team members exerting more effort working towards individual goals if the norm is one of competitiveness (Ellemers et al., 2004), so a balance must be found between the team's norms for collective rather than competitive working and creating a shared identity that encourages *inter*group advantage instead of *intra*group performance goals. Additionally, the current prominence of a particular identity (such as with the team or organisation) encourages a person to try and embody the norms of the group. They will want to be seen as embodying the norms, and thus more prototypical of the group, and feel that they are working to maintain or increase the perceived status of their group (Haslam et al., 2000).

Since identities are flexible and context dependent, performance may be influenced by the identity that is contextually relevant at the time, or is most salient. This means that managers have an opportunity to shape the norms and relative salience of group values to get the most from team members. For example, creating a shared identity for the team with norms for intergroup competition and valuing collaboration could lead to social labouring where team members are inclined to work to achieve their team's goals, increasing their team's status relative to other teams, and to work for the collective rather than the individual.

Practical applications

A wealth of research suggests that organisational identity can influence several workplace outcomes, but it is also important to consider how best to harness this in practice. As explained above, a person's sense of self is strongly influenced by identification with groups, teams, or social structures. Applied to organisations, this means that broadly the organisation can align its purpose, values, and culture to create an identity which employees can associate with their sense of self. This creates a core though the organisation which allows leaders to influence teams towards achieving the organisation's strategic objectives.

Organisations can display their identity through branding and uniforms, or even the way that workspaces are decorated. This can act as a very overt way to ensure that the identity is made salient within the workplace. Furthermore, having the core values displayed around buildings can act as a reminder of the values with which employees feel identified. Given that the strength of identification is also linked to belonging to the group and other members, the degree to which other employees also live the values of the organisation and display in-group favouritism can also help to maintain strong identification. This would be even more important for leaders and managers to show that they are prototypical of the group. This means that managers may benefit from reminding their teams of the shared values and creating team-based values and norms that can be espoused in the context of the smaller team.

The need to belong is fundamental to humans, who spend large amounts of their time at work. It therefore makes intuitive sense that being able to foster a sense of belonging through shared identity in the workplace would have positive effects on performance. This benefits both the organisation and the employees. As detailed in the happy-productive worker hypothesis (see Chapter 5 for more details), employees who are happy and healthy at work are more productive.

Future directions in the field: virtual teams

With advances in technology and through global social and political changes to working practices many organisations offer the opportunity for employees to work flexibly, virtually, and in geographically distributed teams – and this may become the norm. To-date, much of the research cited above considers more traditional ways of working, primarily focusing on co-located employees working in the same physical environment. It is therefore important to consider the potential impact of distributed, virtual, and hybrid working patterns on identity development and the ability of organisational leaders to harness the positive outcomes associated with strong organisational identification.

There may be differences in the impact of distributed and virtual working depending on whether the team already has an identity before being distributed or is formed virtually from the beginning. However, research to date has highlighted problems with virtual teams. In fact, Au and Marks (2012) found that perceived cultural differences created additional problems for virtual teams that led to greater use of stereotypes and more conflict between team members. It is, however, thought that creating a shared set of values and working to enhance identification can moderate this effect. This means that having a shared identity in virtual teams may help resolve or prevent interpersonal conflicts between team members (Hinds & Mortensen, 2005).

Little research has yet identified whether and how best to manage the development or formation of shared identity in the creation of virtual teams; however, wider research on virtual teams emphasises the importance of communication, developing trust, and knowledge-sharing opportunities (Hallier & Baralou, 2010; Hinds & Bailey, 2003). These are also important elements in the creation of a shared identity, so there may be a lot of overlap between virtual and collocated teams in this context. However, it may also be that completely virtual teams are not the most efficient working pattern, and there may need to be opportunities for face-to-face interactions at various stages through the team life cycle to allow for the benefits of shared identity when the team is dispersed. Opportunities for social interactions are important for helping team members feel that they belong. The added benefit of allowing social interactions to be a valid part of working relationships is the opportunity for knowledge exchange and greater interpersonal spill-over into productivity.

As virtual and hybrid working patterns increase it will be important for organisational psychologists to ensure research is being undertaken to understand the challenges virtual teams face, and the potential benefits of developing and maintaining strong identification between members. This may require additional support for leaders to manage such relationships and shifts in organisational culture to appreciate the importance of balancing interpersonal social and professional relationships. In particular it will be useful to keep up to date on potential changes to policy regarding hybrid and flexible working and what impact this may have on managing team relationships.

Conclusion

In this chapter the application of SIT to organisational team dynamics has been explored. Whilst there is a wealth of evidence that a strong sense of identification with the organisation has generally positive effects, there is also an avenue of research that should not be ignored, suggesting that in relation to identification there can be too much of a good thing.

Organisational identification can have a positive influence on workplace processes such as:

- increased motivation to work for the good of the team;
- higher ability for leaders to influence when they are perceived as more typical of the group and its norms and values;
- reduced intentions to leave the organisation;
- more willingness to go the extra mile at work;
- higher levels of engagement and job satisfaction.

However, there are also potential pitfalls that must be acknowledged in relation to strong organisational identification, these include:

- negative impact on wellbeing and potential for burnout owing to a strong attachment to the organisation and willingness to work more;
- spending more time focused on work, in turn, negatively impacting life satisfaction.

Similarly, the impact that organisational identification has on leadership processes can be both positive and negative. Whilst there are benefits of the leader being seen as the most typical member of the group to enhance leadership influence and likelihood of being chosen as a leader, this can also allow the leader credit to behave badly. Furthermore, the benefit to team members of a prototypical leader is the strengthening of the team's values and identity, although on the other hand, this can also mean that the leader deviates from the existing group norms and can lead the team in a new direction which may stray from individuals' personal values and self-identity.

With this in mind there is a balance to be had in managing belonging, interpersonal relationships, and team identification to get the best outcomes in terms of employee wellbeing, productivity, and engagement. This highlights the importance of organisational psychologists maintaining an understanding of the science they are using in practice.

Explore further

- SIGN website: https://sign.centre.uq.edu.au/
- Ashforth, B.E. & Mael, F. (1989). Social identity theory and the organization. *The Academy of Management Review*, 14(1), 20–39. https://doi.org/10.2307/258189
- Hogg leadership paper: Hogg MA. (2001). A social identity theory of leadership. *Personality and Social Psychology Review*. 5(3):184–200. doi:10.1207/S15327957PSPR0503_1

References

Abrams, D. & Hogg, M.A. (2006). *Social identifications: A social psychology of intergroup relations and group processes*. Abingdon: Routledge.

Abrams, D., Randsley de Moura, G., Marques, J.M. & Hutchison, P. (2008). Innovation credit: When can leaders oppose their group's norms?. *Journal of Personality* and *Social Psychology*, 95(3), 662.

Abrams, D., Randsley de Moura, G. & Travaglino, G.A. (2013). A double standard when group members behave badly: Transgression credit to ingroup leaders. *Journal of Personality and Social Psychology*, 105(5), 799.

Ashforth, B.E. & Mael, F. (1989). Social identity theory and the organization. *Academy of Management Review*, 14(1), 20–39.

Au, Y. & Marks, A. (2012). 'Virtual teams are literally and metaphorically invisible': Forging identity in culturally diverse virtual teams. *Employee Relations*, 34(3), 271–287.

Avanzi, L., van Dick, R., Fraccaroli, F. & Sarchielli, G. (2012). The downside of organizational identification: Relations between identification, workaholism and well-being. *Work & Stress*, 26(3), 289–307.

Bello, D., Leung, K., Radebaugh, L., Tung, R.L. & Van Witteloostuijn, A. (2009). From the editors: Student samples in international business research. *Journal of International Business Studies*, 40, 361–364.

Branković, M., Pavlović, M., Žeželj, I., Vladisavljević, M., Jovanović, O. & Petrović, N. (2015). Social identity complexity and inclusiveness as predictors of intergroup emotions. *Primenjena Psihologija*, 8(4), 363–378.

De Moura, G.R., Abrams, D., Retter, C., Gunnarsdottir, S. & Ando, K. (2009). Identification as an organizational anchor: How identification and job satisfaction combine to predict turnover intention. *European Journal of Social Psychology*, 39(4), 540–557.

Ellemers, N., De Gilder, D. & Haslam, S.A. (2004). Motivating individuals and groups at work: A social identity perspective on leadership and group performance. *Academy of Management Review*, 29(3), 459–478.

Giessner, S.R. & van Knippenberg, D. (2008). 'License to fail': Goal definition, leader group prototypicality, and perceptions of leadership effectiveness after leader failure. *Organizational Behavior and Human Decision Processes*, 105(1), 14–35.

Hallier, J. & Baralou, E. (2010). Other voices, other rooms: Differentiating social identity development in organisational and Pro-Am virtual teams. *New Technology, Work and Employment*, 25(2), 154–166.

Haslam, A.S., Powell, C. & Turner, J.C. (2000). Social identity, self-categorisation, and work motivation: Rethinking the contribution of the group to positive and sustainable organisational outcomes. *Applied Psychology: An International Review*, 49(3), 319–339.

Haslam, S.A. & Ellemers, N. (2011). Identity processes in organizations. *Handbook of Identity Theory and Research*, 715–744.

Hinds, P.J. & Bailey, D.E. (2003). Out of sight, out of sync: Understanding conflict in distributed teams. *Organization Science*, 14(6), 615–632.

Hinds, P.J. & Mortensen, M. (2005). Understanding conflict in geographically distributed teams: The moderating effects of shared identity, shared context, and spontaneous communication. *Organization Science*, 16(3), 290–307.

Hogg, M.A. (2001). A social identity theory of leadership. *Personality and Social Psychology Review*, 5(3), 184–200.

Hollander, E.P. (1985). Leadership and power. In G. Lindzey & E. Aronson (Eds.), Handbook of social psychology (Third Edition). New York: Random House.

Judge, T.A., Piccolo, R.F. & Kosalka, T. (2009). The bright and dark sides of leader traits: A review and theoretical extension of the leader trait paradigm. *The Leadership Quarterly*, 20(6), 855–875.

Karanika-Murray, M., Duncan, N., Pontes, H.M. & Griffiths, M.D. (2015). Organizational identification, work engagement, and job satisfaction. *Journal of Managerial Psychology*, 30(8), 1019–1033.

Li, Y., Fan, J. & Zhao, S. (2015). Organizational identification as a double-edged sword. *Journal of Personnel Psychology*, 14 (40). https://doi.org/10.1027/1866-5888/a000133 .

Pratt, M.G. & Rafaeli, A. (1997) Organizational Dress as a Symbol of Multilayered Social Identities, *Academy of Management Journal*, *40*(4), 862–898.

Ramiah, A., Hewstone, M. & Schmid, K. (2011). Social identity and intergroup conflict. *Psychological Studies*, *56*, 44–52.

Rast III, D.E., Gaffney, A.M., Hogg, M.A. & Crisp, R.J. (2012). Leadership under uncertainty: When leaders who are non-prototypical group members can gain support. *Journal of Experimental Social Psychology*, *48*(3), 646–653.

Rast III, D.E., Hogg, M.A. & Randsley de Moura, G. (2018). Leadership and social transformation: The role of marginalized individuals and groups. Journal of Social Issues, *74*(1), 8–19.

Reicher, S., Haslam, S.A. & Hopkins, N. (2005). Social identity and the dynamics of leadership: Leaders and followers as collaborative agents in the transformation of social reality. *The Leadership Quarterly*, *16*(4), 547–568.

Steffens, N.K., Haslam, S.A., Reicher, S.D., Platow, M.J., Fransen, K., Yang, J. ... & Boen, F. (2014). Leadership as social identity management: Introducing the Identity Leadership Inventory (ILI) to assess and validate a four-dimensional model. The Leadership Quarterly, *25*(5), 1001–1024. https://doi.org/10.1016/j.leaqua.2014.05.002.

Tajfel, H.E. (1978). *Differentiation between social groups: Studies in the social psychology of intergroup relations*. Academic Press.

Tajfel H. & Turner J. (1979). An integrative theory of intergroup conflict. In W.G. Austin, S. Worchel (Eds.) *The social psychology of intergroup relations* (pp. 33–47). Monterey, CA: Brooks/Cole.

Travaglino, G.A., Abrams, D., de Moura, G.R., Marques, J.M. & Pinto, I.R. (2014). How groups react to disloyalty in the context of intergroup competition: Evaluations of group deserters and defectors. Journal of Experimental Social Psychology, *54*, 178–187.

Turner, J.C., Hogg, M.A., Turner, P.J. & Smith, P.M. (1984). Failure and defeat as determinants of group cohesiveness. British Journal of Social Psychology, *23*(2), 97–111. https://doi.org/10.1111/j.2044-8309.1984.tb00619.x

van Knippenberg, D. (2000). Work motivation and performance: A social identity perspective. *Applied Psychology: An International Review*, *49*(3), 357–371.

van Knippenberg, D. & Hogg, M.A. (2001). Social identity processes in organizations. *Group Processes & Intergroup Relations*, *4*(3), 185–189.

Wegge, J., van Dick, R., Fisher, G.K., Wecking, C. & Moltzen, K. (2006). Work motivation, organisational identification, and well-being in call centre work. *Work & Stress*, *20* (1), 60–83.

Wietrak, E., Rousseau, D. & Barends, E. (2021) *Work motivation: An evidence review. Scientific summary*. London: Chartered Institute of Personnel and Development.

Williams, K.D. & Jarvis, B. (2006). Cyberball: A program for use in research on interpersonal ostracism and acceptance. *Behavior Research Methods*, *38* (1), 174–180.

Chapter 10

Well-being and work in focus

Mindfulness at work

Jutta Tobias Mortlock

Overview

This chapter links with the British Psychological Society's (BPS's) area of well-being and work. It provides an overview of what mindfulness is and how it contributes to workplace well-being. We will introduce some of the core scientific concepts related to workplace mindfulness, including the mechanisms of action that drive the effectiveness of mindfulness for people at work and several different workplace-relevant mindfulness literatures. We will consider the current scientific debates in mindfulness at work and offer some suggestions for future mindfulness research and practice. The chapter concludes with a set of practical recommendations for applying mindfulness at work.

Learning outcomes

By the end of this chapter you will:

- know what mindfulness is and how it is defined in the scientific literature;
- understand the link between mindfulness and well-being at work;
- be aware of the current debates in workplace mindfulness;
- be able to apply several key practical approaches to bringing mindfulness into workplaces.

What is mindfulness?

Over the last 40 years, a distinct set of scientific mindfulness literatures has emerged, largely in silos. These mindfulness 'schools of thought' range from individual mindfulness for stress reduction to collective mindfulness for entire organisations, and from mindfulness for self-regulation to mindfulness for self-exploration. Mindfulness is practised in schools, in workplaces, in prisons, and in the military (van Dam et al., 2017). On news-stands, you can find mindfulness periodicals for teens and seniors alike, alongside magazines for mindful eating, mindful exercise, and mindful environmentalism.

But what exactly is mindfulness? To date more than 33 definitions of mindfulness have been published in the scientific literature (Nilsson & Kazemi, 2016). The most well-known

DOI: 10.4324/9781003302087-12

was coined by Jon Kabat-Zinn: 'paying attention in a particular way: on purpose, in the present moment, and nonjudgmentally' (Kabat-Zinn 1994, pp. 3–4). Kabat-Zinn is the founder of the world's most well-known and extensively researched Mindfulness-Based Intervention (MBI); the Mindfulness-Based Stress Reduction (MBSR) program. In the late 1970s, Kabat-Zinn brought his knowledge of Buddhism to his research and teaching on stress reduction at the Massachusetts Institute of Technology (MIT).

MBSR was originally designed as 'participatory medicine', bringing together contemplative traditions and clinical medical science, to help hospital patients suffering clinical or mental health conditions to find relief (Kabat-Zinn, 2011). Kabat-Zinn's seminal work spawned the so-called 'first-generation' of MBIs, rooted in Buddhist traditions and designed for secular community settings, aiming to be 'maximally accessible to people with diverse values and religious affiliations' (Crane et al., 2017, p. 991). This first generation of mindfulness training approaches was designed to serve three specific purposes: as a tool for self-regulation, a tool for self-exploration, and a tool for self-liberation (self-liberation refers to proactively considering issues that transcend the self, including holding a desire to be of compassionate service to others; Shapiro, 1992).

Hospital patients signed up to participate in MBSR and to practise mindfulness meditation in order to cultivate wise, transformative awareness, and 'to do something *for themselves* as a complement to their more traditional medical treatments' (Kabat-Zinn, 2011, p. 288, *emphasis in original*). In short, the first wave of scientific interest in mindfulness focused on helping clinical patients help – or even heal – themselves through mindfulness meditation.

So what is meditation? The terms mindfulness and meditation are routinely used interchangeably, even in seminal mindfulness publications (c.f. Creswell, 2017; van Dam et al., 2017), yet they are not one and the same. Kabat-Zinn defined 'meditation' operationally (an operational definition describes what people actually do), as 'self-regulation of attention' (leaning on Goleman and Schwartz's 1976 definition). This means that Kabat-Zinn explains mindfulness as a meditative practice of self-regulating one's attention in the present moment in a particularly non-judgmental and purposeful way. Much prominent mindfulness research today is focused on formal meditation practice, frequently using the breath as an anchor to develop awareness of sensations, emotions, thoughts, and physical reactions, including through exercises such as mindful eating or scanning the body (Kabat-Zinn, 2005).

However, mindfulness meditation need not involve a specific format, for example sitting cross-legged in silence for a period of time with one's eyes closed (incense optional). In fact, mindfulness is a 'way of being' (Kabat-Zinn, 2011, p. 284) or a state of mind that is familiar to anyone and can arise organically at any time, not only in conjunction with formal guided meditation practice (Reina & Kudesia, 2020).

Box 10.1   Mindful reflection for willing readers

Bring to mind the last time you were mindful. Consider the following questions: What led up to this point? How were you being in the situation you were in, to yourself, and to anyone around you? How did this feel? What impact did this have, on how you felt, on any decisions you took, on anyone else?

What can you learn from this reflection about how being mindful may be helpful to you?

If we want to fully understand mindfulness at work, and foster it in organisations, understanding its potential in supporting workers in being and doing well, we need to further explore its link with well-being.

Mindfulness and well-being

Kabat-Zinn argued that mindfulness is transformative and has the potential to overcome suffering and generate insight, wisdom, and compassion for individuals, communities, and our global society (Kabat-Zinn, 2011).

The terms 'suffering', 'insight', 'wisdom', and 'compassion' are not commonly used in workplaces or in organisational psychology. A more contemporary term for 'suffering' is (painful, unwanted) 'stress'. A simpler way to understand the purpose of mindfulness is that it helps people learn skilful ways to manage unwanted stress, and thus improve their well-being: this is why mindfulness is so strongly associated with well-being.

Over the past 40 years Kabat-Zinn and hundreds of other behavioural scientists and clinical psychologists explored the connection between mindfulness meditation and mental health so extensively that there are thousands of scientific studies on the subject today. Researchers at Oxford University demonstrated that mindfulness meditation can work just as effectively against chronic depression as antidepressants (Kuyken et al., 2015). This is a ground-breaking insight. Chronic depression is often based on chemical alterations in the brain, assumed to be ameliorated most effectively by external chemicals such as antidepressants; that mental exercise such as mindfulness meditation can achieve the same result speaks to the extensive link between mind and body. We can strengthen this connection through mindfulness, validly and reliably, and this is why mindfulness is interesting for science as well as for practice.

The effectiveness of MBIs in generating individual stress management skills is fairly well proven. Meta-analyses of MBIs with non-clinical samples indicate significant stress reduction (Chiesa & Serretti, 2009), increased well-being (Eberth & Sedlmeier, 2012), and higher quality of life (Khoury et al., 2015).

MBIs are increasingly popular as a way to enhance individuals' well-being in the contemporary workplace, but let's not forget that the use of mindfulness goes back to the fifth century BC. According to Buddhist scholar Bhikkhu Bodhi, Buddhism is rooted in the teachings of the Buddha, who lived in northeast India at that time. He created 'a system of training that leads to insight and the overcoming of suffering' (Bodhi, 2011, p. 20) and gained popularity and spread throughout Asia in the centuries that followed. This system of training focuses on altruistic concern for the welfare of all sentient beings (Flanagan, 2011).

To unpack the link between mindfulness and well-being further, let's examine the purpose of mindfulness in its original context. At the heart of Buddhist principles and practices is a discipline that is called 'mindfulness' today. This discipline consists of two parts: (1) objectively paying attention to and being aware of one's experience, and (2) clearly comprehending this experience by interpreting it in a meaningful way, specifically focusing on generating wisdom and compassion (Bodhi, 2011).

This second part of Buddhist mindfulness practice has a strong ethical component. Buddhists call this 'right mindfulness': presence of mind, coupled with clear ethically informed comprehension and with social responsibility (Purser & Milillo, 2015). A quote from the Buddha's original and preserved discourses illustrates this way of being vividly: 'right mindfulness… [is] contemplating the body in the body, ardent, clearly comprehending, mindful, having removed covetousness and displeasure in regard to the world' (cited in Bodhi, 2011, p. 20). Crucially, to transform suffering, according to Buddhist principles, we must refrain from 'unwholesome' psychological motivations in relation to self, others, and the world at large, such as greed or hatred (Monteiro et al., 2015).

Here's the 21st-century description of what this means: in order to genuinely improve our well-being through mindfulness, we need to learn to (1) observe our experience objectively, and (2) develop the mental discipline of choosing thoughts and actions that are ethically and morally helpful, not only towards us but also towards others. Succinctly put, mindfulness seems to be about more than self-help.

Core concepts relevant for workplace mindfulness

To grasp the potential of mindfulness for employees, we need to understand how mindfulness works. We also need to discuss the less well-known scientific workplace-relevant mindfulness literatures, in addition to exploring and debating 'first-generation' MBIs based on MBSR. Each of these topics will be covered below.

The mechanisms of action that make mindfulness work

While the general public often (mis)understands mindfulness as temporary relief from life's challenges and as a way to avoid engaging with difficulty (Choi et al., 2021), leading mindfulness scholars to argue that mindfulness contains two key elements: grounding one's awareness in present-moment attention, and an attitude of open-minded acceptance or discernment (Bishop et al., 2004; Creswell, 2017; Van Dam et al., 2017). This overlaps considerably with the two-part Buddhist discipline of mindfulness outlined above.

Present-moment awareness is achieved through attention regulation, typically through formal meditative practice. An attitude of acceptance is strongly linked to metacognition, defined as the process of monitoring and adjusting how one processes information (Fernandez-Duque et al., 2000). More specifically, acceptance is the result of metacognitive capacity, in other words the capability to shift perspective from within one's subjective experience onto that experience (Bernstein et al., 2015). Metacognition has been discussed by several mindfulness scientists over the years. Shapiro et al. (2006) for example emphasised the pivotal role of reperceiving in mindfulness, the process of learning to attend to moment-to-moment experience without judgment by shifting perspective in relation to thought. Subsequently, Bernstein et al. (2015) argued that reperceiving is synonymous to decentring, the process through which metacognitive capacity develops.

Three interrelated psychological processes generate metacognitive capacity: (a) meta-awareness, which means being aware that one is aware; (b) disidentification from one's experience; and (c) reduced reactivity to (especially difficult) thought content (Bernstein et al., 2015). Together these metacognitive processes produce acceptance.

Why does this matter for workplaces? Mindfulness at work is about more than present-moment attention. Recall that mindfulness can arise organically in everyday life (Reina & Kudesia, 2020). We all know that it is possible to notice different aspects about situations in our lives, which in turn can change our relationship with them. Consider the last time you felt the urge to check your email whilst dealing with a difficult work challenge, but became aware that interrupting your concentration may not be fully in line with your professional aims. The act of noticing this urge made you *mindful* of the choices available to you in that moment (whether you acted on that state of mindfulness or not is a different matter).

Furthermore, the aim of mindfulness in organisations needs to be more than a psychological property of individuals. This is because being mindful in a workplace context is not necessarily about being aware, nice, or even friendly – instead, the core function of workplace mindfulness is to generate a suitable context for developing metacognitive capacity, embedded in a collective response to organisational challenges (Kudesia, 2019).

Ellen Langer's socio-cognitive approach to mindfulness

Around the same time as Kabat-Zinn started developing MBSR, another scholar pioneered a different mindfulness school of thought using a different approach to generating mindfulness: Ellen Langer at Harvard University.

Langer defines mindfulness as 'openness to novelty' (Langer, 1989), conceptualising it as an everyday socio-cognitive practice of consciously noticing information in the present situation and how it is automatically (mindlessly) categorised, in order to become more actively engaged in the present (Langer et al., 1978; Langer, 1989).

The basic process underlying the effectiveness of Langerian mindfulness consists of helping individuals clarify and change their relationship with themselves and with the situation at hand by proactively seeking alternative interpretations of situations and stimuli, which fosters feeling comfortable with ambiguity and an increased sense of self-acceptance. Langerian mindfulness is related to metacognitive capacity because an awareness of more than one perspective in any given situation is key to a state of mindfulness. Langer and colleagues argue that 'one of the most natural methods of reducing self-evaluation and replacing it with acceptance is to assume a mindset of mindfulness rather than mindlessness' (Langer, 1989; cited in Carson & Langer, 2006, p. 29). Indeed, the benefits of non-meditative mindfulness practices for reducing anxiety and depression and increasing physical well-being and longevity are extensively documented (Alexander et al., 1989; Haigh et al., 2011; Pagnini et al., 2015).

This type of mindful mental practice is conceptually similar to what is called 'analytical meditation' in Eastern contemplative traditions, to help individuals discipline their minds and gain new insight, as distinct from 'concentrative meditation' (Dalai Lama, 2005, p. 109). In particular, Langerian mindfulness draws extensively on parables, intellectual puzzles, and humour, to help individuals accept and change their relationship with themselves and with uncertainty (Carson & Langer, 2006).

Box 10.2   Mindful socio-cognitive practice for willing readers

Reflect – in writing – on different aspects of the topic 'being enthusiastic about mindfulness', in three steps.

1   Write down what might be positive if you adopted such an attitude (for example, the potential benefits to you and / or others, and so on).
2   Now, write down what might be negative if you adopted this attitude (for instance, what information might you be sceptical about, how would you relate to certain people, and so on).
3   Finally, look over what you've written, and then write down what your most productive attitude towards reading the rest of this chapter is. What (if any) new choices became available to you?

What can you learn from doing this exercise?

Everyday mindfulness as described by Langer (1989) allows for more openness to all the options that life has to offer – even providing a feeling of empowerment (Langer et al., 1978).

The innovation offered by the Langerian socio-cognitive approach to mindfulness is that people can practise mindfulness *in situ* by focusing on context and the person's environment (Langer, 1989). In other words, Langerian mindfulness is an 'everyday' process that does not involve taking a break from active engagement with the situation at hand in order to direct attention inward and engage in meditative practice focused on the breath or other intrapsychic experience. This mindful process of actively drawing novel distinctions is said to promote cognitive flexibility in relation to the situation at hand (Pagnini et al., 2016). Cognitive flexibility is the capability of adaptively and flexibly responding to particular situations, rather than thinking rigidly or on autopilot (Hayes et al., 1999; Shapiro et al., 2006).

Collective mindfulness

So far, we have covered a range of different mindfulness approaches that specify individuals' mental relationship with their inner world; their own thoughts, feelings, and judgments. But mindfulness can also infuse the mental space between two or more people, in that we can become mindful *of each other*: consciously aware and encountering each other with an attitude of cognitive flexibility (for example, by giving each other the benefit of the doubt at work). In fact, there is another core mindfulness literature that is less intrapsychic in orientation and instead more focused on social and situational awareness: focused *collective* mindfulness. This literature is dedicated to studying team processes of shared cognition and action that help teams and entire organisations uncover and overcome unexpected stressors and thus 'manage the unexpected' (Weick et al., 1999).

In contrast to a focus on *individual* stress management through MBSR and related mindfulness training programs, collective mindfulness is a social construct, defined as the 'capacity of groups and individuals to be acutely aware of significant details, to notice errors in the making, and to have the shared expertise and freedom to act on what they notice' (Weick et al., 2000, p. 34). In other words, employees acting mindfully on a collective scale manage stress *collectively*: they are able to anticipate, detect, and appropriately respond to unexpected, stressful problems (Vogus et al., 2014; Weick et al., 1999).

Collective mindfulness arises out of specific social practices, actions, and communication patterns that liken the 'collective mind' of a group of individuals who organise mindfully to a flock of birds flying in unison, with each bird constantly paying attention not only to their own direction, but also to every other member of the flock, and constantly aligning individual action with the overall direction of the collective (Weick & Roberts, 1993).

Because collective mindfulness is enacted through a dynamic process of social action and interaction, it is also referred to as *mindful organising* (MO, 2016; Sutcliffe et al., 2016), to emphasise its non-static, ever-evolving nature. Originally, the concept of MO was developed to explain how High-Reliability Organisations (HROs) develop capacity to avoid catastrophic failure and perform in nearly error-free ways despite operating in extreme, stressful conditions; however, its scope has expanded to also apply to teams and organisations that are capable of being aware of the status quo in order to improve it, refusing to operate on 'auto pilot' (Fiol & O'Connor, 2003; Sutcliffe et al., 2016).

Five collective mindfulness processes generate MO:

1 Sensitivity to operations, i.e. being committed to checking on a daily basis whether the organisation's activities are aligned with its goals and strategy, or if people's actions are in fact focused on something else entirely in completing daily tasks. This often happens when the leaders are not paying close attention to daily reality for their employees. Imagine a high-end hotel that aims to provide a superior customer experience, but suffering from chronic understaffing and high turnover: this strategy is not feasible unless leadership is 'sensitive' to the operational reality that an understaffed workforce cannot deliver superior service.

2 Preoccupation with failure, i.e. proactively noticing and discussing potential problems. Many people in groups and work teams talk about problems, but 'preoccupied' here means 'fascinated' or 'actively engaged' whenever difficulty or problems are being discussed or addressed. Most teams find it emotionally uncomfortable to discuss difficulty; a collectively mindful team in contrast makes conscious time for these discussions because of a shared understanding that this is essential for avoiding (or at least learning from) disasters.

3 Reluctance to simplify, i.e. a commitment to not brush difficult or uncomfortable issues under the carpet. Similar to the process mentioned just above, this is a shared mindset in a team that complexity is welcome, that uneasy problems with no simple solutions are worth discussing openly, and that whistle-blowers are always encouraged to speak up. This is because a team that organises mindfully is aware that such discussions are essential for anticipating, as well as responding to, unexpected stressful challenges.

4 Commitment to resilience, i.e. consciously making contingency plans for the possibility that team members may not be able to function 100% of the time. This is based on a shared mindset that it is ludicrous to imagine that every team member will always 'function', like a cog in a machine, without ever falling sick or leaving. It involves sharing knowledge about which and how individuals and teams work, it involves work sharing and work shadowing, and it means the organisation has enough 'slack in the system' to function even if critically important team members drop out.

5 Deference to expertise, i.e. giving the final say in important decisions to the person who is most qualified to make this decision, independent of rank, role, or years of experience (Weick et al., 2000). This collective mindfulness process is about paying attention to the diversity of skills or expertise available in any group or team, and drawing on this when making decisions, rather than having the most senior or most highly ranked team member decide *on autopilot*. Imagine a software design team with team members' ages ranging from 21 to 65; it's likely that the 21-year-old will be more qualified to understand complex social media challenges than the 65-year-old. A collectively mindful team would be aware of this and 'defer to' (or at least involve) the junior team member in the decision-making process.

While MO may appear to align closely with standard management practice, leading collective mindfulness experts emphasise that teams who organise mindfully 'are motivated to work for the benefit of others and are more receptive to others' perspectives and incorporate those perspectives into their work' (Vogus et al., 2014, p. 592). The origin of this interpersonal mindset stems from pro-sociality; attitudes and behaviours intended to benefit others (Batson & Powell, 2003), and the capacity to be emotionally ambivalent, i.e. capable of experiencing positive and negative emotions at the same time, for example feeling hope as well as doubt (Vogus et al., 2014).

This is an important point: while MBIs to date are focused on the self, in that they intend to serve as tools for self-regulation, self-exploration, and self-liberation (Shapiro, 1992), the underlying pro-sociality in the collective mindfulness literature reflects the original other-orientation of traditional mindfulness practice (Lopez, 2010) and its strong emphasis on ethical action (c.f. Bodhi, 2011).

To date, the collective mindfulness scholarship has largely bypassed prominent mindfulness science debates. This is probably because collective mindfulness is rooted in management science, rather than a combination of contemplative and clinical science. In addition, it conflicts with the assertion that mindfulness can only be understood from the inside out, as an embodied practice and first-person experience of awareness that is not about intellect or cognition, and instead nurtured through the second-person perspective of a highly skilled trainer (Kabat-Zinn, 2011). Finally, currently little is known in the peer-reviewed literature about mindfulness interventions targeting not only individual mindfulness but also aiming to generate collective mindfulness in organisations (an exception is Tobias Mortlock et al., 2022). This means that organisations interested in evidence-based methods to bring mindfulness to their employees tend to rely on 'first-generation' MBIs, at least as a starting point for their learning and development initiatives.

In sum, mindfulness in organisations can indeed reduce stress and improve well-being for individuals and entire workplaces – but it is a concept (and a phenomenon) that is more multi-faceted than individuals or groups meditating at work. Concretely, this means you might see individuals take time out from work to meditate, either at their desks or in dedicated group settings, or you might notice individuals or teams engaging in metacognitive practices, for example by asking themselves or each other questions relating to the five collective mindfulness processes outlined above.

Current debates

Issues associated with 'first-generation' MBIs

There is a growing body of scientific evidence suggesting that first-generation MBIs may not be as transformative or unequivocally beneficial as previously assumed: there appears to be a systematic publication bias in the majority of scientific mindfulness journals, linked to overstating the effectiveness of MBIs, especially over the medium or long term (Coronado-Montoya et al., 2016).

In addition, longitudinal evidence into the effectiveness of MBIs are rare. A workplace-focused exception is van Berkel et al.'s (2014) evaluation of a Randomised Controlled Trial (RCT) of an MBI targeting work engagement, mental health, mindfulness, and need for recovery, reporting no effect of the intervention after 6 or 12 months.

Furthermore, workplace mindfulness interventions based on MBSR that target outcomes beyond individual stress reduction do not seem unequivocally effective. For example, employees appear to experience lower work motivation after 15 minutes of mindfulness meditation designed to improve their well-being at work (Hafenbrack & Vohs, 2018); critical-thinking performance after 6 weeks' use of the Headspace™ app appears not to increase (Noone & Hogan, 2018); and there seems to be conflicting evidence on the effect of mindfulness on prosocial motivation (Hafenbrack et al., 2020; Hafenbrack et al., 2021).

Finally, leading scholars argue that mindfulness sometimes even causes suffering (Baer et al., 2019). At least 20 case studies exist in the scientific press that document adverse effects of mindfulness meditation (Van Dam et al., 2017). Polyvagal theory illuminates why this adverse effect of mindfulness practice may occur (Porges, 2011). Our autonomic nervous system determines our automatic response to stress, and it adapts with life experience. If an individual has consciously or unconsciously experienced trauma (e.g. an emergency worker or trauma victim but potentially also someone who has experienced overwhelming stress, prejudice, or discrimination), he or she will have experienced this as a life-threatening state of 'freeze'. Any subsequent experience reminiscent of freeze is avoided at all cost, and that can include silent sitting meditation as this may simulate a state of freeze. Conversely, Polyvagal theory also explains why other-orientation (a hallmark of collective mindfulness processes as outlined previously) is an effective antidote to stress, because trust-based social engagement *automatically* calms us down. Social engagement not only benefits others but also improves the actor's own well-being (Aknin et al., 2013; Klein, 2017) and is hence a powerful antidote to stress, both by reaching out to others for help when stressed, and by providing empathy and comfort to those feeling stressed (Porges, 2011).

Issues associated with future directions

Experts argue that mindfulness scientists and practitioners should use more context-sensitive approaches for MBIs in workplaces (Rupprecht et al., 2019), for integrating more diverse schools of thought in workplace mindfulness research (Selart et al., 2020), and for moving on from 'essentially replicating clinical mindfulness research in the workplace' (Reb et al., 2020, p. 3).

In particular, scholars call for a shift away from continuing to 'bend' first-generation MBIs to ever more contexts and instead 'blend' more diverse evidence-based mindfulness processes (Kudesia, 2019). Researchers and practitioners should collaborate in designing and evaluating alternative training formats to MBSR-based mindfulness training, especially those combining individual with collective mindfulness processes to reflect the multi-level nature of mindfulness in organisations.

Additionally, online delivery of mindfulness training is bound to increase in future. While we know that online MBIs may be effective in certain cases (Spijkerman et al., 2016), it is as yet unclear whether and when online delivery of mindfulness training is more appropriate than offering face-to-face mindfulness training to people at work (Kuster et al., 2017). Important current research questions include what combination of asynchronous delivery of mindfulness training with synchronous (online or face-to-face) training with a facilitator can help improve worker well-being (Sanderson et al., 2021). More research is needed in particular as online mindfulness training delivery is likely to be particularly cost-effective and scalable for organisations in the long term.

Practical applications

Figure 10.1, below, is a map of workplace-relevant scientific mindfulness literatures, based on Tobias Mortlock (2023). The map is organised into four quadrants and offers suggestions for practical applications. Three of these four quadrants map on to the three-fold purpose of first-generation MBIs, as mentioned at the top of this chapter: self-regulation, self-exploration, and self-liberation (Shapiro, 1992); the final quadrant is entitled 'prosocial engagement', leaning on Vogus et al. (2014), who argued that pro-sociality is at

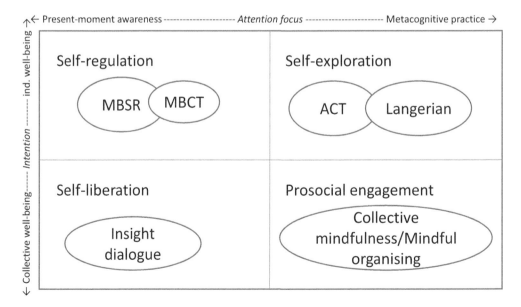

Figure 10.1 A visual map of key workplace mindfulness literatures organised by purpose, attention focus and intention orientation.

the heart of collective mindfulness, and on Porges (2011), who demonstrated that social engagement is *automatically* a highly effective stress antidote.

Figure 10,1 is organised as follows: The horizontal axis represents attention focus, specifically ranging from present-moment awareness to metacognitive capacity. The vertical axis represents an intention orientation ranging from improving individual well-being to improving collective well-being.

Mindfulness to increase self-regulation

In the top left-hand quadrant are two approaches to help self-regulation: MBSR, largely focusing on enhancing individual well-being predominately through non-judgmental present-moment awareness training, and mindfulness-based cognitive therapy (MBCT), designed to treat persistent depression (Segal et al., 2002). MBCT mirrors MBSR in format and delivery but has a stronger emphasis on cognitive therapy and evidence suggests that it may be particularly effective in promoting psychological health and well-being (Querstret et al., 2020).

Much mindfulness practice aiming to help increase self-regulation is focused on our five senses, e.g. paying attention to how we breathe in and out, noticing bodily sensations, listening to the sounds surrounding us, or slowly eating a raisin by noticing its appearance, smell, and taste fully. This is because when we consciously perceive our experience of the present through any of our five senses, our body automatically down-regulates our autonomic nervous system's stress arousal. In practice, this means consciously slowing down whenever you notice feeling stressed, and focusing on what you can see/hear/feel/smell, or even taste, even just for one moment.

Mindfulness to increase self-exploration

Self-exploration is concerned with understanding one's mind better, in particular making sense of the often conflicting thoughts and emotions many of us experience. Mindfulness practice focused on developing metacognitive capacity, such as the Langerian socio-cognitive approach to mindfulness outlined above, is particularly helpful.

Structured reflection is a metacognitive practice because it helps individuals change their relationship to their thoughts and emotions and provides a sense of perspective, often through written reflections on their daily experience. The list below is based on Carson and Langer's (2006) suggestions for enhancing mindful self-acceptance:

- Consider yourself as a 'work in progress'. Write about what may/may not, be true about who you are and what you are good/bad at. What new possibilities can open up for you?
- Add humour. Uncover even tiny aspects of the situation that could be considered funny, strange, or outright bizarre. How might this help you accept the situation a little more?
- Consider alternative understandings of what is 'problematic' about you. In how many ways and in how many different contexts might a 'negative' aspect of you be beneficial?
- Reflect on significant events daily. What new perspectives can you see when reviewing what you have observed during the day?
- Keep a journal of joyful moments. List what you are grateful for and look at this list often.

In the same quadrant, also targeting self-exploration, is Acceptance and Commitment Therapy (ACT). ACT (which we introduced in Chapter Five) deserves a special mention here because it combines mindfulness, acceptance, and metacognitive processes to help individuals change their behaviour in line with important values rather than changing cognition and affect itself (Hayes, 2004). The core aim of ACT is to help individuals develop psychological flexibility – the ability to make choices about where to focus your attention – rather than mindfulness per se, and it achieves this through combining mindful acceptance with committing to values-based action (Flaxman et al., 2013).

Mindfulness to increase prosocial engagement

The quadrant on the bottom right of Figure 10.1 combines an attention focus on developing metacognitive capacity at a collective level and aims to improve collective well-being.

Collective mindfulness emerges indirectly as a consequence of prosocial interactions (Vogus et al., 2014) so practical applications in this quadrant aim to develop a (micro) culture of prosociality, open-mindedness, and psychological safety (c.f. Yu & Zellmer-Bruhn, 2018). This needs to be tackled as a social endeavour – mindfulness practised as a team sport (c.f. Tobias Mortlock et al., 2022). In practice this means people at work need to jointly develop metacognitive capacity through engaging with each other prosocially, so that they become able to collaborate effectively in the face of unexpected stressful challenges.

The following three practices may be particularly effective to create the affective foundation for collective mindfulness, based on Tobias Mortlock et al.'s (2022) empirical evaluation of a team-focused mindfulness intervention:

- Cultivate a perception shift so that people at work see themselves as interdependent, rather than independent of each other, in particular when it comes to dealing with difficulty. This can be achieved for example by having people explore how they might proactively support each other in relation to an upcoming work challenge.
- Promote high-quality interpersonal relationships. We all know how good it feels when someone has our back – yet typically, people at work today feel less socially connected, hence they are more reluctant to reach out to others in the face of stressful challenges. Allocating and protecting time to developing meaningful social connections is simple yet effective here, for example having co-workers interview each other using Aron et al.'s (1997) interpersonal closeness questionnaire.
- Cultivate *idea doubt*. Idea doubt is about doubting the validity of one's own judgments. However, we tend to judge others more harshly when we feel stressed (Yu & Zellmer-Bruhn, 2018). Jointly uncovering how quickly we tend to judge others when under pressure, for example by reflecting on Argyris's (1991) Ladder of Inference, or by completing 'user manuals' for working with each other in a team, helps create a behavioural norm of interrupting the impulse to judge others, hence promoting a team climate of *giving everyone the benefit of the doubt*.

Mindfulness to increase self-liberation

In the final quadrant, on the bottom left, we focus on self-liberation. Self-liberation is, as mentioned before, about reflecting on the issues beyond the self, such as ethical action and being of compassionate service to others. It is strongly linked to the other-oriented motivations that form an essential part of wisdom traditions yet that are often overlooked in 'first-generation' mindfulness debates (Van Doesum et al., 2013).

A practical approach to increasing self-liberation is to engage in *insight dialogue*, an interpersonally oriented meditation practice founded by Gregory Kramer (2007) that combines awareness, wisdom, and the natural relatedness that humans share, to cultivate insight into the causes of human suffering and how to overcome it collectively.

The following six guidelines inform insight dialogue and can be practised in pairs:

Pause: step back from habitual thoughts and reactions and into the present moment.
Relax: calm the body and mind, accept whatever sensations, feelings, thoughts that are there.
Open: become aware of the space and spaciousness in the relational moment.
Attune to emergence: allow the experience to unfold as it emerges without an agenda.
Listen deeply: listen with a relaxed and open-minded awareness and receptivity.
Speak the truth: articulate the truth of your experience with discernment.

Conclusion

To sum up, mindfulness in organisations is a cross-level endeavour, ranging from individual mindfulness meditation and individual metacognitive practice to more socially oriented collective mindfulness processes, all aiming to help individuals, teams, and organisations improve well-being by learning to manage stress and challenges more effectively.

Current debates in the literature reveal that there are some issues with so-called first-generation MBIs, and indicate that mindfulness scientists and practitioners may benefit from blending diverse mindfulness practices more.

Future directions in mindfulness science and practice are likely to combine individual with collective mindfulness training more, and explore untapped possibilities of offering mindfulness training online or in blended fashion.

The ultimate aspiration of mindfulness in organisations is to help prompt a shift in work culture towards a sense that people at work are interdependent, that they support each other, and that stress management is a collective responsibility rather than something that needs to be shouldered by individuals in isolation of others. In this way, scientists-practitioners may genuinely broaden the scope of mindfulness to generate wisdom in today's world of work.

Box 10.3   Case study: mindfulness in the United Kingdom Parliament

In 2013, the British MP Chris Ruane started a collaboration with The Mindfulness Initiative, a not-for-profit mindfulness thinktank, to bring mindfulness to United Kingdom parliamentarians. He enrolled the Oxford Mindfulness Centre to offer an 8-week mindfulness training program based on MBCT to interested politicians and their members of staff. Since then, over 300 Members of Parliament and over 500 members of their staff have received mindfulness training. Chris Ruane says one of the most important skills he has learned through his mindfulness practice is to recognise his own biases in real-time: 'When I am pointing that finger at other people quite often my hypocrisy-o-meter sends it straight back to me between the eyes saying "Chris, you have done that as well" ', he explains (Oxford Mindfulness Foundation, n.d.). The Mindfulness Initiative supported the creation of the UK Mindfulness All-Party Parliamentary Group (MAAPG) in 2014, a cross-party group of UK politicians working together to review research evidence on mindfulness and to develop policy recommendations. The MAAPG produced the Mindful Nation UK report in 2015 following a 12-month inquiry including eight parliamentary hearings. The Mindful Nation UK report is the first policy document of its kind and makes policy recommendations on applying mindfulness-based interventions in the areas of education, health, the workplace, and the criminal justice system. The Mindfulness Initiative regularly produces policy documents based on mindfulness science. Of particular relevance for people at work is the toolkit 'Building the case for mindfulness in the workplace', published in 2016 (The Mindfulness Initiative, n.d.).

References

Aknin, L.B., Barrington-Leigh, C.P., Dunn, E.W., Helliwell, J.F., Burns, J., Biswas-Diener, R., Kemeza, I., Nyende, P., Ashton-James, C.E. & Norton, M.I. (2013). Prosocial spending and well-being: Cross-cultural evidence for a psychological universal. *Journal of Personality and Social Psychology, 104*, 635–652.

Alexander, C.N., Langer, E.J., Newman, R.I., Chandler, H.M. & Davies, J.L. (1989). Transcendental meditation, mindfulness, and longevity: An experimental study with the elderly. *Journal of Personality and Social Psychology, 57*(6), 950–964. https://doi.org/10.1037/0022-3514.57.6.950

Argyris, C. (1991), 'Teaching smart people how to learn', *Harvard Business Review*, May–June, 99–109.

Aron, A., Melinat, E., Aron, E.N., Vallone, R.D. & Bator, R.J. (1997). The experimental generation of interpersonal closeness: A procedure and some preliminary findings. *Personality and Social Psychology Bulletin, 23*(4), 363–377.

Baer, R., Crane, C., Miller, E. & Kuyken, W. (2019). Doing no harm in mindfulness-based programs: Conceptual issues and empirical findings. *Clinical Psychology Review, 71*, 101–114.

Batson, C.D. & Powell, A.A. (2003). Altruism and prosocial behavior. In T. Millon & M.J. Lerner (Eds.), *Handbook of psychology: Personality and social psychology* (Vol. 5, pp. 463–484). John Wiley and Sons, Inc. https://doi.org/10.1002/0471264385.wei0519

Bernstein, A., Hadash, Y., Lichtash, Y., Tanay, G., Shepherd, K. & Fresco, D.M. (2015). Decentering and related constructs: A *Critical Review and Metacognitive Processes Model. Perspectives on Psychological Science, 10*(5), 599–617. https://doi.org/10.1177/1745691615594577

Bishop, S.R., Lau, M., Shapiro, S., Carlson, L., Anderson, N.D., Carmody, J., Segal, Z.V., Abbey, S., Speca, M., Velting, D. & Devins, G. (2004). Mindfulness: A proposed operational definition. *Clinical Psychology: Science and Practice, 11*(3), 230–241. https://doi.org/10.1093/clipsy.bph077

Bodhi, B. (2011). What does mindfulness really mean? A canonical perspective. *Contemporary Buddhism*, *12*(1), 19–39.

Carson, S.H. & Langer, E. J. (2006). Mindfulness and self-acceptance. *Journal of Rational-Emotive and Cognitive-Behavior Therapy*, *24*(1), 29–43.

Chiesa, A. & Serretti, A. (2009). Mindfulness-based stress reduction for stress management in healthy people: A review and meta-analysis. *Journal of Alternative and Complementary Medicine (New York, N.Y.)*, *15*(5), 593–600. https://doi.org/10.1089/acm.2008.0495

Choi, E., Farb, N.A.S., Pogrebtsova, E., Gruman, J. & Grossmann, I. (2021). What do people mean when they talk about mindfulness?. *Clinical Psychology Review*, *89*, 102085. https://doi.org/10.1016/j.cpr.2021.102085

Coronado-Montoya, S, Levis, A.W., Kwakkenbos, L, Steele, R.J., Turner, E.H. & Thombs, B.D. (2016) Reporting of positive results in randomized controlled trials of mindfulness-based mental health interventions. *PLOS ONE 11*(4).

Crane, R.S., Brewer, J., Feldman, C., Kabat-Zinn, J., Santorelli, S., Williams, J.M. & Kuyken, W. (2017) What defines mindfulness-based programs? The warp and the weft. *Psychol. Med.*, *47*(6), 990–999.

Creswell, J.D. (2017). Mindfulness interventions. *Annual Review of Psychology*, *68*, 491–516.

Dalai Lama, T.G. (2005). *The Essential Dalai Lama: His important teachings*. London: Penguin.

Eberth, J. & Sedlmeier, P. (2012). The effects of mindfulness meditation: A meta-analysis. *Mindfulness*, *3*(3), 174–189. https://doi.org/10.1007/s12671-012-0101-x

Fernandez-Duque, D., Baird, J.A. & Posner, M.I. (2000). Executive attention and metacognitive regulation. *Consciousness and cognition*, *9*(2 Pt 1), 288–307. https://doi.org/10.1006/ccog.2000.0447

Fiol, C.M. & O'Connor, E.J. (2003). Waking up! Mindfulness in the face of bandwagons. *The Academy of Management Review*, *28*(1), 54–70. https://doi.org/10.2307/30040689

Flanagan, O. (2011). *The Bodhisattva's brain: Buddhism naturalized*. Cambridge, MA: MIT.

Flaxman, P.E., Bond, F.W. & Livheim, F. (2013). *The mindful and effective employee: An acceptance and commitment therapy training manual for improving well-being and performance*. New Harbinger Publications.

Goleman, D.J. & Schwartz, G.E. (1976). Meditation as an intervention in stress reactivity. *Journal of Consulting and Clinical Psychology*, *44*(3), 456–466. https://doi.org/10.1037/0022-006X.44.3.456

Hafenbrack, A.C., Cameron, L.D., Spreitzer, G.M., Zhang, C., Noval, L.J. & Shaffakat, S. (2020). Helping people by being in the present: Mindfulness increases prosocial behavior. *Organizational Behavior and Human Decision Processes*, *159*, 21–38.

Hafenbrack, A., Lapalme, M. & Solal, I. (2021). Mindfulness meditation reduces guilt and prosocial reparation. *Journal of Personality and Social Psychology*, *123*(1), 28.

Hafenbrack, A.C. & Vohs, K.D. (2018). Mindfulness meditation impairs task motivation but not performance. *Organizational Behavior and Human Decision Processes*, *147*, 1–15.

Haigh, E.A.P., Moore, M.T., Kashdan, T.B. & Fresco, D.M. (2011). Examination of the factor structure and concurrent validity of the Langer Mindfulness/Mindlessness Scale. *Assessment*, *18*(1), 11–26. https://doi.org/10.1177/1073191110386342

Hayes, S.C. (2004). Acceptance and commitment therapy, relational frame theory, and the third wave of behavioral and cognitive therapies. *Behavior Therapy*, *35*(4), 639–665.

Hayes, S.C., Strosahl, K.D. & Wilson, K.G. (1999). *Acceptance and Commitment Therapy: An experiential approach to behavior change*. New York, NY: Guilford Press.

Kabat-Zinn, J. (1994). *Wherever you go, there you are: Mindfulness meditation in everyday life*. New York: Hyperion.

Kabat-Zinn, J. (2005). *Coming to our senses: Healing ourselves and the world through mindfulness*. New York: Hyperion.

Kabat-Zinn, J (2011). Some reflections on the origins of MBSR, skillful means, and the trouble with maps. *Contemporary Buddhism*, 12:1, 281–306, DOI: 10.1080/14639947.2011.564844

Khoury, B., Sharma, M., Rush, S.E. & Fournier, C. (2015). Mindfulness-based stress reduction for healthy individuals: A meta-analysis. *Journal of Psychosomatic Research*, 78(6), 519–528. https://doi.org/10.1016/j.jpsychores.2015.03.009

Klein, N. (2017). Prosocial behavior increases perceptions of meaning in life. *The Journal of Positive Psychology*, 12, 354–361.

Kramer, G. (2007). *Insight dialogue: The interpersonal path to freedom*. Shambhala Publications.

Kudesia, R.S. (2019). Mindfulness as metacognitive practice. *The Academy of Management Review*, 44(2), 405–423.

Kuster, A.T., Dalsbø, T.K., Luong Thanh, B.Y., Agarwal, A., Durand-Moreau, Q.V. & Kirkehei, I. (2017). Computer-based versus in-person interventions for preventing and reducing stress in workers. *The Cochrane Database Of Systematic Reviews*, 8(8), CD011899. https://doi.org/10.1002/14651858.CD011899.pub2

Kuyken, W., Hayes, R., Barrett, B., Byng, R., Dalgleish, T. et al. (2015). Effectiveness and cost-effectiveness of mindfulness-based cognitive therapy compared with maintenance antidepressant treatment in the prevention of depressive relapse or recurrence (PREVENT): A randomised controlled trial. *Lancet, 386*(9988), 63–73.

Langer, E.J. (1989). *Mindfulness*. New York: Perseus Books.

Langer, E.J., Blank, A. & Chanowitz, B. (1978). The mindlessness of ostensibly thoughtful action: The role of 'placebic' information in interpersonal interaction. *Journal of Personality and Social Psychology*, 36(6), 635–642.

Lopez, D.S. Jr. (2010). *Buddhism and Science: A Guide for the perplexed*. Chicago and London: The University of Chicago Press.

The Mindfulness Initiative (n.d.). Building the case for mindfulness in the workplace. Accessed from www.themindfulnessinitiative.org/building-the-case-for-mindfulness-in-the-workplace on 30/12/2022

Monteiro, L.M., Musten, R. & Compson, J. (2015). Traditional and contemporary mindfulness: Finding the middle path in the tangle of concerns. *Mindfulness*, 6(1), 1–3. doi:10.1007/s12671-014-0301-7

Nilsson, H. & Kazemi, A. (2016). Reconciling and thematizing definitions of mindfulness: The big five of mindfulness. *Rev Gen Psychol, 20*(2): 183–193.

Noone, C. & Hogan, M.J. (2018). A randomised active-controlled trial to examine the effects of an online mindfulness intervention on executive control, critical thinking and key thinking dispositions in a university student sample. *BMC Psychology*, 6(1), 13. https://doi.org/10.1186/s40359-018-0226-3

Oxford Mindfulness Foundation (n.d.). Mindfulness for parliamentarians. Available at www.oxfordmindfulness.org/parliament-courses/, accessed on 30/12/2022.

Pagnini, F., Bercovitz, K. & Langer, E. (2016). Perceived control and mindfulness: Implications for clinical practice. *Journal of Psychotherapy Integration*, 26(2), 91–102.

Pagnini, F., Phillips, D., Bosma, C.M., Reece, A. & Langer, E. (2015). Mindfulness, physical impairment and psychological well-being in people with amyotrophic lateral sclerosis, *Psychology and Health*, 30(5), 503–517, DOI: 10.1080/08870446.2014.982652

Porges, S.W. (2011). *The polyvagal theory: Neurophysiological foundations of emotions, attachment, communication, and self-regulation*. New York: W.W. Norton.

Purser, R.E. & Milillo, J. (2015) 'Mindfulness revisited: A Buddhist-based conceptualization', *Journal of Management Inquiry*, 24(1), 3–24. doi: 10.1177/1056492614532315

Querstret, D., Morison, L., Dickinson, S., Cropley, M. & John, M. (2020). Mindfulness-based stress reduction and mindfulness-based cognitive therapy for psychological health and well-being in nonclinical samples: A systematic review and meta-analysis. *International Journal of Stress Management*, 27(4), 394–411.

Reb, J. Allen, T. & Vogus, T.J. (2020). Mindfulness arrives at work: Deepening our understanding of mindfulness in organizations. *Organizational Behavior and Human Decision Processes*. 159, 1–7.

Reina, C.S. & Kudesia, R.S. (2020). Wherever you go, there you become: How mindfulness arises in everyday situations. *Organizational Behavior and Human Decision Processes*, 159, 78–96.

Rupprecht, S., Koole, W., Chaskalon, M., Tamdjidi, C. & West, M.A. (2019). Running too far ahead? Towards a broader understanding of mindfulness in organizations. *Current Opinion in Psychology*, 28, 32–36.

Sanderson, K., Bartlett, L., Martin, A., Kilpatrick, M., Otahal, P. & Neil, A.L. (2021). Effects of a mindfulness app on employee stress: Results of a randomised controlled trial in an Australian public sector workforce.

Segal, Z.V., Williams, J.M.G. & Teasdale, J.D. (2002). *Mindfulness-based cognitive therapy for depression: A new approach to preventing relapse.* Guilford Press.

Selart, M., Schei, V., Lines, R. & Nesse, S. (2020) Can mindfulness be helpful in team decision-making? A framework for understanding how to mitigate false consensus. *European Management Review*, 17, 1015–1026.

Shapiro, D.H. (1992). A preliminary study of long term meditators: Goals, effects, religious orientation, cognitions. *Journal of Transpersonal Psychology*, 24(1), 23–39.

Shapiro, S.L., Carlson, L.E., Astin, J.A. & Freedman, B. (2006). Mechanisms of mindfulness. *Journal of Clinical Psychology*, 62(3), 373–386. https://doi.org/10.1002/jclp.20237

Spijkerman, M.P., Pots, W.T. & Bohlmeijer, E.T. (2016). Effectiveness of online mindfulness-based interventions in improving mental health: A review and meta-analysis of randomised controlled trials. *Clinical Psychology Review*, 45, 102–114. https://doi.org/10.1016/j.cpr.2016.03.009

Sutcliffe, K.M., Vogus, T.J. & Dane, E, (2016) Mindfulness in organizations: A cross-level review. *Annu. Rev. Organ. Psychol. Organ. Behav.*, 3:55–81.

Tobias Mortlock, J., Carter, A. & Querstret, D. (2022). Extending the transformative potential of mindfulness through team mindfulness training, integrating individual with collective mindfulness, in a high-stress military setting. *Frontiers in Psychology*, 13, 867110. www.frontiersin.org/articles/10.3389/fpsyg.2022.867110/abstract.

Tobias Mortlock, J. (2023). Next-generation mindfulness: A mindfulness matrix to extend the transformative potential of mindfulness for consumer, organizational, and societal wellbeing. *Journal of Consumer Affairs*, 57, 721–756. https://doi.org/10.1111/joca.12543

Van Berkel, J., Boot, C.R., Proper, K.I., Bongers, P.M. & Van der Beek, A.J. (2014). Effectiveness of a worksite mindfulness-related multi-component health promotion intervention on work engagement and mental health: results of a randomized controlled trial. *PloS one*, 9(1), e84118. https://doi.org/10.1371/journal.pone.0084118

Van Dam, N.T., Van Vugt, M.K., Vago, D.R., Schmaltz, L., Saron, C.D., Olendzki, A., Meissner, T., Lazar, S.W., Kerr, C.E., Gorchov, J., Fox, K.C.R., Field, B.A., Britton, W.B., Brefczynski-Lewis, J.A. & Meyer, D.E. (2017). Mind the hype: A critical evaluation and prescriptive agenda for research on mindfulness and meditation. *Perspectives on Psychol Sci*, 13(1): 36–61.

Van Doesum, N.J., Van Lange, D.A.W. & Van Lange, P.A.M. (2013). Social mindfulness: Skill and will to navigate the social world. *Journal of Personality and Social Psychology*, 105(1), 86–103.

Vogus, T.J., Rothman, N.B., Sutcliffe, K.M. & Weick, K.E. (2014). The affective foundations of high-reliability organizing. *Journal of Organizational Behavior*, 35(4), 592–596.

Weick, K.E. & Roberts, K.H. (1993). Collective mind in organizations: Heedful interrelating on flight decks. *Adm.. Sci Q.*, 38, 357–81.

Weick, K.E., Sutcliffe, K.M. & Obstfeld, D. (1999). Organizing for high reliability: processes of collective mindfulness. In R.I. Sutton & B.M. Staw (Eds.), *Research in Organizational Behavior* (Vol. *21*, pp. 81–123). https://doi.org/10.1.1.465.1382

Weick, K.E., Sutcliffe, K.M. & Obstfeld, D. (2000). High reliability: The power of mindfulness. *Lead. 17*, 33–38

Yu, L. & Zellmer-Bruhn, M. (2018). Introducing team mindfulness and considering its safeguard role against conflict transformation and social undermining. *Acad. Manag. J., 61*, 324–347. doi: 10.5465/amj.2016.0094

Work design, organisational change and development in focus

Latest developments in organisational psychology

Jane Stewart

Overview

This chapter provides an introduction to contemporary developments in organisational psychology. It is focused on the British Psychological Society's areas of work design, organisational change and organisational development and begins by discussing four key, current economic and social influences on work and organisations. The chapter moves on to provide an overview of some of the latest research in organisational psychology, covering a range of topics including the changing nature of where and when we work, the role of technology and the continuing challenge to improve equality, diversity and inclusion. It also briefly discusses the growth of the responsible business movement and communications in teams and organisations. It closes with reflections on potential future areas of interest and attention

Learning outcomes

By the end of the chapter, you will:

- understand the wider contextual factors influencing current organisations and organisational psychology;
- know about some of the latest research on:
  - when and where work takes place and the impact of technology;
  - workplace equality, diversity and inclusion;
  - the growth in the responsible business movement;
  - employee voice, silence and psychological safety;
- be aware of possible future areas of interest in organisational psychology.

The context

Organisations do not exist within a vacuum. They are shaped by and interact with their legal, social and political contexts. We will start by identifying some of the recent contextual themes influencing work and organisations including: the Fourth Industrial

DOI: 10.4324/9781003302087-13

Revolution; the increasing importance of addressing stubborn inequalities and exclusionary practices; the longer-term impact of a global pandemic; and the growth of critical organisational psychology as a field of study.

Fourth Industrial Revolution

If the first three phases of industrial revolution refer to the widespread use of steam, electricity, and computing, then the Fourth Industrial Revolution relates to the use of technology such as robots, artificial intelligence, big data and communication methods via online social platforms (Schwab, 2016). This latest revolution brings with it two workplace challenges. First is the impact on the way individuals work with technology and the impact on their experience of work, well-being, inclusion and equality. For example, the widespread use of video calling, laptops and smartphones enable people to be available or engage in work outside of the traditional office space. Software's ability to track an individual's activity whilst they are 'online' means organisations can collect data about employees' work. This provides opportunities for improvements and efficiencies but also presents ethical issues around worker surveillance. The second challenge is changes to roles available and the skills and competencies an individual may require to perform their role (Ghislieri et al., 2018).

These advances have also impacted the labour market, in terms of both the work available and the work sought by individuals. For example, advances in technology have led to more accessible technology allowing workers to undertake 'non-standard' employment such as subcontracting, freelancing, gig working and dispatch work (Min et al., 2019). These contracts offer more autonomy for workers who can decide when and how they work; but this independence comes at a cost. Work like this reduces opportunities for social connection, which may increase isolation and decrease support. In most cases it also means lower income security and stability which limits access to affordable debt such as mortgages. For many workers, this kind of work structure is also more costly since workers are unlikely to receive sick pay or annual leave, and may have to pay for uniforms, vehicles, training and other expenses (Fleming, 2017). It is worth noting that the negative elements of gig work have a more significant impact on lower income workers or those who rely on gig work as their main source of income.

Whilst the growth in gig work spans different hourly labour rates and income levels, in the UK and US it is more common in workers under 35 (Department of Work and Pensions, 2018), who are more likely to be on lower incomes and in greater need of affordable debt and sociable workplaces.

Campaigning and action on racism, bigotry, inequality, discrimination and bias

Discrimination in the workplace continues to present a significant challenge. One survey suggested that one in three UK adults reports experiencing discrimination when applying for a job, and a growing number of employment tribunals are initiated on the grounds of race, sexual orientation and disability (CIPHR, 2021). Changes to law and government policy mean companies in the UK are required to be transparent about pay and address discrimination, yet organisations' ongoing failure to successfully engage a fully diverse workforce continues to puzzle researchers (Liu, 2021). A 2017 UK government-initiated review on race argues the issue is structural, explaining:

> In the UK today, there is a structural, historical bias that favours certain individuals. This does not just stand in the way of ethnic minorities, but women, those with disabilities and others.
>
> (Baroness McGregor-Smith, 2017, p. 2)

One explanation for the slow progress towards equality is that the policy changes have simply altered the nature of the problem, rather than reducing or eliminating it altogether. There does seem to be a long-term decreasing trend in overt racism and discrimination, but this apparent improvement masks more subtle but no less insidious behaviour. Unconscious bias and the practice of hiring for 'cultural fit' mean that hiring managers are more likely to employ workers who are similar to them or other existing employees. This may not feel as egregious as the direct discrimination of earlier years, but it has the same impact, perpetuating existing segregation and limiting diversity.

Recent campaigning movements such as #BlackLivesMatters, Equal Pay Day and #metoo have strengthened public focus on issues of exclusion and discrimination. There is a rising awareness that compliance with legal requirements alone won't be sufficient to address the issues. This growing discussion of structural discrimination is accompanied by an increasing need for research and evidence-based practitioners to address these complex issues.

A global pandemic and the ongoing influence on organisations and work

In the first few months of 2020, the COVID-19 pandemic presented a challenge to modern workplaces like nothing before. Labour markets were severely disrupted and millions of workers lost their jobs or found themselves on furlough. Roles and functions were classified as *essential* or *non-essential* (McKinsey, 2021) and only essential workers could leave their homes to work. This also increased the demand for workers undertaking dispatch or gig work in the rapidly expanding food and goods delivery sector.

Wide-ranging government policies covering restriction of movement, economic activity and social interaction led to significant organisational changes. Over the following two years COVID-19 single-handedly demanded changes to how people worked, where they worked and what they did for work. The changes were more dramatic and imposed more quickly than anything seen for decades. Whilst the pandemic may be over and the strict lockdown policies have all been reversed, there are a number of lasting workplace pandemic legacies.

First, the pandemic and associated restrictions in most countries accelerated existing trends such as remote working. With movement restrictions, organisations were forced to find ways to enable all workers to complete their duties from their own homes using technology that may have previously been only partially adopted or not used at all (Malhotra, 2021). Some of the most obvious technologies to be adopted more widely included computer-to-computer video calling, team file sharing, online chat functions and cloud storage. This shift has translated into more remote and hybrid roles available.

Second, because whole families were also having to stay at home, workers were presented with significant additional challenges in their temporary workplace – their home – due to the blurred boundaries of work and home (Kossek et al., 2021). People had to simultaneously care for and educate children, whilst navigating the relationship challenges of sharing a work, home and pandemic experience with partners and other family members. After restrictions lifted, many of these challenges remained at least in part, for those still working partly or fully from home – for example when children were not well enough for school or when partners also continued to work from home.

Finally, some organisations and leaders capitalised on the disruption from the pandemic: businesses pivoted to offer their services by delivery and expanded their home services to meet the needs of people under home restrictions. For example, smaller local restaurants offered cook-at-home packs and other companies (such as US clothing firm Hanes) switched to producing face-coverings during the pandemic. These organisations (and leaders) showed how decision-making and actions allowed them to be resilient in the face of global change (Sarkar & Clegg, 2021).

Improved digital and communication tools enabled real-time research during the pandemic. This allowed us to track the changes and examine the impact of these changes like never before and has led to a broad range of research emerging in the following years. You can find more thoughts on where this might lead in the later section on *future trends*, but it is worth noting that this chapter only captures a tiny fraction of the research that was undertaken during this period.

Box 11.1   Reason's Swiss Cheese Model and COVID-19

During the COVID-19 pandemic, to keep people safe, many workplaces turned to the accident prevention Swiss Cheese Model; a popular human factor model first developed in the late 1980s and 1990s. The period during and after the most severe movement restrictions and pandemic-related hospitalisations saw a spike in interest in the role of organisations in harm prevention. This stimulated a wave of research exploring the topic of workplace safety and harm prevention, and how workplaces responsible for public health and safety (such as hospitals) can apply organisational psychology to improve patient and staff safety.

The Model – During the 1980s and 1990s, Reason developed his work on human error (Reason, 1990) including the accident prevention tool, the Swiss Cheese Model. The model proposes multiple layers of potential defence to workplace accidents and that they can be thought of as multiple slices of Swiss cheese, with the holes in each slice representing, what he describes as, active or latent failures in each layer of defence (Reason, 1998). For an accident to take place, it must pass through these holes in the multiple layers of defence.

These holes can relate to active failures (e.g. a human error made by someone directly involved with the activity) and latent failures, relating to decisions and actions taken by individuals not directly engaged in the activity such as back-office roles. The model shifts attention away from focusing on the frontline individual, to also looking at the wider system and organisational factors responsible for adverse events. The model has been used extensively in industries from medicine, construction and transportation. It is often used as a framework to review accidents and incidents of harm, analysing an organisation's layers of defence and identifying the holes in those layers, and is then used to inform plans to close the 'holes' therefore reducing the likelihood of future accidents and near-misses.

The model during COVID-19 – During COVID-19, the Swiss Cheese Model was used extensively for a variety of purposes including:

- designing and analysing return to work plans in everything from higher education (Ryan et al., 2022) to construction in Singapore (Gan & Koh, 2021);
- informing hospital preparedness plans in Korea (Noh et al., 2020) and elsewhere (Sarin et al., 2020); and
- shaping mitigation plans against online misinformation (Bode & Vraga, 2021).

The model was shared by the media on TV and international newspaper sites, to help the public and specifically workers understand why multiple risk reduction activities (for example hand washing, wearing masks and reduced socialisation) would be more effective than any one single action (Christakis, 2020) in reducing the spread of COVID-19 in communities and workplaces. Further, the successful use of this and associated models presented new options for those thinking about other types of harm prevention and safety in the workplace.

The rise of critical organisational psychology

There has been a steady growth in critical organisational psychology research since the first major wave of books and research articles emerged in the latter part of the twentieth century. Critical organisational psychology (COP) aims to improve our understanding and experience of organisations and work by 'challenging core mainstream assumptions, and also by championing the ideas and views that do not fit within the current trajectory of mainstream research' (McDonald & Bubna-Litic, 2017, p. 599).

Critical Theory is widely used in COP and has been described as an organised effort to step back, identify what is happening under the surface of societies and then use that knowledge to seek change. Thayf and colleagues describe the work in this field as:

conscious and systematic efforts, to take a reflective distance from reality in order to reveal what is hidden behind it, and then get involved in society to seek change for the better social conditions, i.e., a just society.

(Thayf et al., 2021, p. 40)

Specifically, researchers use critical theory as a tool to seek out problematic assumptions in organisational psychology about people and practices. It is also used to identify and address power imbalances in workplaces (McDonald & Bubna-Litic, 2017). This approach involves discovering the experiences of individuals and groups previously ignored or disguised in research and bringing those experiences into the field (Alvesson et al., 2009).

Why does this matter? It's important to challenge existing research and the beliefs that underpin established knowledge in the world of organisational psychology. This might take the form of raising awareness of the implicit assumption that managers are mostly right and not influenced by self-interest, or it may question whether employee engagement leads to workers contributing more effort than they are paid for. It could also be challenging the assumptions in the study of individual differences and the development and adoption of a range of psychometric tests that you can measure and that can quantify a person's personality without accounting for the context.

Perhaps most interestingly, there is a growing body of research exploring how work may contribute to growing inequality. Increasingly, researchers challenge the idea that individuals are treated the same and experience work in the same way irrespective of their identity groups such as gender, ethnicity or socio-economic background (van Dijk et al., 2020). Individuals who already have some privilege are likely to build on their existing advantages whilst simultaneously believing that workplaces operate as meritocracies.

Contemporary research topics

In the following sections we will discuss several contemporary research topics looking at: when and where work happens; challenges of improved technology; responsible business; equality, diversity and inclusion; and psychological safety.

When and where work happens

Significant technological advances have resulted in an increasing demand of 'temporal autonomy' for workers. Temporal autonomy simply refers to the autonomy or control workers have over where and when they work (Malhotra, 2021) meaning that most people who work remotely experience some 'temporal autonomy' (Mazmanian et al., 2013). This trend began in the decades before the global pandemic, accelerated dramatically during the lockdown months, and is expected to continue to grow in the coming years.

This autonomy creates questions for researchers and practitioners, such as what it means for boundaries between work and personal life, and how distance from the organisation and team impacts individual and team performance. For example, research shows that individuals who are relatively emotionally stable and are given higher levels of work autonomy are best placed to meet the stresses associated with remote work (Perry et al., 2018).

Understanding the benefits and challenges of remote working is more important than ever, since it has its pros and cons. The benefits of greater employee autonomy, reduced office costs and (in some cases) increased productivity are tempered by increasing worker isolation and reduced opportunities for informal learning. Hybrid working may also lead to unfair advantages through presenteeism, because workers based in the office may end up with more opportunities (Charalampous et al., 2019). Helpfully, a body of emerging research offers useful suggestions for people who manage remote workers. For example when managers set clear expectations about regularity of communication, there appears to be higher levels of performance and lower risk of burnout in remote workers (Shockley et al., 2021).

Covid-19 restrictions offered an unusual opportunity to expand our knowledge of the impact of remote and hybrid work. But these were unusual times and the research that was conducted occurred whilst people were experiencing the strain and uncertainty of a global pandemic and extensive personal freedom limitations when some workers even felt that their homes were being 'requisitioned' by organisations as workplaces (Jenkins & Smith, 2021). It is therefore important that any research conducted during this period should be considered with the knowledge that the circumstances were highly irregular and workers were experiencing multiple stressors and lacked choice in their own situations.

Challenges of improved technology

Workplace technology has been the subject of researchers' interest for some time. The benefits are extensive with the widespread availability of computers, internet connections, printers and smartphones revolutionising many professions over the last three decades. Job types have come and gone as more administration can be automated, and organisations now have access to huge amounts of data about the way in which work is executed to help inform decisions about productivity. People can collaborate for better outcomes without travel (think doctors in different countries discussing MRI scans or test results before a procedure) and disabled workers are able to access work easily, thanks to improved assistive technology tools including voice-activated devices and text-to-speak software.

Here though, we briefly explore some of the challenges that technology brings to workers, including the inability to disconnect and maintain boundaries from work, the burden of digital tool upkeep and the depleting effects of technology on working practices.

The 'Always On' culture refers to the inability to disconnect from work because of tools that enable access to tasks and materials outside of main working time and location. Being 'available' can be problematic for workers who find it hard to switch off with email alerts and messages. Despite some evidence of positive improvements in employees' experience of work technology, employee well-being and team relationships seem to suffer (McDowall & Kinman, 2017). Whilst technology gives people the autonomy over *when* they access work, it also leads to people who never switch off. This is known as the 'autonomy paradox'. Individuals battle with the competing desire to be a 'good' employee versus their desire to access work at a time that best suits their well-being (Mazmanian et al., 2013).

Another significant challenge is known as digi-housekeeping. This refers to workers having to maintain their digital tools, such as deleting junk mail, charging laptops and troubleshooting printers. These tasks exist 'invisibly' in workers' time, adding to the burden of work without organisations acknowledging the time or effort. It is argued '… these need to be more explicitly acknowledged as essential activities to be scheduled into daily timetables' (Whiting & Symon, 2020, p. 1093).

Finally, the growth in remote working has been accompanied by an increase in the use of communication tools such as video conferencing and online meeting tools. This has led to an increased demand for research on the impact of these tools. Initial findings on 'zoom fatigue' showed that individuals' experience of video conferencing is more exhausting than other meeting mediums but that better meeting management may mitigate against this (Nesher Shoshan & Wehrt, 2022).

Responsible business

Employees increasingly expect their organisations to be values-driven and to have a purpose beyond profit (Korn Ferry, 2021). The emergence of organisations that have a 'hybrid' purpose has attracted interest (Blasi & Sedita, 2022). Benefit corporations, commonly known as 'B-Corps', have developed where business owners own and manage organisations that aren't solely driven by profit. Specifically, B-Corps seek to deliver against up to five distinct areas (Governance, Workers, Community, Environment and Customers) with a focus on social and environmental targets, as well as financial ones (Liute & De Giacomo, 2022). They are sometimes described as driven by a 'triple bottom line': profit, people and the planet. These are profit-making organisations that enshrine their commitment to the greater good in their governance documents. The growth of these responsible businesses disrupts the traditional categories of public, private and not-for-profit sectors.

Read more about the development of one B-Corp in Box 11.2.

Box 11.2   Case study: becoming a B-Corp

(From an interview, Carrier et al., n.d.)

There are currently over 6000 B-Corp organisations in 89 countries, covering 159 industries and employing over 500,000 workers. This is a case study of one early adopter organisation in the UK.

About COOK – COOK is a British food company making hand-made frozen meals since 1997. The company started as a small family firm with ambitions to create impact beyond financial success, growing to over 100 shops and around 1300 staff across the UK. James Perry, current co-Chair, and founders Edward Perry and Dale Penfold were determined to make COOK something different. James Perry was motivated by a disappointing experience working at a FTSE-100 listed food and drink company, where he experienced the deployment of an aggressive strategy to achieve better shareholder value. When asked what is different about being an employee at COOK, Perry said: 'The person is more important than their employment relationship with the company'.

Initial Challenges – The team faced significant challenges from investors about the viability of a food manufacturing company driven by a triple bottom line (profit, people and planet). Perry, who believed that the dominant, profit-making, shareholder business model was problematic (and served the interests of capital rather than society), hoped there was a better way. COOK decided to sell direct to customers partly to avoid the power and influence of UK supermarkets and maintain the decision-making control of how they ran the company, priced and managed production. That approach provided space to operate outside the mainstream approach in the industry; however, the company continued to feel isolated and unsure how best to continue to grow their impact beyond generating profit.

Finding the B-Corp Movement – Perry was in San Francisco in 2010 at a conference, when he encountered the B-Corp movement for the first time. Describing it as 'the moment he found out they weren't alone', he returned to the UK and worked with his brother and Penfold to map out how COOK might become a B-Corp and to enshrine the organisation's commitment to people and the wider community and environment in the governance, policies and operations of the company.

Certification – The team established their current B-Corp Impact Score and began mapping the gap between that and the minimum score of 80 to become certified. After changing their governance, employee policies, practices and several other operating elements, COOK was certified as one of the first UK B-Corp organisations in 2013 with a B Impact Score of 80.2.

Since Certification – COOK has increased its B-Corp impact score to 104.1 (at the time of writing) and was recognised by Best Companies as the number one food and drink company to work for in the UK in 2021; with last reporting figures showing £85mn in sales and £7.5mn in profit. COOK is also certified by the Living Wage Foundation with higher salaries limited to 15 times that of the lowest paid worker and has delivered 2.5 million free school meals through one of its many community initiatives.

Equality, diversity and inclusion

Whilst public awareness of issues of equality, diversity and inclusion (EDI) continues to grow, stubborn issues of inequality and exclusion persist. There is a clear need to move beyond what is often seen as 'box-ticking' compliance activity. Many organisations are seeking to better understand and address issues of exclusion, inequality and prejudice. Some of the ways in which organisational psychology can play a role are discussed here.

Organisations that want to support marginalised groups can draw lessons from recent research in several ways. The demand for better insight into inclusive recruitment practices continues, aiming to address the inherent bias in many recruitment techniques and improve selection processes to increase the diversity of applicants. It's useful to know that having a higher proportion of women or minorities involved in selection results in higher numbers of women and minority applicants (Kazmi et al., 2022). Whilst this may not demonstrate causation, or indeed be applicable in all countries or industries, insights such as these can play some role in supporting HR practitioners to make more evidence-based decisions.

Organisations are increasingly aware that understanding the experiences of different groups can ensure that policies and procedures incorporate a wider range of views, and have a positive impact on the whole organisation. The UK equalities act recognises different protected characteristics (age, disability, gender reassignment, marriage and civil partnership, pregnancy and maternity, race, religion or belief, sex, and sexual orientation) and workers in these groups have traditionally been underrepresented in existing research. More recently there has been a shift towards *intersectionality* which acknowledges the experiences of people who have more than one marginalised charac-teristic. For example, this might highlight that the experiences of Black women will be different from those of *White* women, and also from Black *men*.

Workplace allies and trade unions can play a part in reducing exclusionary practice. They might offer organisations insights into how to execute EDI workplace interventions more effectively, for example, helping with the wording and framing of inclusion pol-icies in the wider workforce, and understanding the micro-dynamics of ally mobilisation (Wang et al., 2021). Similarly, recognising the moderating role of trade union activity on ethnic minority employees' perceptions of workplace equality can help strengthen the case for increasing union activity (Seifert & Wang, 2018)

Psychological safety

Interest in the concept of psychological safety at work has continued to grow since Edmondson published her research on the topic, defining psychological safety as a belief that speaking up with ideas, questions, concerns, or mistakes is expected and feasible' (Edmondson, 1999). In simple terms, psychological safety can be understood as a team environment where team members feel included and safe to learn, contribute and chal-lenge the status quo. It can help organisations in two key ways, providing leaders with a structure to think about their own underlying beliefs for what is expected and encour-aged in workplace conversations; and offering a clear focus for improving the quality of workplace conversations.

In recent research, the Productive Conversation Matrix (illustrated in Figure 11.1) is presented as a way to differentiate how employee voice and silence can be considered in terms of the quality and usefulness of the conversations. The model proposes four

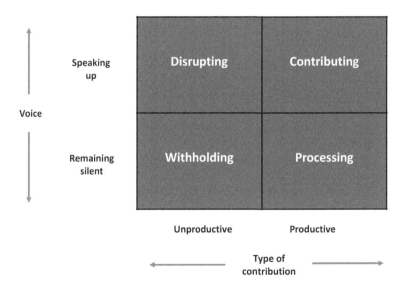

Figure 11.1 The Productive Conversation Matrix (Edmondson & Besieux 2021; permission granted from Informa Limited).

categories of behaviour, each with a different outcome. Employees either speak up or stay silent and each act can be considered productive or unproductive. The different outcomes for the team are defined as 'disrupting', 'contributing', 'withholding' and 'processing'. By differentiating in this way, the researchers (Edmondson & Besieux, 2021) offer useful ideas for individuals to think about, and ultimately create, psychologically safe teams. By understanding and applying these tools to their own workplaces, leaders, managers and employees can better identify, and therefore address, undesirable speaking up behaviours, as well as actively encourage productive speaking up behaviours that contribute to the positive development of the team.

Future challenges

The world of work continues to develop and change with new challenges emerging all the time. Just some of the future challenges that may need addressing are discussed below.

Measuring employee outcomes or inputs. Over the last three decades businesses and researchers have aimed to address stagnant productivity in many global economies. Employees are increasingly judged on the value they add to the organisation, rather than the number of tasks they undertake, and some organisations have started to measure an employee's contribution to outputs and outcomes rather than measuring the amount of time worked or the quantity of work completed. This new focus on measuring the quality rather than the quantity of employees' contributions further supports those wanting to work from home: if performance is being measured via value-add then concerns about time and place of work is less relevant as there is no need to regulate the time they clock in and clock off.

New employment patterns. In addition to changes to when and where we work, some organisations have been experimenting with other practices. Flexible or unlimited annual leave is an enormously attractive perk, and in a labour market where organisations are competing for the best talent, this kind of policy could significantly impact recruitment and retention. The most obvious risk with such a policy is that employees could take advantage of the offer, shirking their duties, and leaving colleagues to cover for them. However, this could be addressed with a clear policy outlining expectations. More worrying could be that a culture of presenteeism develops, where people actually end up taking *less* annual leave. Employees might not take leave for fear of falling behind with their work or because it might suggest a lack of commitment or a poor work ethic.

Other organisations have been experimenting with a 4-day week, where employees remain on full pay but work reduced hours. Recent studies suggest that this might increase well-being and staff retention, and decrease the number of sick days. Perhaps more surprisingly, the policy appears to have no detrimental impact on productivity – people are achieving the same in 4 days that they used to in 5, partly because workers have more energy and partly because the number of meetings they have to attend reduces. On the downside, however, the 4-day week may be difficult to introduce in front line roles and would have a more detrimental impact within the service industry, or at schools. One study showed that pupils' school attainment went down when the school closed one day a week (Laker & Roulet, 2019; Thompson, 2021).

Box 11.3   Case study: flexible working in a cosmetics company

Ali manages a team of three marketing executives at an international cosmetics company. The company adopted a flexible working policy six months ago, allowing staff to work from home three days a week. Since the shift to flexible working, Ali has noticed a number of changes in the team. All three team members initially seemed pleased with the change but are now reporting frustrations and appear to be working longer hours.

Ali sits down with the company organisational psychologist, to review the team's adoption of the new policy. Ali shares the concerns he has about his team and, using the BPS consultancy cycle, they agree an approach, roles and timelines to investigate further and take action if appropriate. Together, they agree Ali will meet with the team and request they complete a daily diary detailing what took up their time and how they felt about each task.

The data is shared with Ali and the organisational psychologist. They review it together and make the following observations:

- each time a team member moved work location, digi-housekeeping tasks, such as troubleshooting Wi-Fi problems and software or charging devices, appeared to take up more time than Ali had expected;
- team members reported spending significantly more time on screen on days working from home, often skipping breaks, attending more meetings and working into the evening;
- team members reported frustration with coming into the office, only to find none of the rest of the team were in that day and that their work tasks could have been completed at home.

Together, Ali and the organisational psychologist discuss the challenges, and consider how individuals could be provided better resources to meet the demands of their roles. They decide various actions that could help the team and Ali decides to try the following:

- identifying a regular team meeting slot for the team to attend in the office, with topics focused on co-creation work and areas with high levels of interdependence;
- introducing the option for team members to block out up to two hours each day in their diary as focus time, where they don't need to attend meetings;
- approving the purchase of additional laptop power cables for team members.

After three months, Ali discusses the impact of the changes with his team. Everyone agrees that all the changes have been helpful. Team members identify that the policy of two days per week in the office continues to be a source of frustration, as they feel it is too arbitrary and are still unclear on the rationale for this. Ali requests that the organisational psychologist consider investigating whether this was an issue in other departments, to inform their thinking about whether it is a broader issue and something that could benefit from being raised with senior management. In the meantime, Ali sought permission from their manager to give the team more autonomy and flexibility by changing the requirement for office-based working from two days per week to nine days in a month, allowing more temporal autonomy for team members over where they work.

Purpose in work. There has been an increase in research and practitioners writing about how individuals find purpose and experience engagement in their work. At first glance, this seems like a positive step – we know that purpose leads to higher job and life satisfaction, so it is surely a good thing to encourage. But critical theorists have proposed that this focus is a facet of a capitalist, exploitative approach to management. They argue that the focus on purpose is simply a way to get more out of employees – taking advantage of their intrinsic motivation to get them to work harder and put up with worse conditions.

As the landscape settled after the disruptions from the pandemic, many employees reviewed the purpose of work in their lives and balanced it against the employment opportunities available to them. This period became known in popular press as the 'Great Resignation' or 'Great Reshuffle' (Kuzior et al., 2022). This was fuelled, at least in part, by workers delaying moving jobs during the pandemic, wanting to retain a remote or hybrid element to work, a better work-life balance and in response to workplace stress.

Whether this trend will continue is unknown as individuals continue to review the purpose of work in their lives (income and income security, job satisfaction, community, collective effort) and balance that against what employers are seeking (time working, presence in specific locations, engagement and commitment). This rebalancing of the exchange of labour for pay and working conditions is likely to present a number of questions about the relative weight individuals give to preferred remote, flexible or hybrid working patterns versus pay and benefits.

Role clarity. The pace of change in technology is such that a role can change almost as soon as an individual starts a new job, and yet, there is little evidence that employees are given space and time to keep role descriptions updated. Role clarity is an underlying contributor to high-performing teams and to individual, team and organisational performance and satisfaction. As the pace of change in workplaces is sustained, understanding the influence of ongoing role clarity on performance and how role clarity is experienced by workers could help organisations more consistently maintain or improve team performance.

Beyond the big economies. As countries continue to develop outside of the world's biggest economies, their demands for organisational psychologists and associated research will continue to grow. A greater diversity of themes of interest may emerge. Another impact of technological advancements is the ability for researchers to connect with organisations and workers across the globe, with the potential for fruitful collaborations. This broadening access to research participants should ensure more empirical research in a broader range of cultures enabling everything from exploring the experience of working in war-affected locations to the impact of culture variations on homeworking policy success.

Conclusion

The experience of work is changing rapidly. Where we work, when we work and the way in which we use technology are all constantly evolving and organisational psychologists can play a major role in helping individuals and organisations navigate these shifts. In addition, organisations are still looking for effective ways to remove exclusionary practices, build and maintain purpose-driven, responsible businesses and communicate effectively. In this chapter, we have explored some of the current developments and research themes in organisational psychology. It is useful to remember that these are a snapshot of some of the current developments at the time of writing and that, as the economic and social context of organisations and work shifts, so do the needs, interests and behaviours of the people working within them.

Explore further

If you are keen to explore some of these themes further you may find the following resources useful.

Podcasts

- Talking About Organisations is an academic-led podcast exploring some of the most influential research in organisations and management and deep dives into key research papers with useful summaries and interesting discussions.
- The Department 12 podcast explores current issues relating to the field of organisational psychology itself.
- My Pocket Psych and World of Work Project cover a range of useful topics for employees and managers seeking out new ways of thinking about and improving their own experience of work.

Blogs And Books

- You can learn more about the B-Corp movement on their website www.bcorporat ion.net and more about developing an anti-racist workplace here: https://timesu pfoundation.org/work/equity/guide-equity-inclusion-during-crisis/building-an-anti-racist-workplace/
- For learning more about psychological safety there is no better place to start than Dr Amy Edmondson's easy to read 'Fearless Organisation' https://fearlessorganizat ion.com/the-fearless-organisation.
- The UK-based What Works Well-being is a great place to hear about the latest research coming out and has a whole section on the workplace https://whatwor kswellbeing.org/.
- Finally, if you want to explore more of the discussion around inclusion, exclusion and associated topics like anti-racism then listening to John Amaechi being interviewed on Adam Grant's great 'WorkLife' podcast from Ted is an interesting place to start. www.ted.com/podcasts/worklife/building-an-anti-racist-workplace-transcript

References

Alvesson, M., Bridgman, T. & Willmott, H. (Eds.). (2009). *The Oxford handbook of critical management studies*. Oxford Handbooks.

Blasi, S. & Sedita, S.R. (2022). Mapping the emergence of a new organisational form: An exploration of the intellectual structure of the B Corp research. *Corporate Social Responsibility and Environmental Management*, 29(1), 107–123.

Bode, L. & Vraga, E. (2021). The Swiss cheese model for mitigating online misinformation. Bulletin of the Atomic Scientists, 77(3), 129–133.

Carrier, J., Stewart, J. & Perry, J. (n.d.). Cook: A B-Corporation case study of responsible business (No. 66). Retrieved 8 May 2022, from https://thewowpodcast.libsyn.com/james-perry

Charalampous, M., Grant, C. A., Tramontano, C. & Michailidis, E. (2019). Systematically reviewing remote e-workers' well-being at work: A multidimensional approach. *European Journal of Work and Organizational Psychology*, 28(1), 51–73.

Christakis, D.A. (2020). School reopening—the pandemic issue that is not getting its due. *JAMA Pediatrics*, 174(10), 928–928.

CIPHR (2021). Workplace Discrimination Statistics. Marlow: CIHRP. https://www.ciphr.com/workplace-discrimination-statistics/

Department of Work and Pensions. (2018). *Characteristics of those in the gig economy*. UK Government.

Edmondson, A. (1999). Psychological safety and learning behavior in work teams. *Administrative Science Quarterly*, 44(2), 350–383.

Edmondson, A.C. & Besieux, T. (2021). Reflections: Voice and silence in workplace conversations. *Journal of Change Management*, 21(3), 269–286.

Fleming, P. (2017). The human capital hoax: Work, debt and insecurity in the era of Uberization. *Organization Studies*, 38(5), 691–709.

Gan, W.H. & Koh, D. (2021). COVID-19 and return-to-work for the construction sector: Lessons from Singapore. *Safety and Health at Work*, 12(2), 277–281.

Ghislieri, C., Molino, M. & Cortese, C.G. (2018). Work and organizational psychology looks at the fourth industrial revolution: How to support workers and organizations?. *Frontiers in Psychology*, 9, 2365.

Jenkins, F. & Smith, J. (2021). Work-from-home during COVID-19: Accounting for the care economy to build back better. *The Economic and Labour Relations Review*, 32(1), 22–38.

Kazmi, M.A., Spitzmueller, C., Yu, J., Madera, J.M., Tsao, A.S., Dawson, J.F. & Pavlidis, I. (2022). Search committee diversity and applicant pool representation of women and underrepresented minorities: A quasi-experimental field study. Journal of Applied Psychology, 107(8), 1414.

Korn Ferry (2021). Future of Work trends, 2022: a new era of humanity. Los Angeles: Korn Ferry.

Kossek, E.E., Dumas, T.L., Piszczek, M.M. & Allen, T.D. (2021). Pushing the boundaries: A qualitative study of how stem women adapted to disrupted work–nonwork boundaries during the COVID-19 pandemic. *Journal of Applied Psychology*, 106(11), 1615.

Kuzior, A., Kettler, K. & Rąb, Ł. (2022). Great Resignation – ethical, cultural, relational, and personal dimensions of Generation Y and Z employees' Engagement. *Sustainability*, 14(11), Article 11. https://doi.org/10.3390/su14116764

Laker, B. & Roulet, T. (2019). Will the 4-day workweek take hold in Europe. Harvard Business Review.

Liu, C. (2021). Why do firms fail to engage diversity? A behavioral strategy perspective. Organization Science, 32(5), 1193–1209.

Liute, A. & De Giacomo, M.R. (2022). The environmental performance of UK-based B Corp companies: An analysis based on the triple bottom line approach. *Business Strategy and the Environment*, 31(3), 810–827.

Malhotra, A. (2021). The postpandemic future of work. Journal of Management, 47(5), 1091–1102.

Mazmanian, M., Orlikowski, W.J. & Yates, J. (2013). The autonomy paradox: The implications of mobile email devices for knowledge professionals. *Organization Science*, 24(5), 1337–1357.

McDonald, M. & Bubna-Litic, D. (2017). Critical organisational psychology. In B. Gough (Ed.), *The Palgrave handbook of critical social psychology* (pp. 597–619), London: Palgrave Macmillan. https://doi.org/10.1057/978

McDowall, A. & Kinman, G. (2017). The new nowhere land? A research and practice agenda for the 'always on' culture. *Journal of Organizational Effectiveness: People and Performance, 4*, 256–266.1-137-51018-1_29

McGregor-Smith (2017). Race in the *workplace*. London: Department for Business and Trade and Department for Business, Energy & Industrial Strategy. https://assets.publishing.service.gov.uk/government/uploads/system/uploads/attachment_data/file/594336/race-in-workplace-mcgregor-smith-review.pdf

McKinsey (2021) The future of work after Covid-19. London: McKinsey & Company. www.mckinsey.com/featured-insights/future-of-work/the-future-of-work-after-covid-19

Min, J., Kim, Y., Lee, S., Jang, T.W., Kim, I. & Song, J. (2019). The Fourth Industrial Revolution and its impact on occupational health and safety, worker's compensation and labor conditions. *Safety and Health at Work*, 10(4), 400–408.

Mutambudzi, M., Niedzwiedz, C., Macdonald, E.B., Leyland, A., Mair, F., Anderson, J., Celis-Morales, C., Cleland, J., Forbes, J., Gill, J., Hastie, C., Ho, F., Jani, B., Mackay, D.F., Nicholl, B., O'Donnell, C., Sattar, N., Welsh, P., Pell, J.P., … Demou, E. (2021). Occupation and risk of severe COVID-19: Prospective cohort study of 120 075 UK Biobank participants. *Occupational and Environmental Medicine*, 78(5), 307–314. https://doi.org/10.1136/oemed-2020-106731

Nesher Shoshan, H. & Wehrt, W. (2022). Understanding 'Zoom fatigue': A mixed-method approach. *Applied Psychology*, 71(3), 827–852.

Noh, J.Y., Song, J.Y., Yoon, J.G., Seong, H., Cheong, H.J. & Kim, W.J. (2020). Safe hospital preparedness in the era of COVID-19: The Swiss cheese model. International Journal of Infectious Diseases, 98, 294–296.

Perry, S.J., Rubino, C. & Hunter, E.M. (2018). Stress in remote work: Two studies testing the Demand-Control-Person model. *European Journal of Work and Organizational Psychology*, 27(5), 577–593.

Reason, J. (1990). *Human Error*. Cambridge: Cambridge University Press

Reason, J. (1998). Safety culture: Some theoretical and practical issues *Work Stress, 12* (3) pp. 202–216

Ryan, B.J., Muehlenbein, M.P., Allen, J., Been, J., Boyd, K., Brickhouse, M., … & Brickhouse, N. (2022). Sustaining university operations during the COVID-19 pandemic. *Disaster Medicine and Public Health Preparedness*, 16(5), 1901–1909.

Sarin, A., Bhatnagar, V., Neelakantan, A. & Khandare, M. (2020). Best practices with optimal outcomes during COVID-19 pandemic-A Swiss Cheese Model experiment in the naval training command. *Journal of Marine Medical Society*, 22(2), 266–266.

Sarkar, S. & Clegg, S.R. (2021). Resilience in a time of contagion: Lessons from small businesses during the COVID-19 pandemic. *Journal of Change Management*, 21(2), 242–267.

Schwab, K. (2016). *The Fourth Industrial Revolution*. Geneva: World Economic Forum

Seifert, R. & Wang, W. (2018). Race discrimination at work: The moderating role of trade unionism in English local government. *Industrial Relations Journal*, 49(3), 259–277.

Shockley, K.M., Allen, T.D., Dodd, H. & Waiwood, A.M. (2021). Remote worker communication during COVID-19: The role of quantity, quality, and supervisor expectation-setting. *Journal of Applied Psychology*, 106(10), 1466–1482.

Thayf, H.S., Syamsuddin, M.M. & Supartiningsih, S. (2021). Critical management studies: Introducing a new perspective. *International Journal of Creative Business and Management*, 1(1), 38–48.

Thompson, P.N. (2021). Is four less than five? Effects of four-day school weeks on student achievement in Oregon. *Journal of Public Economics, 193*, 104308.

van Dijk, H., Kooij, D., Karanika-Murray, M., De Vos, A. & Meyer, B. (2020). Meritocracy a myth? A multilevel perspective of how social inequality accumulates through work. *Organizational Psychology Review, 10*(3–4), 240–269.

Wang, C.S., Whitson, J.A., King, B.G. & Ramirez, R.L. (2021). Social movements, collective identity, and workplace allies: The labeling of gender equity policy changes. *Organization Science, 32*(5), 1–12. https://doi.org/10.1287/orsc.2021.1 492

Whiting, R. & Symon, G. (2020). Digi-housekeeping: the invisible work of flexibility. *Work, Employment and Society, 34*(6), 1079–1096.

Part III

Professional practice

Chapter 12

Professionalism in organisational psychology

Ethical and reflective practice

Julia Yates

Overview

This chapter introduces two related but distinct aspects of professionalism in organisational psychology: working ethically and reflective practice. The chapter starts with a focus on ethics. Working ethically is integral to all aspects of organisational psychology work, research and practice, and in this chapter, we explain the importance of ethical practice, introduce the Universal Declaration of Ethical Principles for Psychologists and discuss ethical dilemmas and ethical maturity. In the second part of the chapter, we will explore the concept of reflective practice, discuss its value and introduce two simple frameworks that readers can use to help reflect on their own practice.

Ethical and reflective practice are clearly quite separate, but they are closely bound together in that reflection leads both directly and indirectly to ethical practice. It contributes directly to ethical practice by allowing psychologists to reflect on their practice to assess the ethical basis for their own actions, and to help them make ethical choices. Indirectly, reflection enhances ethical practice by supporting competence, which is a key pillar of ethical practice. Reflection thus is both a constituent part of ethical practice and a core aspect of the process of ethical decision making.

Learning outcomes

By the end of this chapter you will:

- know about the key aspects of ethical and reflective practice;
- understand the contributions that both ethical and reflective practice can make to clients, practitioners and the profession;
- be aware of models and frameworks that can help you develop your own ethical and reflective practice;
- appreciate the particular ethical context of research.

DOI: 10.4324/9781003302087-15

Ethics

Discussions about values and ethics have been documented since the time of the Ancient Greeks, and were no doubt going on well before then. Values are broad ideas of what matters – what is important to us. They don't always govern what we do, but they influence how we feel about our actions after the event. Ethics are the practical application of our values (Iordanou et al., 2016). They are more specific than values and generally refer to a set of rules or a code that directs the action we take or the decisions we make (Beckett et al., 2017).

Ethics are important to us as professionals, offering benefits to our clients, to ourselves and to our profession more broadly. They ensure safety and protect our clients, help us to manage boundaries, lead to higher quality and more authentic practice, and maintain and boost the reputation of our profession. But ethical practice is not always straightforward.

One valuable tool to help professionals navigate stormy ethical waters is a good ethical framework – a clear set of professional guidelines which outline our professional values and can give us some clear guidance as to the most appropriate professional response in any situation. In addition to an ethical framework, we also need to develop our own sense of ethical maturity which can help us to work out what to do when the guidelines are not enough and we find ourselves facing a situation not covered by the frameworks. Let us look at each of these in turn.

Ethical frameworks

For as long as professions have grouped together, they have been working towards developing ethical codes. Pettifor and Sawchuk (2006) suggest that professional ethical codes generally orientate themselves around two fundamental goals, aiming to ensure that professionals do no harm, and encouraging them to do some good. Going a little further, Lane (2011) argues that many of these codes of conduct cover very similar ground addressing three issues:

- *Purpose*: Who are we, why are we here and what are we trying to do?
- *Perspective*: What is the shared knowledge base and assumptions of our profession?
- *Process:* How do we work and how do we interact with our clients?

In 2008, in Paris, the International Union of Psychological Sciences developed its own code. This draws on a number of ethical frameworks going back as far as Hippocrates' oath of ethics, and incorporates codes from different professions, including medicine and law. Their Universal Declaration of Ethical Principles for Psychologists covers four key principles which represent a moral framework intended to 'guide and inspire psychologists worldwide toward the highest ethical ideals in their professional and scientific work' (International Union of Psychological Science, 2008).

1. Respect for the dignity of persons and peoples

This principle puts the worth of all people at the heart of psychological practice and emphasises that everyone is entitled to respect, regardless of their demographic or personal characteristics, background or experiences. This is a core attitude, underpinning all professional interactions.

2. Competent caring for the well-being of persons and peoples

The second of the principles is linked directly to our work as psychologists and proposes that psychologists should work for the benefit of individuals, groups of people and humanity at large. At a basic minimum it holds that psychologists should do no harm, but also suggests that psychologists need to be competent and well-equipped to do the work they are doing, and should be aware of themselves and the impact of their actions.

3. Integrity

The declaration highlights the importance of integrity to the advancement of scientific knowledge, arguing that if researchers are not honest and open about their research, we cannot be confident that their findings are trustworthy. It also highlights the role that professional integrity plays in ensuring public confidence in the profession, perhaps harking back to some of the shameful ethical practices witnessed in the early decades of psychological research when researchers didn't always treat their participants with the respect and care that we would expect now (see the Box below for a summary of the Stanford Prison Experiment). The essence of integrity here is described as open, complete and clear communication.

4. Professional and scientific responsibilities to society

This final principle proposes that at the heart of all psychologists and psychological endeavours should be a drive to improve things – people, organisations, communities and societies. This entails adherence to ethical standards, high-quality training and the self-reflection of individual psychologists and the profession as a whole.

This Universal Declaration was developed through collaboration with psychologists from around the globe. It aims to transcend borders, but whether this is a realistic goal is a moot point. Parsonson and Alquicira (2019) argue that ethics are inevitably bound up in context and culture. Ethical codes generally reflect the ethical assumptions within any given culture, and as such they change over time, as political, economic and social trends influence attitudes in different ways. Comparing the ethical codes for psychologists in a range of different countries, Parsonson and Alquicira note that whilst there were significant similarities (all seemed to value respect, responsibility and integrity), there were differences in priorities, with some countries particularly valuing social justice and others focusing more on competence. They also point out that most of the published ethical codes are written from an individualistic perspective, and psychologists working with clients from collectivist cultures might need to consider their codes from a different cultural perspective.

The Universal Declaration is of course, not the only ethical code you could consider. The British Psychological Society (BPS) has its own Code of Ethics, which, drawing heavily on the University Declaration, focuses on four primary ethical principles: respect, competence, responsibility and integrity, and offers more specific and practical standards of the behaviour expected of its members. Other professional bodies, for example the Chartered Institute of Personnel and Development, or the Association for Coaching, will offer their own codes, and you may also want to explore any industry-specific codes linked to where you work. These ethical frameworks are designed to help us make good professional choices and all psychologists, in all professional contexts, should sign up and adhere to an ethical framework.

The codes will help to guide your behaviour, and will also offer some assurance to your clients; but sometimes, an ethical code isn't enough. Throughout your working lives, you will encounter situations that aren't explicitly addressed by the codes and you will have to find ways to resolve ethical tensions. In these situations, a psychologist will need to reach their own conclusions, drawing on their own personal sense of ethical maturity.

Ethical dilemmas and ethical maturity

In a review of the literature, Pettifor and Sawchuk (2006) conclude that the ethical dilemmas most often encountered by psychologists are those linked to confidentiality, dual relationships and payment sources. Issues of confidentiality arise when psychologists feel under pressure to break client confidentiality, for example, whether to release professional notes to a lawyer or disclose that a third party has sexually abused a client, or whether parents should be told that their child has sought counselling.

Dual relationships prove problematic when psychologists feel that they are blurring the lines between professional and personal relationships, and might struggle to know whether they should offer their professional skills to friends, whether they should agree to meeting a client outside the office, or what to do if they find themselves romantically attracted to a client.

Finally, dilemmas linked to sources of payment include instances where a psychologist wonders about the morality of taking money from a client who is struggling financially or from an organisation whose values they don't agree with, or whether they are giving sufficient value for their charges.

Whilst these may be some of the most common, a wide range of different ethical dilemmas can arise. Ethical practice entails an alignment of values within a nested system. It relies on the alignment of our personal and professional values, the values of our clients and the values of the profession. When these value systems line up, ethical choices are straightforward, but all too often, we can find that some of these values clash, and it may be difficult to work out what to do.

These ethical dilemmas or clashes of values can take many different shapes. A clash could arise between your professional values and those of the people you are working with. A coach asked to do some work with an oil company might feel a clash between their client's values (promoting the use of fossil fuels) and their personal values (trying to slow down climate change). A clash between personal and professional values might arise for a coach who wants to earn money for their family (personal value) but doesn't feel suitably skilled to take on a particular contract (profession's value).

In these situations, adherence to an ethical code may not be enough and alongside our commitment to an external framework, we need to strive towards what practitioners call 'ethical maturity'. This is described by Hawkins and Smith (2013) as the increased capacity to embrace ethical complexity and deal with appropriate respect and fairness to all partners involved in a situation. A more detailed definition comes from Carroll and Shaw (2012) who describe it as:

> having the reflective, rational, emotional and intuitive capacity to decide whether actions are right and wrong, or good and better, having the resilience and courage to implement those decision, being accountable for ethical decisions made and being able to learn from and live with the experiences.
>
> (Carroll & Shaw, 2012, p. 30)

Delving deeper still, Van Nieuwerburgh (2020) offers us a useful model of ethical maturity, which he describes as a 'virtuous circle' (Figure 12.1)

Van Nieuwerburgh suggests that core to ethical maturity is confidence in your own principles and values. This confidence then allows you to be more aware of and open to what he describes as 'moments of choice', which are situations where you are facing an ethical dilemma or are struggling to decide which is the right choice to make. Your personal set of values, along with your professional ethical code, then helps you to make courageous choices, choosing the right option rather than the easy one. A clear decision-making process here would mean that you would be able to articulate the rationale behind the choice you made and offer a clear justification for the decision. Time spent reflecting on your choice would then allow you to make peace with the decision you made, and would ensure that you could capitalise on anything you learnt from it, which then leads to increased ethical maturity through a clearer sense of your own principles and values.

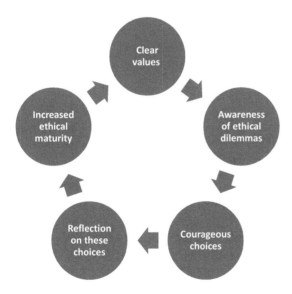

Figure 12.1 Virtuous cycle of ethical maturity (adapted from Van Nieuwerburgh, 2020).

Ethics in research

The principles of ethical practice outlined above should be applicable in any professional context, but there are additional ethical issues to consider when it comes to conducting research. There are some quite shameful accounts of studies in the early days of psychological research in which the researchers did not take due care of their participants, causing them unexpected, unnecessary and unethical distress (see Box 12.1 for more details). In response, there is now a fairly robust set of systems in place to ensure that all psychological research is properly considered. There are two key questions to consider when conducting psychological research: a) what impact could involvement have on the participants and b) what is going to happen to the participants' data?

In terms of the participants, you need to make sure they feel completely comfortable about getting involved, know exactly what to expect and are taking part freely and willingly. You need to think about any issues that might make them feel obliged to get involved, and ensure you mitigate against these – for example, you can make sure that a survey is anonymous, or that line managers never find out who was involved or who chose not to take part. You should also spend some time thinking about whether the involvement could trigger any negative thoughts or feelings, and then consider how you frame the research and what support you could put in place afterwards, should the participants decide that it would be useful to talk their feelings through with a professional. As far as participants' data is concerned, the key considerations are around confidentiality and anonymity. Participants need to be assured that anything they tell you – in a survey, or in person – will not be made public, so data needs to be stored securely and any identifying information and all participant details need to be removed.

Some organisations, and all universities, will have their own ethical approval processes for research or codes of conduct that you need to adhere to – do make sure that you find out what is required before you start. The BPS has its own guide on conducting ethical research which is a good starting point for anyone embarking on a research project. This stresses the principles of scientific integrity, social responsibility, maximising benefits and minimising harm, and encourages researchers to consider risk, valid consent, confidentiality, giving advice, deception, power dynamics and the debrief.

As well as being good ethical practice, these steps will improve the quality of your research – ensuring that people involved genuinely want to help, and making sure that they feel comfortable being open and honest with you. You can read more about this in Chapter 13 which focuses on research in organisations.

Box 12.1   The Stanford Prison Experiment

The ethical hoops we have to jump through before we can conduct even the simplest of studies can sometimes feel disproportionate, but some of the research conducted in the early days of psychology explains the somewhat over-zealous approach we take now.

In 1973 Zimbardo conducted the (in)famous Stanford Prison Experiment (Haney et al., 1973), to explore whether the way prison guards treated prisoners was a result of the characteristics of prison guards or the nature of the context – as he described it, was prison-guard brutality dispositional or situational? Volunteer participants for the study were randomly assigned to either 'prisoner' or 'guard' roles and were expected to spend 14 days and nights in a mock prison. Zimbardo himself acted as the prison governor.

The participants were given no guidelines for behaviour, and Zimbardo and his colleagues just sat back and watched the participants' interactions. Within hours of the start of the experiment, the prison 'guards' had started to harass and mistreat the 'prisoners', and before too long were administering humiliating and dehumanising punishments, including withholding food from them, stripping them naked and removing the beds from their cells. The 'prisoners' also quickly fell into their roles and after some early rebellions were quashed, became more and more submissive. The experiment was terminated after just six days because of the emotional breakdowns of the prisoners and the excessive aggression of the guards, and with hindsight Zimbardo himself realised that even he had been consumed by the experiment, wholeheartedly adopting the role of the prison governor, and losing all sense of objectivity.

The study violated several ethical principles (which would not be allowed today) including participants not being fully informed, deception, significant psychological harm and incidents of humiliation and distress. It revealed fascinating psychological insights, but the harm done to the participants and the reputation of the profession wasn't worth the insights the research brought.

Reflective practice

I mentioned earlier in the chapter that reflection is a core part of ethical practice. It is only through reflection that a practitioner can identify and work through their ethical moments of choice: ethical maturity and resolution will not happen without reflection. But reflective practice is more than a route to resolving ethical dilemmas, also helping practitioners to identify and build on good practice, and to identify and eliminate unhelpful behaviour. Reflection thus enhances competence, which, as we saw earlier in the chapter, is a core aspect of most ethical codes.

What is reflective practice?

Reflection is, in essence, good quality thinking, or as Paul (1985) rather neatly describes it: 'thinking about your thinking... in order to make your thinking better' (p. 11). Thinking is obviously something we can just do in an informal or unstructured way, but reflecting in a more organised way is likely to improve the quality of your thoughts and therefore the contribution your reflection makes to your practice. Although it is widely recognised as an important part of professional practice and research, defining it, and identifying how it works and what impact it has, has proved somewhat challenging to researchers. In this section, an overview of what reflection is and what benefits it can bring is offered, followed by two examples of reflective frameworks to help you structure your reflection.

One insightful quote which sums up the importance of reflection comes from John Dewey, one of the most influential writers in this field, who points out that 'we do not learn from experience; we learn from reflecting on experience' (Dewey, 1933). It's such an obvious point, but beautifully highlights that the value to be gained from experience can only be realised through the process of reflection: without that, the experience counts for very little. In a similar vein, Carroll (2010) describes it as the process that turns information and knowledge into wisdom. Other definitions highlight different key elements of the process, and core to most are curiosity and criticality towards one's own practice (e.g. Gates & Sendiack, 2017).

Delving a little deeper, Dewey describes reflective thinking as 'the turning over of a subject in the mind and giving it serious consideration' (1933, p. 3). It can bring clarity and certainty to situations that are muddy and ambiguous and can provide people with confidence about their conceptualisation of a situation. Schon's seminal work on reflection (Schon 1983, 1987) distinguishes between reflection-in-action – the thinking and analysis that happens during activity, from reflection-on-action, which is the thinking and analysis that happens afterwards. Reflection-in-action is often triggered by a surprise event or reaction and requires a practitioner to go beyond their usual approaches or change tack. For a practitioner to draw on a range of ideas in-action, and to store any new ideas they generate in the moment, they need to spend some time thinking about what they do, what works and what alternative approaches could be available to them. This more thoughtful, deliberative process is reflection-on-action and it is this that forms the starting point for our contemporary notions of reflective practice.

Reflection can lead to a new understanding through reframing a situation, and it is this reconceptualisation that can lead you to identifying alternative approaches that you could use another time. Carroll (2010) describes reflection as a vital tool to prevent us from mindless, routine practice, seeing it as the process that can give us choices and ensures that we don't fall into bad habits. Its aim is to get practitioners to examine their actions, thoughts and feelings, in order to develop insights that can improve their practice (York-Barr et al., 2006).

Box 12.2 Biases, blind spots and the evidence-base

One of the commonly stated hopes or expectations of reflection is that it can help us to identify our biases. It is generally accepted that eliminating biases altogether is impossible as they are a fundamental aspect of human cognition, but it is often assumed that through introspection, we can at least go some way towards limiting the influence these biases have on our behaviour. This notion is certainly supported by our professional bodies (e.g. BPS, 2017) and reports from practitioners who feel that reflection helps them to understand and address their biases (e.g. MacLean et al., 2019).

However, the evidence-base for this isn't quite so compelling (Lilienfeld & Basterfield, 2020), with research suggesting that we have limited access to our own higher-order cognitive processes, and a tendency to a 'bias blind spot' in which we imagine others to be far more prone to biases than ourselves (Pronin et al., 2004). The evidence thus suggests that we are both biased and blind to our biases. It has even been suggested that introspecting might reduce awareness of our own biases: we look inward to seek biases, don't find any (because of our inability to access our own high-order processes) and assume we have none, thus fuelling our bias blind spots (Hansen & Pronin, 2012).

How to reflect

There are myriad different approaches to reflective practice. It is generally thought to be more useful when done through a structured process, with dedicated time set aside on a regular basis. Reflection can take the form of writing – keeping a diary or journal in which you describe and analyse your experiences, talking to others, or just thinking things through by yourself. One practical approach that can aid your reflection is to record your own professional practice (with your clients' express permission, of course). If you can video or audio record yourself in a coaching session, running a workshop or giving feedback to a client and watch it back, it can provide a great opportunity for you to see what your practice looks like from the outside, as well as reflecting on how it felt from the inside. You might be able to notice reactions and responses in your clients that you may not have spotted at the time, and develop a better understanding of the dynamics in the session.

If you find that reflecting on your own only seems to take you so far, it may be worth considering some more formal supervision. Supervision offers a confidential and structured space in which a colleague (or a group of colleagues) can facilitate deeper reflection. Supervision is a working alliance between professionals where supervisees offer an account of their work, reflect on it, receive feedback and are given ideas or guidance if appropriate. The object of this alliance is to enable the practitioner to gain in ethical competency, confidence and creativity to help them to give the best possible service to clients (Inskipp & Proctor, 2001). Supervision can take different forms. Traditional supervision is a regular, one-to-one conversation with a qualified supervisor working in your field, but peer supervision may be easier and more straightforward to arrange and can still offer a safe, confidential space within which to reflect.

Reflective frameworks

There are numerous different frameworks you can use to help structure your thoughts to ensure that you cover all angles and make the best use of your reflection time. Rolfe at al. (2001) offers one of the simplest and most memorable models, which invites the reflector to answer three questions:

• What?
  Describe the incident – what happened and what did you do?

- So what?
  Think about the impact of your behaviour. How did it make you feel? What impact did it have on your client(s) or the session? How do you think it made them feel?

- Now what?
  What could you or would you do differently another time? Why would you make that change and what impact do you think it might have?

The case study in the box below gives an example of how this framework could be used.

Box 12.3   Case study: a reflective diary entry following a coach's ethical dilemma

What?

My friend Lily has asked me to coach her. Our relationship means a lot to me and taking care of my friendships is one of my most important personal values, so I really want to help. Lily has been struggling with this particular issue for a long time – we have had many coaching-type conversations over the years but I can see that what she now needs is some dedicated time with a good coach to help her to move forwards. I know Lily doesn't have many options – she can't really afford to pay for professional coaching and this issue really needs to be resolved as it's making her life difficult. I want to help her, but my professional code tells me, quite clearly, that you shouldn't coach your friends.

So what?

I feel quite torn. My values as a human being are that you should help people if you can, and as a friend, that you should go out of your way to do whatever you can to offer support, and what is the point of all my years of training if I can't help someone I care about? Plus, I don't know how I could explain my rationale – I think it would be very hard to say no without sounding selfish and unsupportive. On the other hand, coaching a friend flouts professional guidelines, and it doesn't always work – so much of the magic of coaching lies in the non-judgemental, confidential safe space that a coach can create, and Lily and I know each other far too well to believe that I wouldn't have a view, or a judgement, on her actions. I think I care too much about her to not interfere, which would then risk making the coaching worse than useless. So I'm left with a dilemma: do I risk damaging the friendship by refusing to help, or risk causing some harm (and possibly damaging the friendship anyway) by offering to help?

Now what?

The more I think about it, the clearer that I am that I have to say no to Lily. I'm not the right person to help her not because I don't care enough, but because I care too much. But I need to think very carefully about how to handle this – it matters to me that she understands why I'm making this choice, and that she knows I value her. I've got a few ideas. I could put together a series of exercises for her – I have a few techniques that I think might really help and I can give her some materials that she can use herself to see if they generate any useful insights. This will also make me feel a bit better because I will feel that I am at least trying to do something to help, even if it's not what she was hoping for. I also need to think about the form of words to use to explain my choices – I need to convey my message clearly and empathically. Finally, I'm going to reach out to my coaching network to see whether anyone has any ideas about low-cost coaching – someone might know of an organisation who could help, or might be happy to offer Lily a discount or a deal in return for a favour from me. I'm not looking forward to the conversation with Lily, but I feel sure that it's the right choice, and I'm sure that Lily will understand.

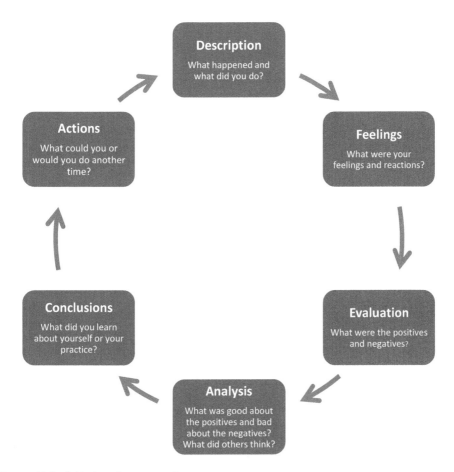

Figure 12.2 Gibbs's reflective cycle.

One of the most widely used frameworks for reflection is Gibbs's reflective cycle (1988). This is similar to Rolfe et al.'s model, but is more detailed and explicit, ensuring that your reflection covers more breadth. It consists of six steps which are illustrated in Figure 12.2. These are just two examples from dozens of frameworks for reflection you will be able to find online, any of which can help you to structure your thinking, to help you to think more deeply and more clearly.

Conclusion

This chapter has introduced two aspects of good psychological practice: ethical and reflective practice. The two approaches are quite distinct but are linked: ethical decisions rely on reflective thinking, and reflection additionally serves to enhance competence. They are skills that will improve with practice, but they are not easy and won't happen automatically. Both require focused effort and dedicated time and the quality of your thinking in both areas will be deepened through the use of models. The importance of these aspects of professional practice cannot be overstated; both will make you a stronger practitioner and have positive consequences for your clients and employers, and for the profession.

Explore further

Ethical Codes: British Psychological Society Code of Ethics: www.bps.org.uk/news-and-policy/bps-code-ethics-and-conduct; The Universal Declaration of Ethical Principles for Psychologists: www.iupsys.net/about/declarations/universal-declaration-of-ethical-principles-for-psychologists/

Iordanou, I., Hawley, R. & Iordanou, C. (2016). *Values and ethics in coaching*. London: Sage. Although this book focuses on the practice of coaching, the insights are relevant to a wide range of specialisms.

Schon, D.A. (1983). *The reflective practitioner: How professionals think in action*. New York: Basic Books. This one is a little old, but probably remains the key text on professional reflective practice.

The Stanford Experiment: www.youtube.com/watch?v=760lwYmpXbc&t=9s. This is a YouTube video that tells the story of this experiment, including clips of Zimbardo himself explaining what happened.

References

Beckett, C., Maynard, A. & Jordan, P. (2017). *Values and ethics in social work*. London: Sage.

British Psychological Society (BPS). (2017). *Practice guidelines*, Leicester: British Psychological Society. www.bps.org.uk/sites/bps.org

Carroll, M. (2010). Levels of reflection: On learning reflection. *Psychotherapy in Australia*, 16(2), 24–31.

Carroll, M. & Shaw, E. (2012). Ethical maturity: Making difficult life and work decisions. *Psychotherapy in Australia*, 18(3), 30–44.

Dewey, J. (1933) *How we think: A restatement of the relation of reflective thinking to the educative process*. Boston, MA: Heath

Gates, N.J. & Sendiack, C.I. (2017). Neuropsychology supervision: Incorporating reflective practice. *Australian Psychologist*, 52(3), 191–197.

Gibbs, G. (1988). *Learning by doing: A guide to teaching and learning methods*. Oxford, UK: Oxford Brookes University, Further Education Unit

Hansen, K.E. & Pronin, E. (2012). Illusions of self-knowledge. In S. Vazire & T.D. Wilson (Eds.), *Handbook of self-knowledge* (pp. 345–362). New York: The Guilford Press.

Haney, C., Banks, C. & Zimbardo, P. (1973). Interpersonal dynamics in a simulated prison. *International Journal of Criminology and Penology*, 1, 69–97.

Hawkins, P. & Smith, N. (2013). *Coaching, mentoring and organizational consultancy* (2nd edn.). Maidenhead: McGraw Hill Education.

Inskipp, F. & Proctor, B. (2001). Group supervision. In J. Scaife, (Ed.) *Supervision in the mental health professions: A practitioner's guide* (pp. 99–121). Hove: Brunner-Routledge.

International Union of Psychological Science. (2008). *Universal declaration of ethical principles for psychologists*. Montreal, Quebec, Canada: IUPsyS. www.iupsys.net/about/declarations/universal-declaration-of-ethical-principles-for-psychologists/#:~:text=The%20Universal%20Declaration%20of%20Ethical,their%20professional%20and%20scientific%20work

Iordanou, I., Hawley, R. & Iordanou, C. (2016). *Values and ethics in coaching*. London: Sage.

Lane, D. (2011). Ethics and professional standards in supervision. In T. Bachkirova, P. Jackson & D. Clutterbuck (Eds.), *Coaching and mentoring supervision: Theory and practice* (99–104). Maidenhead: McGraw-Hill.

Lilienfeld, S.O. & Basterfield, C. (2020). Reflective practice in clinical psychology: Reflections from basic psychological science. *Clinical Psychology: Science and Practice*, 27(4), e12352. https://doi.org/10.1111/cpsp.12352

MacLean, N., Neal, T., Morgan, R.D. & Murrie, D.C. (2019). Forensic clinicians' understanding of bias. *Psychology, Public Policy, and Law*, 25(4), 323–330. https://doi.org/10.1037/law0000212

Parsonson, K.L. & Alquicira, L.M. (2019). International psychology ethics codes: Where is the 'culture' in acculturation? *Ethical Human Psychology & Psychiatry*, 20(2), 86–99.

Paul, R. (1985). The spirit and justice: A model for reflection and action. *Transformation*, 2(2), 5–8.

Pettifor, J.L. & Sawchuk, T.R. (2006). Psychologists' perceptions of ethically troubling incidents across international borders. *International Journal of Psychology*, 41(3), 216–225.

Pronin, E., Lin, D.Y. & Ross, L. (2002). The bias blind spot: Perceptions of bias in self versus others. *Personality and Social Psychology Bulletin*, 28(3), 369–381. https://doi.org/10.1177/01461 67202286008

Rolfe, G., Freshwater, D. & Jasper, M. (2001) *Critical reflection in nursing and the helping professions: a user's guide*. Basingstoke: Palgrave Macmillan.

Schon, D.A. (1983). *The reflective practitioner: How professionals think in action*. New York: Basic Books.

Schon, D.A. (1987). *Educating the reflective practitioner*. San Francisco: Jossey–Bass.

Van Nieuwerburgh, C. (2020). *An introduction to coaching skills: A practical guide*. London: Sage.

York-Barr, J., Sommers, W., Ghere, G. & Montie, J. (2006). Reflective practice for continuous learning. In J. York-Barr, W. Sommers, G. Ghere & J. Montie (Eds.), *Reflective practice to improve schools. An action guide for educators*. CA, Corwin: Thousand Oaks.

Chapter 13

Research design and evidence-based practice

Jennifer Gerson, Lynsey Mahmood and Lara Zibarras

Overview

The British Psychological Society (BPS) considers research methods an underpinning topic that sits at the centre of their core areas for organisational psychology. To be Scientist Practitioners, we need to understand the scientific research that translates into good practice. The purpose of this chapter is to give you a brief introduction to the world of research design and evidence-based practice. In this chapter, we will introduce the foundations of using scientific evidence to underpin the practice of organisational psychology and discuss what it means to be a scientist practitioner. Organisational psychologists often need to interpret, design, and conduct research to explain and understand behaviour in a work setting. This chapter will introduce quantitative and qualitative research design. We will walk you through the cycle of research, discuss different types of study designs, and briefly introduce methods of data analysis. Later in the chapter, we will also discuss some current issues in the field. Research design is a broad area and has entire books written about it, so the aim of this chapter is to provide the foundations of commonly used research methods.

Learning outcomes

By the end of this chapter, you will:

- have an overview of evidence-based practice;
- understand the scientist practitioner model;
- appreciate research design and the research process;
- be aware of current issues in the field of research methods including the replication crisis, open science and WEIRD samples.

What is evidence-based practice?

Organisational psychology is a discipline based in scientific practice. This means that organisational psychology practitioners base their decisions on a range of evidence. Academic literature is one source of evidence, but it is not the only one. Evidence to

DOI: 10.4324/9781003302087-16

support decision making can also come from non-academic literature such as government reports and white papers; from reports from regulatory organisations; from expert or practitioner experience; and from organisation metrics. The key to effective evidence-based practice is using a variety of evidence to support decision making, rather than relying on only one source. It is important to gain a holistic view of the problem and potential solutions to guide the organisation towards the best possible decision. This is why it is important for organisational psychologists to be Scientist Practitioners.

The Scientist Practitioner model

The Scientist Practitioner model asserts that an organisational psychologist has a solid understanding of scientific research and can apply that to the organisational context. There is a tendency for scientists to work in academic silos and practitioners to work in organisations, without bridging the gap between the two, and that is why being a Scientist Practitioner is so valuable. We can understand the research and evidence, and then apply it to the organisation so that the best and most effective decisions can be made. In some cases, organisational psychologists will conduct their own research within an organisation or evaluate the impact of an intervention, so the science underpinning their work must include research methods.

Designing research in organisational psychology

Broadly speaking, organisational research will be either quantitative (using numbers) or qualitative (using words). The decision about which to use is usually determined by what you want to discover, i.e. what your research question is, but practical logistics might also play a part. Mixed methods – using a combination of qualitative and quantitative – is also popular when organisations have the resources. Let us look in more detail at these two different approaches.

Qualitative research

At its most basic level, qualitative research involves analysing non-numerical data – most often language, but it can also examine behaviour and images. The goal is to gain insight into people's beliefs, attitudes and perceptions of particular events or experiences. This enables the researcher to understand the world from the other person's perspective. Thus, qualitative studies rely on personal accounts and focus more on the 'why' than the 'what' of people's experiences. Qualitative research can be inductive or deductive. Inductive research starts with the data and examines what the data can tell us about a phenomenon or help to answer the research question. Deductive qualitative research starts with the theory and looks for clues in the data that help us to better understand the theory.

Qualitative data collection methods rely on collecting data that focuses on the participant's first-hand experience of what is being studied. As such, researchers might use observation (where the researcher observes the participants in situ), interviews, focus groups or case studies (we cover this in greater detail later in the chapter). The number of participants you would use in a qualitative study tends to be relatively small – you might conduct three or four focus groups with six participants in each, or you might conduct 20 in-depth interviews. Since participants are often identified based on who can give the most in-depth answers, this kind of approach may be particularly subject to biases and ethical issues, so it is particularly important for qualitative researchers to be both rigorous and self-reflective. Chapter 12 deals with ethical and reflective practice in more depth.

Quantitative research

While qualitative research can be inductive or deductive, quantitative research is always **deductive**. This means that it is concerned with *testing theories*. In quantitative research, researchers use experiments or surveys with a larger number of participants to identify patterns to test the theories. Unlike qualitative research, quantitative methods are less interested in the experience of each participant, and more interested in what can be deduced about all participants as a group.

In quantitative research, the set of people who participate in your study are known as a **sample**. Samples are small subsets of the **population,** which is all the people who fall into the category of what is being studied. For example, if you were conducting a study on job stress within a large engineering company that employs 2000 engineers, you might randomly choose 100 engineers to complete a survey. In this case, the 100 engineers are your *sample*, and they belong to the *population* of 2000 engineers who work for the company. As researchers, it's unlikely you'll collect data from the entire population, so the goal of good quantitative research design is to conduct rigorous enough research so that findings can be generalised to the population. Let's first cover some basics and present the cyclical process of qualitative and then quantitative research.

The process of research

Research is a cyclical process, which is explained by the Problem-Plan-Data-Analysis-Conclusion problem-solving cycle (Spiegelhalter, 2019, see Figure 13.1). We use this cycle as a framework to explore foundational information about each stage of this process, giving a broad introduction to research design.

- The process starts with the identification of a *problem* that needs solving, or a question which a researcher wants to understand.
- Once a problem has been identified, the next stage of the cycle is to *plan* how this question could be investigated systematically. This involves identifying how to measure or explore abstract concepts, which concepts to measure, choosing an appropriate study design and planning how, when, where and with whom the study will be conducted.
- Once the research has been planned, the next stage is to collect *data*. This stage involves collecting the data for your study, data management and sometimes data cleaning (although this can also be done in the next step) or transcribing qualitative data.
- Once data has been collected, we move to data *analysis* where we finish sorting and cleaning the data, visualise the data using graphs and tables, and apply statistical analysis or qualitative analysis to look for patterns.
- Finally, once the data has been analysed, we move to the *conclusion* stage, where the results are interpreted, conclusions are drawn and our results are communicated to

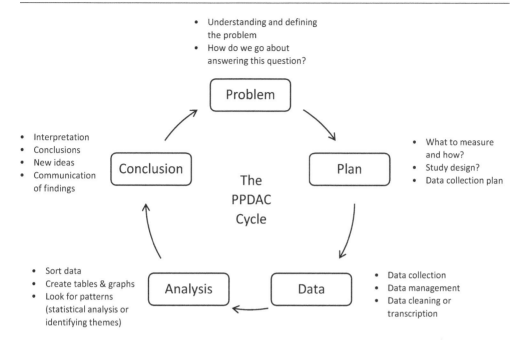

Figure 13.1 An adapted version of the PPDAC cycle, Spiegelhalter, 2019.

our audience (usually other academics or an organisation). In this stage, we may also get ideas for new research questions through the discovery of unexpected patterns or phenomena the research could not explain, which restarts the research cycle.

In the sections that follow, we first present this cyclical process (in Figure 13.1) focusing on qualitative research; and then we present this cyclical process focusing on quantitative research.

The qualitative research process

1 Problem – developing a qualitative research question

Developing a good research question is the first stage of designing research. **Research questions** are *'what'*, *'how'* or *'why'* questions about your topic of interest that guide your research. Qualitative research questions tend to be broad, particularly with inductive studies. The researcher needs to keep an open mind and not second guess the possible findings. However, the research question still needs to be precise and represent exactly what the researcher wants to examine. A good qualitative research question might be 'What are the barriers and enablers for work-life balance for parents?', or 'What impact do senior managers feel their coaching has had on their leadership behaviours?'.

To identify a good research question, you need to explore the academic literature in your area of interest to identify gaps in the literature (i.e., things that science does not already know about your topic). For your research to be original, your question needs to ask something that other researchers have not already examined. Authors of academic literature often make suggestions at the end of their papers about things for further investigation (look in the discussion section, or sometimes under its own subheading called 'Future research').

Qualitative research is exploratory and tries not to pre-judge the results. Therefore, we do not include hypotheses in qualitative research. Instead, we include a research question to help plan and guide the qualitative research.

2 Plan – planning qualitative research

For qualitative research projects, once we have identified our research question, the next stage of the process is to identify our research paradigm. A research **paradigm** is the philosophical framework which we base our research design upon, and includes our ontology, epistemology and research methodology. **Ontology** *asks the question, 'What is reality?'*. **Epistemology** *asks the question, 'How can we know reality?'*. **Research methodology** *asks the question, 'How can we go about discovering the answer to our research question?'*. There are a few common epistemologies which are used in qualitative research to guide the researcher to determine the appropriate research methodology, including phenomenology, which is concerned with the individual participant's lived experience, and critical realism, which aims to uncover an objective reality through exploring people's interpretations of events.

Once we have determined our research paradigm which helps us plan the research, the next step is to determine which data collection method will best suit our research question.

3 Data – collecting qualitative data

Common data collection methods for qualitative research include observation, interviews, focus groups and the critical incident technique (Flanagan, 1954). These are outlined below.

Observation is a data collection method where a researcher observes the participants in their 'natural environment' (sometimes called *in situ*). The purpose of this is to capture information about the culture, relationships and environment participants are a part of. There are different types of observational methods, ranging from the researcher attempting to be as unobtrusive as possible and simply take notes (naturalistic observation), to the researcher embedding themselves into the environment to speak with the participants and observe as part of the group (participant observation).

Interviews involve collecting information on a particular topic from a single participant by asking them questions. Interviews range from being very structured, through to more informal and unstructured.

1 **Structured interviews** are almost like an in-person questionnaire. The researcher asks the participant a set of questions (without deviation), with little opportunity to explore ideas beyond the questions. The data can be collected face to face or through a written survey. Face-to-face data collection, even with a structured interview, will usually yield

more and richer data, but a survey can be an efficient way to gather qualitative data from a larger number of participants.

2 **Semi-structured interviews** are more open and flexible. There are some pre-determined questions, but the researcher may follow up interesting ideas with additional questions. This is the most common way to structure a research interview as the researcher can make sure that the data collected is relevant to the research question, and can respond to and follow up on the specific experiences of each participant, taking the interview in an unanticipated but valuable direction.

3 **Unstructured interviews** are very exploratory. The researcher may have one overarching theme to cover, and the questions emerge from the on-going discussion.

4 **Narrative interviews** are used when a researcher has one area of interest. For example, they might ask the participant: 'please tell me the story of your life'. Whilst the participant speaks, the narrative is not interrupted. It's only after the story that the researcher might ask for clarification or expansion.

When conducting interviews in practice, regardless of the interview structure, it is helpful to start with an easy, rapport-building question or two. The key questions themselves must each cover just one idea, and should not lead the participant in any direction. Finally, it's best practice to avoid ending the interview on a difficult topic, and to provide the participant with the opportunity to ask questions or make further comments. Interviews are useful because they are flexible, and can be used for different roles and contexts. However, they rely on the interviewer's skill to elicit information from participants and rely on a participant's memory and recall which may be flawed.

A focus group is *a group interview* which makes 'explicit use of the group interaction to produce data and insights' (Morgan, 1997, p. 2). Focus groups can range in size (often around 4–7 people) and participants are chosen to help answer a specific research question. Most often groups are chosen so that participants have a shared perspective (e.g. similar job level or team). A facilitator will guide the conversation so that the discussion revolves around a particular topic. The idea is to obtain ideas and perceptions from the participants in a non-threatenin\g environment.

In organisational psychology, focus groups can be used in both research and practice (for example an intervention). The data that is collected via a focus group can be done in isolation, may be supplementary data, or may be one part of a multi-method approach. The main benefits of using focus groups are that you can gain data from a number of participants in a relatively short period of time, and they encourage employee participation and give insight into complex topics. The disadvantages include identifying and then assembling the right people, group issues such as conformity, and maintaining 'focus' on the specific topic. There is also a risk with focus groups that they homogenise the data – participants with more extreme or outlying views are less likely to voice them in front of others, so the data may not be as trustworthy as that obtained through interviews.

Critical Incident Technique (CIT) is a research method where the researcher asks the participant to describe an event when a behaviour impacted a specific outcome (either positively or negatively). According to Flanagan (1954), an 'incident' is any observable human activity which allows inferences to be made about the participant. In order to be 'critical', an incident had a specific impact on the outcome. Within organisational psychology, CIT is used in different areas such as job analysis, performance appraisal, or training needs analysis. CIT is often used during interviews or focus groups and the interviewer might ask a question such as: *'Please tell me about a time when you did something that was effective in closing a sale'*. After the respondent replies, they might be probed with questions such as *'What circumstances led up to the incident?'*, *'What was the outcome?'*, *'Why was this behaviour so helpful in closing the sale?'*. A well-written incident is specific, focused on the participant's behaviour, and includes both the context and the outcome. CIT is useful in identifying critical tasks, it's flexible to use because it can be used for different levels and different roles, and it's especially useful for job tasks that are not easily observed. However, some drawbacks of this method are that some respondents are prone to bias and exaggeration, it can be subjective, and time consuming to analyse.

4 Analysis – analysing qualitative data

There are numerous approaches to analysing qualitative data. Some of them are quite procedural – a set of techniques for identifying the meaning within the data (for example thematic analysis or content analysis). Others are broader methodologies, embedded within a whole set of philosophical assumptions (for example Interpretative Phenomenological Analysis – IPA is linked to phenomenology – the study of lived experience).

The most common approaches (for example, IPA, grounded theory, thematic analysis) follow a similar process. The interviews or focus groups are recorded and then transcribed verbatim (i.e. every word the participants say is written down). The researcher needs to familiarise themselves with the data – reading the transcripts several times, perhaps re-listening to the audio transcripts, and re-reading any memos or notes the researcher made during the data collection phase.

The next stage is detailed coding. The researcher needs to look through the data, line by line, phrase by phrase, sentence by sentence and give each bit of the data a code, or a label that describes what they think it means. In the next stage, the researcher examines the codes and starts to group them together – identifying similar or related concepts. In the last stage the researcher takes these new groups of codes and considers the relationships between them, and their relationship with the research question. This should lead to a final set of themes and sub-themes which, together, answer the research question.

5 Conclusion – interpreting qualitative findings

Once the data has been analysed, the final step of the data cycle is to interpret the data and report the findings. With qualitative research you aim to answer your original research question, reporting on your findings and then comparing them with previous research. Often you answer the question: do your findings confirm (or not) previous research? What are the main theoretical and practical implications? It's important to be aware of your audience; especially when you are reporting to clients you must ensure that you answer the question 'so what' – what do your findings mean for this organisation?

The quantitative research process

1 Problem – developing a quantitative research question

Quantitative research questions need to ask about clearly defined concepts that can be measured with numbers or Likert scales. For example, if you were interested in discovering how work-life balance influences job satisfaction, a good quantitative research question might be *'what is the relationship between work-life balance and job satisfaction?'*.

   Once you have identified your research question, the next step in quantitative research is to develop a **hypothesis**. A hypothesis is *a predictive statement which describes the relationship or difference you expect to find* in your research. Writing a good hypothesis is one of the most challenging parts of the research design. *Good hypotheses need to be positively worded, logical, testable, and refutable.* Let's look at each of these elements in detail.

- Positively worded means that your hypothesis must make a statement about the existence of a relationship or difference.
- Logical means that your hypothesis needs to make sense and be based in evidence. As hypotheses are rooted in theory, your hypotheses should be backed up by literature.
- Testable means that the prediction must be about things which can be measured and quantified. To make hypotheses testable, we also need to make sure that our *predictions are specific*. If your hypothesis is vague, it will be difficult to test if the prediction is true.
- Refutable means that it must be possible to obtain results which prove that our hypothesis is wrong.

2 Plan – planning quantitative research

For quantitative research projects, once we have identified our research question and hypotheses, the next stage of the process is to plan how we will go about investigating whether data supports our hypotheses. The first stage of this process is to decide how we will measure our variables. A **variable** is a concept, trait or characteristic we can measure or manipulate in a research study. While sometimes variables are things which can be directly measured, often variables are concepts which cannot be measured directly, such as personality. To measure these variables, they first need to be **operationally defined.** An operational definition is a way of describing how a variable will be defined to make it measurable in your study. Let's see an example. If we wanted to measure height, we would need to describe how we define height in our study so other researchers could replicate our work. Are we measuring height in feet? Centimetres? Without an operational definition, it will be difficult for other scientists to compare their findings to ours, and difficult for our readers to understand what our results mean. So here, our operational definition might be something like 'height is measured using feet and inches'.

3 Data – collecting quantitative data

Once we have defined our variables, the next step is to decide what type of study design to use in order to collect our data. In general, designs can be categorised as experimental, cross-sectional or longitudinal.

Experimental designs are studies conducted in a tightly controlled environment (often a lab) where researchers manipulate one of the variables in order to determine whether it influences another variable. In experiments, the variable being manipulated is known as the **independent variable**, and the variable which is affected by change in the independent variable is called the **dependent variable**.

Experiments can use either a between-participants design, or a within-participants design. In between-participant designs, participants are randomly assigned to either a control group or an experimental group. Participants in the control group are given an activity which runs the same amount of time as the experimental group's activity, but is not relevant to the experiment, while the experimental group is given an activity which manipulates the independent variable. Both groups then take the same measure for the dependent variable, and the researcher uses statistical analysis to determine whether there is a difference between the two groups brought about by the manipulation of the independent variable. For example, if we were interested to find out whether spending time with puppies made people happy, we could randomly assign participants to one of two conditions; the control group would be given 10 minutes to complete a jigsaw puzzle, while the experimental group would be given 10-minutes with puppies. After both groups completed their tasks, participants could fill in a happiness questionnaire. This would allow us to test whether the group who spent time with puppies were happier than the control group.

You may see these designs referred to as **randomised controlled trials (RCTs)**. RCTs are frequently used to test interventions. In within-participants designs, all of the participants experience both conditions. After each condition, the dependent variable is measured for all participants, allowing researchers to determine whether there was a change in the dependent variable between conditions using the same set of people. If we look back at our previous example, if we wanted to use a within-participants design to investigate whether puppies made people happy, then participants in our experiment would first spend 10 minutes completing a jigsaw puzzle, and then take a happiness questionnaire, and afterwards would spend 10 minutes with puppies and take the happiness questionnaire a second time. This would allow the researchers to compare the happiness between each condition for the same set of participants. Experimental designs are often considered the gold standard for research as they allow us to determine **causality**, which means *we can determine which variable causes the other*.

However, depending on the variables of interest, experimental designs are not always possible. For designs to be considered a true experiment, it must be possible to manipulate the independent variable, and possible to randomly assign participants into any group. In cases where independent variables may be things like age, gender or social class, it is not possible to do an experiment as we cannot randomly assign someone to a social class or manipulate variables like age.

In cases like these we can instead conduct a **quasi-experiment**. A quasi-experiment is an experiment which has some characteristics of an experimental design but does not fulfil all the requirements to be classed as a true experiment. For example, if an organisation had been running a training programme on mindfulness every year and wanted to know whether this programme influenced males and females in its organisation in the same way, it would be possible to use this data to compare the effectiveness of the programme for males versus females. This would be considered a between-participants quasi-experimental design, since there were two different groups of participants (males and females), but it was not possible to randomly allocate participants to their group since gender cannot be randomly allocated.

Cross-sectional designs are studies which look at the relationship between two or more variables at a single point in time. Cross-sectional designs look for **correlational relationships**, meaning they look to see if as one variable increases, another variable either increases or decreases with it. Cross-sectional studies are conducted by collecting survey data, and are not able to determine causality. Although it is tempting to assume that if one variable increases with another, they are related, it is important to note that correlation does not equal causation. There are many examples of variables which are correlated by coincidence or are correlated because they are both related to a third variable which has not been measured; these are called **spurious relationships.** For example, there is a strong correlation between the divorce rate in the US state of Maine and the per capita consumption of margarine (Vigen, 2015), but it would be ridiculous to assume that the consumption of an artificial butter product has any effect on marital success.

Longitudinal designs are *studies which examine the relationship between two or more variables with the same participants over multiple points in time,* and can also be conducted by collecting survey data, but over multiple time points. This type of design is still correlational but can give us a better insight into the time order of variables, making them better than cross-sectional designs. Longitudinal designs are often used when researchers want to understand relationships which take place over time but cannot be manipulated or randomly assigned to test experimentally. For example, if a researcher was interested in understanding how education level impacted long-term career prospects, the researcher could conduct a longitudinal survey where they asked the same participants about their education and career once a year for 5 years. This data could then be analysed to identify how education level affects the careers of participants over the 5 years that the data was collected.

Things to consider when choosing a research design

There are many things to consider when choosing a research design. For quantitative analysis, different designs vary in their ability to determine causality and generalise results to the population of interest. These considerations are called validity. **Internal validity** *is the extent to which conclusions can be drawn about whether one variable causes another,* and **external validity** *is the extent to which the research can be generalised.* Different research designs have differing amounts of internal and external validity. For example, a well-designed RCT would have high internal validity, since experimental methods allow us to determine causality, but if the study was conducted on a small, unusual sample, the study might have poor external validity since the sample does not accurately represent the population. For example, if we wanted to measure working attitudes in employees, but our sample was 90% women who work part-time, this would not accurately represent the population who should be roughly 50% women and mostly work full-time.

Other issues to consider when choosing a research design include whether we have access to sample the population we want to study, how and where the data will be collected, and whether the design we choose is realistic (i.e., while it might be ideal to run a longitudinal study where participants respond every day for 3 weeks, will participants take part in that study or will most drop out?). Along these lines, it is important that no matter which design is chosen, that researchers collect the sample size needed for the analysis. When collecting quantitative data, it's good to consider statistical power (i.e., can we get enough participants to run the analysis we need?).

We also need to consider the ethical implications of our research, such as whether participating in the research could harm participants or causes stress or unhappiness. We also need to consider whether it's ethical to withhold an intervention from a control group. In universities and many other organisations, all research must first go through an ethics board to ensure the safety of participants, but ethics of study design should be an important consideration for external organisations as well (see Chapter 12 for more details on this).

4 Analysis – analysing quantitative data

Once quantitative data has been collected, the next step is to analyse the data for statistical patterns. Most quantitative research in psychology uses **Null Hypothesis Significance Testing (NHST)** to determine if results are 'significant', but what does 'significant' really mean? To understand this, we need to understand what a **null hypothesis** is. When we write hypotheses to predict the outcome of a study or experiment, the null hypothesis predicts that there is no relationship between the variables of interest. For example, if we have hypothesised that a mindfulness intervention will significantly lower job stress, then our null hypothesis would state that a mindfulness intervention will have no effect on job stress.

How is the null hypothesis used in statistical testing to look for patterns? When you read research, you might see authors referring to results as 'significant' when the reported p-value is less than.05. The p-value is about the null hypothesis, not the results themselves, and looks to see if there is a higher likelihood that the null is true. A **p-value** represents the probability of finding a specific result if the null hypothesis were true, so when we look for p <.05, we are looking to see if there is less than a 5% chance that we would find this result if the null hypothesis were true (i.e., there is no relationship). This means that NHST is about the probability of accepting the null hypothesis, not about finding an effect in our data. This has made p-values quite controversial, and often misunderstood, with some recent calls for changing the value of p, and others for scrapping the use of NHST altogether (see Box 13.1).

To explore patterns, researchers use descriptive statistics such as the **mean** (*the average of a set of numbers*), the **median** (*the middle number in a set of numbers*) and **standard deviation** (*a calculation which tells us how much a set of scores vary or deviate from the mean*) to describe the sample, as well as NHST methods to look for patterns in correlational data (i.e., correlations, regressions) or differences between groups in experimental data (i.e., t-tests, ANOVA). NHST allows researchers to determine whether the data collected supports the null hypotheses, and if it does not, view it as support for the hypotheses created at the start of the research process. We are then able to (hopefully) use that information to generalise the results to the population in order to answer to the research question.

5 Conclusion – interpreting quantitative findings

Once the data has been analysed, the final step of the data cycle is to interpret the data and report the findings. Data may support or refute the hypotheses, and results can lead to further research questions or new hypotheses which restart the cycle. It is important to acknowledge who the target audience is. When writing up statistical analysis for a client, emphasis needs to be placed on what they can do with the results. The findings need to be situated within their organisational context. It is also important to avoid jargon and ensure that you explain the core concepts and important statistical results in clear, plain language. This is why it is important to find balance between being a Scientist and a Practitioner – it is our job to understand and digest the science, and then make it practical and tangible for the client.

Box 13.1   The trouble with p…

Is a result statistically significant? To find out we check to see if p <.05; however, recently, psychologists have questioned whether the cut-off for p-values should be smaller. In their landmark paper 'Redefine statistical significance', Benjamin and colleagues (2018) argue that p <.05 yields too many false positives (finding statistical significance when there is not an effect in the real world), and that p should be changed to p <.005 for claiming new discoveries in the field of psychology.

In response to this paper, a group of scientists (88 of them!) wrote a rebuttal called 'Justify your Alpha' (Lakens et al., 2018). In the paper, the authors argue that .005 is just as arbitrary as.05, and that instead of a new 'significance' threshold, scientists should choose and justify the alpha level – that is the number used for statistical significance of p-values appropriate for their study before collecting data. They further argue that the use of the term 'statistically significant' should no longer be used, and instead, researchers should include meaningful interpretations of their results and implications of their findings to practice. Some researchers even suggest we should avoid NHST all together and use a different system (Cumming, 2014; Vandekerckhove et al., 2018). Others argue that as p cannot give any indication to how important a finding is, other statistical measures such as effect size should be emphasised instead (Sullivan & Feinn, 2012). The problem with p is nothing new and debate continues, but for now, most researchers still use NHST and p <.05 despite these issues. For an in-depth analysis on why p-values are controversial, have a look at Greenland et al., 2016 in the 'Explore further' section.

Current issues in the field of research methods

There are several current and important issues in the field of research methods that should be considered, notably replication and open science. We turn to these now.

The replication crisis and open science

In 2011, a paper was published in a prestigious psychology journal which claimed to find evidence for the existence of precognition – the ability to predict the future (Bem, 2011). As (to the best of our knowledge) humans are not capable of seeing the future, this shouldn't have been possible. The paper used common experimental methods from social psychology, and this triggered a conversation in the field about the methods and practices in modern psychology research. After all, if these methods could be used to show statistical evidence for something that should not be possible, what did that imply about all the studies that had come before it using the same methods? This prompted psychologists to attempt to replicate the results of prior studies, some of which had been highly influential in their fields, to see if the findings could be replicated. In science, if results represent a phenomenon that is happening in the real world, then other scientists should be able to reproduce those findings most of the time using the same methods but with different participants. This is **replication**.

While in some other disciplines, scientists had been checking each other's work through replication studies, in psychology (and a few other fields), this had not been as common a practice. Bem's 2011 paper prompted a large group of psychologists from around the world to collaborate in an attempt to replicate 100 experiments which had been published in three high-ranking psychology journals (Open Science Collaboration, 2015). While some of these results did replicate, the vast majority did not. In fact, only 36 out of 100 studies replicated, prompting what is now known as the replication crisis.

There are many potential reasons for research failing to replicate. Some of these are just part of the process of science, but others are a result of poor research practices which can be changed to make research better. Below are some reasons that results may not replicate:

1 False positives: As we saw earlier, quantitative research relies on NHST to assess whether results are 'significant'; however, there is always a chance that results are due to chance instead of representing an actual effect, and in this way, some replication failure is a normal part of the scientific process and highlights the need for replication.
2 Small samples: Research conducted on small samples can make it more likely to find a false positive. For example, if researchers were running an experiment by flipping a coin and hypothesised that a coin would land on heads more often than tails; if the coin was only flipped 10 times, it is possible that the coin would land on heads 7 out of 10 flips. Statistically, this would suggest that the hypothesis is correct. But if the coin was flipped 1000 times, any differences in the number of times heads vs tails appear would unlikely be significant. Research studies with larger sample sizes are more likely to yield replicable results.
3 Samples are not representative: Another issue which can cause issues with replication is the ability to generalise the findings of a study to the population. If the initial research is conducted on a sample which does not represent the population, this can pose an issue for replicating the findings with a different set of participants (see Box 13.2).
4 Bad research practices: Another reason for results not replicating is *questionable research practices* (**QRPs**) such as HARKing or p-hacking. **HARKing** stands for

Hypothesising After Results Known and is exactly what it sounds like. Researchers collect data, explore the dataset to find what is significant, and then write their hypothesis *after* they know which relationships are significant. **P-hacking** is the manipulation of data to make p-values significant, and can take many forms, such as collecting additional data until the hypothesised relationship is significant or removing selected data points to change the significance of p. In very rare cases, researchers have also falsified data to get their research published (Aldhous, 2011). Why would researchers engage in these practices? Most don't! However, the academic system tends to reward significant results because publishing journal articles is a measure of career success and tied to getting jobs, grants and promotions, and academic journals are more likely to publish significant results (Fanelli, 2012). This might incentivise questionable research practices. However, psychology is moving more towards open science practices that should help to reduce these problems.

Why does it matter if research does not replicate? Replication is essential to good science. If results are specific to only a small subset of the population, or are a result of QRPs/false positives, it may mean that future theories in the field are grounded in work that does not represent reality. It also can mean organisations spend money trying to implement interventions which don't work.

In response to the replication crisis, psychology has turned to **open science** to mitigate these issues. Open science is *a set of practices which increase the transparency and accessibility of research* (Nosek et al., 2015). These include practices such as pre-registration, open access journal articles, and open data:

- **Pre-registration**: Pre-registration is a process where researchers fill in an online form describing their study in detail before they collect their data. This allows researchers to declare in advance who their participants will be, how many participants they will collect, which variables they will use, what their hypotheses are, and which analysis they will conduct, along with any other information which could impact the outcome of their study. Once the pre-registration is complete, it is published online and later acknowledged in any publications which come from the study. This can prevent a variety of questionable research practices. For example, it would not be possible to create a hypothesis after exploring the results, since the hypotheses are published publicly prior to collecting the data. This can also stop different methods of p-hacking such as continuing to collect data until the results are significant or changing to a different analysis to see if there are significant results with a different test, since these details are published in advance of the data collection.
- **Open-access journal articles:** In the traditional publishing system, journals charge individuals and institutions a fee to access the work published in their journal. This can create barriers to knowledge, as not all individuals have equal access to this knowledge. Some journals have begun publishing open-access articles, which means the fee to journals is paid by the author or the author's affiliated institution upfront, allowing free access to the article for all individuals.
- **Open data:** Like pre-registration, open data ensures that the authors are being open and ethical in their research practices. After collecting and analysing their data, many authors will now deposit their data in an open data repository. This allows other

researchers to access the data, run the same tests, and see if they can replicate the results the authors found in their article. This practice can prevent p-hacking since other researchers can essentially double check the authors' work, discouraging poor practices from occurring.

These practices can help to prevent QRPs and increase transparency in the research process, making research more rigorous and therefore more likely to replicate. These practices are becoming more common in the field, and some journals now require practices like pre-registration or open data in order to publish in their journal.

Box 13.2   Representation in psychology research: psychology is WEIRD

The goal of research is to generalise the results to learn something about the population we are interested in, and sometimes, about humanity as a whole. So, what happens if the samples used in research are not a good representation of human behaviour? This is a fundamental issue in psychology research...the samples are **WEIRD**.

Participants from most research samples come from countries which are *Western, Educated, Industrialised, Rich and Democratic* (Henrich et al., 2010). Research shows that a huge 96% of the samples in the top psychology journals are WEIRD, even though WEIRD cultures represent only 12% of the human population (Henrich et al., 2010).

And even WEIRDer? Most samples are comprised of psychology undergraduate students (Arnett, 2008), a very small subgroup, who arguably, are not a good representation of the population. This represents a serious issue for generalisability, especially since WEIRD and non-WEIRD participants differ fundamentally in aspects as basic as visual perception and the concept of the self (Henrich et al., 2010). So, what can be done to make psychology less WEIRD? Henrich and colleagues suggest that researchers should try to collect data from diverse samples which represent the population of interest, and to explicitly state any issues with generalisability when publishing research. For more on the WEIRD phenomenon, see Henrich et al., 2010 under Explore Further.

Conclusion

Research design and evidence are fundamental to the practice of organisational psychology. In this chapter, we have introduced the scientist practitioner model, discussed the research design cycle and highlighted a few current issues in the field of research design. We hope the skills, definitions and information in this chapter will encourage you to take an evidence-based approach to your practice of organisational psychology.

Box 13.3   Case study: research design in practice – designing research for the fire and rescue service

The Fire and Rescue sector in the UK has been applying an evidence-based approach to research and practice. Whilst this is common in firefighting, it is less common in other areas of the fire and rescue service, including the application of organisational psychology. In some services a greater focus has been placed on taking a Scientist Practitioner approach, and controlling (to some extent) the conditions under which constructs are studied. For example, being able to investigate stress among fire fighters who work in particular stations and therefore attend different types of emergency incidents. This means that interventions can be applied in a more controlled environment where control groups can be a 'wait-list group' who receive the intervention at a later date.

One fire and rescue service in the south-east of England has starting using organisational psychology consultants in-house. This means that different teams work collaboratively with a specialist consultant to ensure they are best placed to provide expertise for the issue. This has resulted in more use of data and evaluation of training, interventions and other activities that are implemented to better plan, review and develop offerings. The researchers support the planning and data analysis parts of the process, which means organisational psychologists must work with the teams to ensure the correct approach is taken to manage their problem or question.

One example of this is in stress management. Fire and Rescue services typically have a number of services available to them to support staff with mental health and well-being. However, the uptake was low among firefighters, and so the well-being manager worked with the organisational psychologists to understand why. It was initially thought that the service was not quite right for firefighters. However, whilst gathering information it was discovered that firefighters thought that using mental health and well-being services may look bad on record; and worse, that needing or using support services may eventually lead to being taken off active service. Therefore, services were being avoided to reduce the chances of this happening.

This highlights the importance of asking the right question before developing solutions. The outcome for this research was to have more in-house, informal support available before being directed towards external services, and developing clearer policies about the use of support services and how a person could get the most benefit from services available. The additional in-house support included well-being champions who were mental-health first-aiders and as such were trained to support colleagues even in somewhat complex cases.

Explore further

For more funny spurious correlations, check out Vigen's website: www.tylervigen.com/spurious-correlations

For more information on WEIRD samples, read:

216   Jennifer Gerson, Lynsey Mahmood and Lara Zibarras

Henrich, J., Heine, S.J. & Norenzayan, A. (2010) The weirdest people in the world?, *The Behavioral and Brain Sciences*, 33(2–3), 61–83; discussion 83–135. doi: 10.1017/S0140525X0999152X.

For more information on problems with p-values:

Greenland, S. *et al.* (2016) Statistical tests, P values, confidence intervals, and power: a guide to misinterpretations, *European Journal of Epidemiology*. Springer Netherlands, 31(4), pp. 337–350. doi: 10.1007/s10654-016-0149-3.

For more information on the open science movement and how to incorporate open science into your own practice: www.apa.org/science/about/psa/2019/02/open-science

References

Aldhous, P. (2011) Psychologist admits faking data in dozens of studies, New Scientist, November.

Arnett, J.J. (2008) The neglected 95%: Why American psychology needs to become less American, *American Psychologist*, 63(7), 602–614. doi: 10.1037/0003-066X.63.7.602

Bem, D.J. (2011) Feeling the future: Experimental evidence for anomalous retroactive influences on cognition and affect. *Journal of Personality and Social Psychology*, 100(3), 407–425. doi: 10.1037/a0021524

Benjamin, D.J. *et al.* (2018) Redefine statistical significance. *Nature Human Behaviour*, 2(1), 6–10. doi: 10.1038/s41562-017-0189-z

Cumming, G. (2014) The new statistics: Why and how. *Psychological Science*, 25(1), 7–29. doi: 10.1177/0956797613504966

Fanelli, D. (2012) Negative results are disappearing from most disciplines and countries. *Scientometrics*, 90(3), 891–904. doi: 10.1007/s11192-011-0494-7

Flanagan, J.C. (1954) The critical incident technique, *Psychological Bulletin*, 51(4), 257–272. www.ncbi.nlm.nih.gov/pubmed/19586159

Greenland, S., Senn, S.J., Rothman, K.J., Carlin, J.B., Poole, C., Goodman, S.N. & Altman, D.G. (2016) Statistical tests, P values, confidence intervals, and power: a guide to misinterpretations, *European Journal of Epidemiology*, 31(4), 337–350. doi: 10.1007/s10654-016-0149-3

Henrich, J., Heine, S.J. & Norenzayan, A. (2010) The weirdest people in the world?. *The Behavioral and Brain Sciences*, 33(2–3), 61–83; discussion 83–135. doi: 10.1017/S0140525X0999152X

Lakens, D. et al. (2018) Justify your alpha. *Nature Human Behaviour*, 2(3), 168–171. doi: 10.1038/s41562-018-0311-x

Morgan, D.L. (1997) Focus groups as qualitative research (Second Edition). Thousand Oaks, CA: Sage.

Nosek, B.A. et al. (2015) Promoting an open research culture. *Science*, 348(6242), 1422–1425. doi: 10.1126/science.aab2374

Open Science Collaboration (2015) Estimating the reproducibility of psychological science. *Science*, 349(6251). doi: 10.1126/science.aac4716

Spiegelhalter, D. (2019) *Learning from data: The art of statistics*. Pelican.

Sullivan, G.M. & Feinn, R. (2012) Using effect size–or why the p value is not enough. *Journal of Graduate Medical Education*, 4(3), 279–282. doi: 10.4300/jgme-d-12-00156.1

Vandekerckhove, J., Rouder, J.N. & Kruschke, J.K. (2018) Editorial: Bayesian methods for advancing psychological science. *Psychonomic Bulletin and Review*, 25(1), 1–4. doi: 10.3758/s13423-018-1443-8.

Vigen, T. (2015) *Spurious correlations*. Hachette Books. www.tylervigen.com/spurious-correlations

Chapter 14

Working in organisational psychology

Hayley Lewis

Overview

The world of organisational psychology is vast, and it can be confusing knowing where to begin. This chapter examines the variety of roles and sectors that organisational psychologists can work in. Often, students and those early on in their careers as organisational psychologists can feel confused and alone. This chapter provides practical guidance, support and ideas sourced from the stories and experiences of those who have been in the field for several years.

Learning outcomes

By the end of this chapter you will:

- know more about the different career paths possible in organisational psychology;
- have learned about the skills and attitudes needed to succeed in the field;
- have some ideas for finding a job after your qualification;
- have learned how to become a successful self-employed practitioner;
- understand the benefits of being a chartered and registered psychologist.

Career paths in organisational psychology

Training in organisational psychology can enable people to go into a variety of roles. You can become a registered occupational psychologist, work in consultancy, or choose to use the skills and knowledge of organisational psychology to become a better leader. The beauty of the profession is that it gives those of us who specialise in this field a deep understanding of what enables people to thrive at work and the factors that help organisations become successful.

In my own 25-year journey, for example, I started working in an in-house psychology consultancy at the BBC, then moved into the public sector to set up an organisational development team, and then moved further away from pure organisational psychology, to work in a variety of operational management and strategic leadership roles covering services such as technology strategy, customer services and marking and communications.

DOI: 10.4324/9781003302087-17

My knowledge and experience as an organisational psychologist gave me an edge when leading complex services and large teams, and my experience in the real world of leading cash-strapped services and dealing with crisis situations has added a richness to my current practice as an independent consultant psychologist.

In other words, the opportunities are endless when you step into the wonderful world of organisational psychology! But before we go any further, let me introduce you to the organisational psychologists who kindly shared their experiences for this chapter:

> **Dr Rachel Lewis** graduated from her MSc in 2004. She is a chartered and HCPC-registered occupational psychologist, working both as an academic at a UK university and as a practitioner in a consultancy specialising in workplace health and well-being.
>
> **Dr Grace Mansah-Owusu** is a chartered psychologist and graduated from her MSc in 2008. She then followed this with a PhD specialising in contemporary career theories and their application to Black knowledge workers in the UK. She now works as a talent management consultant for a large UK-based charity.
>
> **Dr Hannah Matta Haikal** graduated from her MSc in 2007. She is a chartered and HCPC-registered occupational psychologist and currently leads talent strategy for a large telecommunications company in the United Arab Emirates. Hannah completed her professional doctorate in 2021.
>
> **David Melville** graduated from his MSc in 1999. He is a chartered psychologist working as a consultant for a large, global consultancy where he specialises in recruitment, organisational change, and transformation.
>
> **Nadia Nagamootoo** graduated from her MSc in 2004. She is a chartered and HCPC-registered occupational psychologist, now running her own consultancy specialising in diversity, equity and inclusion (DEI).
>
> **Thomas Rice** graduated from his MSc in 2020. He works in the civil service specialising in assessment and selection and is currently working towards gaining his professional doctorate in organisational psychology.

Advice on career paths

It can sometimes be difficult to know where to start when it comes to a career in organisational psychology. Sometimes, this is because there are so many pathways to take. It can also feel daunting to those just starting out in the field as to how to get a foot on the career ladder. In this section, there are lots of ideas for you, based on the experiences of the psychologists who shared their stories for this chapter. Hopefully, their stories will help you feel inspired and optimistic. If they can do it, you can too!

The generalist versus specialist debate

A question you might be asking yourself is, 'Do I specialise straight away, or do I apply for a role which is more general?' The short answer is you need to do what's right for you. One of the main things that all the OPs in this chapter have in common is they have had a mix of breadth and depth throughout their careers. This taps into the concept of T-shaped skills (Figure 14.1), often used by recruiters and hiring managers when looking for the best applicants.

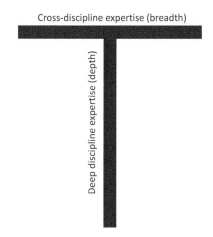

Cross-discipline expertise (breadth)

Deep discipline expertise (depth)

Figure 14.1 T-shaped skills model.

The concept of T-shaped skills was first used by the consultancy McKinsey and Company and further popularised by the journalist David Guest in the early 1990s. The breadth part of the T-shaped skills model focuses on things such as communication, influence, creativity, and understanding of areas outside a specific professional domain. For example, you might already have skills and knowledge in marketing or finance. The depth part of the model is about having deep expertise in one or two areas of a professional field. For example, you might be an organisational psychologist specialising in assessment and selection and organisational change.

Ultimately, the T-shaped skills model reinforces the importance of developing skills other than those in our specific domain. For example, in his first role after his MSc, David says he 'Learned lots about how to work as a professional from different colleagues. For example, how to plan and be organised.'

The T-shaped skills model also highlights the importance of transferable skills. This is something Thomas talks about in his career journey. He worked for seven years before deciding to do his undergraduate degree, followed by his MSc. Thomas's work experience included working for a data management consultancy, where he gained skills around quantitative and qualitative research; and time with an executive search company, where he learned how to communicate with senior stakeholders in the finance profession. These are skills he uses in his current role where his specialism is assessment and selection for part of the civil service. Thomas also recognises that even when we have an area of specialist expertise, everything we do as psychologists is 'intertwined. You can't, for example, look at assessment and selection without looking at training and development.' This kind of understanding only comes about by having a mix of breadth and depth of experience.

For Nadia, the mix of breadth and depth is the reason she thinks she has had a successful career, both as a corporate employee and more recently, as the owner of a consultancy:

I've been able to gain credibility with clients. Prior to becoming a diversity, equity, and inclusion (DEI) specialist, I developed expertise around organisational culture, assessment and selection, and talent management. I'm also an accredited coach and have an executive MBA. There's this breadth of knowledge I've gained over time. I wouldn't be as good at what I'm doing now if I didn't have that breadth to start with.

The importance of adaptability and open-mindedness

As Shakespeare wrote, in Romeo and Juliet, 'What's in a name? That which we call a rose by any other name would smell as sweet.' I use this quote all the time when talking with students about jobs because it reinforces that our job title really shouldn't and often doesn't matter.

Many MSc students can focus too much on the idea that the word 'psychologist' must be in their job title. The reality is that there are very few roles out there which have the word 'psychologist' in the title. When this is added to the fact that around 600 people graduate from organisational psychology MSc, in the UK alone, each year, then that makes those rare roles called 'psychologist' even harder to find. Grace offers up wise advice when she explains:

> [If] the term organisational psychologist or psychologist isn't in your job title it doesn't matter. You're never going to waste what you learn during your MSc. It's applicable in so many settings. People feel 'no, no. I MUST get this psychologist job title', but if you go in with one specific idea and you don't get it, then it's going to be hard for you.

Thomas adds to this by sharing:

> All experience is valid experience. I just knew that the education path of the MSc would help me get into any role. I don't think graduates should just look for organisational psychologist roles. They are few and far between. Look wider for more opportunities. For example, I wouldn't pick a job that said psychologist in the title over the one that didn't if the latter was more interesting.

Hannah's experience during and immediately after her MSc reinforces the value of thinking more widely when it comes to roles. She was already working in a recruitment team, running assessment centres, while she did her MSc. After graduation, Hannah then worked in a tech start-up as an HR assistant, 'doing a bit of everything'. Unfortunately for Hannah, the 2008 global recession struck, and she lost her job. She subsequently found a temporary job in the United Arab Emirates (UAE) supporting development centres for a few months, following which she made the move into local government (UK) as a talent management and organisational development consultant before heading back to the UAE where she spent the rest of her career to-date in a range of HR leadership roles.

It's also important to remember that our priorities will change and evolve over time. Personal circumstances can impact how we feel about our jobs and the decisions we make. The Kaleidoscope Career Model (Mainiero & Sullivan, 2005) suggests that there are three factors which feed into how we approach our careers:

- authenticity – making career choices that allow us to be true to ourselves;
- balance – striving to achieve an equilibrium between our work and personal lives;
- challenge – our need for challenging and stimulating work, as well as career progression.

These three factors are simultaneously active throughout our working lives, but the order of priority will change as our circumstances change. A new parent, for example, may find that the need for balance intensifies and becomes the most important priority, with authenticity and challenge active but in the background. Meanwhile, for someone looking for their first role in the field, challenge might be the most important, with the other two moving into the background.

My own career experience included spending several years in a senior leadership role that didn't suit me. I had ended up in that role partly because challenge had been my primary driver. As I hit my early 40s, I started to dream about setting up as an independent practitioner but kept putting it off. My priorities changed after a huge personal loss, the death of my father and then my mother's subsequent diagnosis of a terminal illness. Challenge shifted into the background and balance moved into the most important position. This change in personal priorities gave me the impetus to make the leap from corporate employee to independent practitioner, running my own business.

A change in personal circumstances is also what led to Nadia setting up her own business, a successful consultancy specialising in Diversity, Equality and Inclusions (DEI). Nadia had her first child while working in local government and it was this life change which gave her the courage to make the move from her role as an organisational development manager, to setting up on her own.

3. The importance of relationships

The word 'networking' seems to instil fear and loathing in many of the students and practitioners I work with. Yet, networking, when done right, has many benefits for us and our careers. As Adam Grant says, in his book *Give and Take: Why helping others drives our success*:

> Extensive research demonstrates that people with rich networks achieve higher performance ratings, get promoted faster, and earn more money. And because networks are based on interactions and relationships, they serve as a powerful prism for understanding the impact of reciprocity styles on success.
>
> (Grant, 2013, p. 34)

If you're a woman, avoiding networking can potentially harm your career progression. For example, one study suggests that when women impose barriers on themselves, such as hesitating when meeting new people, it may mean they under-benefit from situations where networking occurs (Greguletz et al., 2018). One of the main reasons women appear to put these barriers in place is because of anxiety about being seen to exploit relationships. Yet the benefits of networking can be profound. For example, Hannah found that networking, along with continuously building and nurturing her professional relationships, helped with increasing her self-belief.

As Nadia says, 'I would say my network has absolutely accelerated the speed at which I was successful. I don't know any progression I've made without the support of someone.' She adds, 'I was proactive. I found people who would act as my sponsors, my mentors, my coaches, my general network. I went to networking events where organisational psychologists hung out and built relationships and hung on to those relationships.'

If you're someone who perhaps feels anxious about approaching people then Rachel has some words of advice: 'I'm not one for networking but I try to treat everyone I meet in a positive way so that enables me to go back and speak to them if I need to.'

While Grace emphasises the importance of not leaving your network to chance when she suggests: 'Build networks, create networks.' This is something that Thomas echoes when he says:

> Ask people for coffee dates. Take up all sorts of opportunities. LinkedIn is also a tool to meet people so use it that way. You're not pestering. You don't go to networking events to meet people you know. You go to also meet new people and learn from others.

Advice I give to students and new practitioners is to follow up online when you meet a new person and keep the connection going. A good habit to get into is to send someone you've met in real life a LinkedIn connection request. I normally do this 24 to 48 hours after I've met someone virtually or in person and I always add a personalised note. But it doesn't end there. Once a week, I contact someone among my LinkedIn connections to see how they're doing and offer to meet for a coffee. And there are times where I send a connection an article, or even one of my sketchnotes, that I think they'd find helpful because of something I know they've been working on.

All the psychologists interviewed talked about the importance of mentors, as part of their network. For example, Thomas talked about having a 'community of mentors' and Nadia emphasised how vital mentorship was in her journey: 'When I was doing the executive MBA and then setting up my business, mentors helped me in that space of uncertainty.'

Before approaching people at random, ask yourself what you want from a mentor. It's important you're clear that you are asking for a favour. This can help the person you approach to make an informed decision as to whether they're the best mentor for you. If you already work in an organisation, they may have a mentoring scheme in place and, therefore, it's always worth approaching the HR department to see if they can help. If there isn't such a scheme in your organisation, then it's time to tap into your network. Here are some examples to get you started:

- **University and college networks** – if you are a current student, then your university might have a mentoring scheme you can sign up to. However, if that's not quite right for you, how about asking lecturers? As a lecturer on a MSc programme, I have been asked to be a mentor by around a dozen students over the past few years and I've said yes to many of these. Where I haven't been able to, due to my lack of capacity, I've introduced the student to someone in my professional field who I think might be a good mentor for them.
- **Senior managers in your company** – if your organisation doesn't have a formal scheme then why not send an email to a senior manager who you think could help? If you're a bit reluctant then you could always speak to your own line manager for assistance.
- **LinkedIn** – if you are already connected to someone who you think matches what you need, then drop them a note via direct messaging. As a mentor, believe me when I say that you really won't be irritating. It's always lovely and a real honour to be asked. As the saying goes, 'If you don't ask, you don't get.' If you aren't connected to a person

on LinkedIn but you want them to be your mentor, why not use your own connections? LinkedIn shows you who in your network is connected to someone you're not. You can ask your connection to introduce you. (*Note – this is always far better than sending a generic connection request with no context. Please don't send random connection requests to strangers you've never met, particularly asking them to be your mentor. This can be irritating and come across as unprofessional – something you don't want!*)

The importance of continuous learning

Albert Einstein allegedly once said: 'The more I learn, the more I realise how much I don't know', and so it is for the lifelong learner. There is always new research and new ways of doing things to learn about in OP. As Nadia says:

> Things change in organisational psychology. I graduated in 2004. If I continued applying my 2004 knowledge, it's just not relevant. We need to stay relevant as practitioners. We need to keep up to date. I pride myself as being a bridge between theoretical and applied sides of organisational psychology. It gives the client confidence. I don't think you can influence if you're outdated.

Thomas reiterates this:

> When I first walked out of my MSc, I thought 'okay I've ticked that studying box' but that's not enough. I don't think you can successfully work in organisational psychology without continuously learning. It's beyond CPD. The evidence-based nature of what we do means we're always learning, still reading, still gaining knowledge.

Staying relevant and planning for the future was one of the reasons Hannah made the decision to do a doctorate:

> I wasn't feeling close to my profession as an organisational psychologist. I was an HR practitioner but not an OP. I felt myself drifting from the field, even though I'd done chartership. I wanted to hone my research skills and do great work founded in evidence and take this to the workplace. And lastly, because I want opportunities later in my career, perhaps more autonomy and flexibility, and this will give me more credibility as an independent practitioner and weave in some academia work as well.

And this doesn't have to be about digging into research journals, although that's important. David suggests it's about: 'Asking good questions but also watching and listening. Look at the people around you and notice their strengths. What is making them strong and good at what they do? What can you learn from them?'

The importance of personal values

All the psychologists in this chapter talked about the importance of knowing and standing by their core values. When we think of personal values, we think of what matters to us most in life (see Box 14.1). When we are clear in our core values, they can act as a motivator to act, as well as serve as standards for how we live our life. For example, Rachel advises 'listening to your values and underlying drive' when it comes to making decisions. This is echoed by Hannah:

> Values have been important in making decisions about the kind of companies I want to work for. This is also important when you think about our code of ethics and how we should operate as psychologists. This affects how we make decisions, how we approach issues. In terms of guiding my career path, those core values are variety, adventure, and making a difference. These have shaped which opportunities I've picked, along with the industry I'd want to be part of.

For Nadia, her purpose and values have been influenced, in part, by her heritage:

> I'm a first gen UK-born with my family coming from Mauritius from a low socio-economic background. My privilege stems from my education. Throughout my life there have been times where I've been the 'only' in the room. What I've found through my work in diversity, equity and inclusion is something deeply purposeful for me.

Box 14.1   Find out your core values

The Values Project is a collaboration between The University of Western Australia and Pureprofile. It is a multi-year programme which aims to help people understand how their values can shape and influence the things that matter most to them in life. Among the academics working on The Values Project is Professor Shalom Schwartz, one of the world's leading experts on individual- and culture-level values, whose research has been used in more than 80 countries.

You can learn more about your core values by doing the free survey at www. thevaluesproject.com

Understanding your core values is important because it can help you make important decisions, such as which organisations to apply for and which not to. It can also help you to identify the kind of jobs that will excite and energise you, and those which may not.

Advice for finding your first job as an organisational psychologist

If you're still an undergraduate and haven't started your MSc, you might want to take inspiration from Nadia's story:

> I started looking for work experience in my holidays as an undergrad. A very small organisational psychology consultancy said yes. By my final year of undergrad, I'd already worked out where I wanted to do my MSc and that I wanted to travel and for that, I needed money. I pitched to them, 'Do you need someone like me?' I worked as the office manager but it didn't matter to me. I was in the environment and learning lots.

If you've already been working in another field or sector, take inspiration from Rachel's and Thomas's stories:

> My first role after my MSc was as a senior consultant in an organisational psychology consultancy. I could get that because of my previous consulting experience in marketing. It helped that I was able to bring in my different skills, such as being able to draw up project plans, speak to clients etc.
>
> (Rachel)

> I worked during my MSc and was self-funded. Throughout my MSc I knew I wanted to transition into the development field. While I was writing my dissertation I applied to a job with a recruitment company, focused on executive search in the finance sector. I liked the idea of selection and assessment along with data and numbers. I thought it was a good entry role. It was a temporary role for four months and a bit like an internship. It helped me overcome barriers of speaking to people at all levels, learning how to be professional, how to give advice to C-suite members. It was good entry experience. That was when I moved to the data and insights company toward the end of my MSc. They focused on reputation and getting opinions of stakeholders, employees for example. I did a lot of quantitative survey projects and qualitative interviews, depending on what the client wanted, and I gained lots of transferable skills.
>
> (Thomas)

If you're finding the job market tough because of the economic climate, take inspiration from Grace, who had a variety of roles during the global recession and then decided to do a PhD:

> I thought 'I'll finish my MSc and get a shiny consultancy role.' I graduated from my MSc in 2008, at the same time as the global financial recession. It was a tough time to get a role. I got a role in a recruitment agency before I finished my MSc. It was a temporary role for five months and I was managing a large account. I then went on to do some temping in an admin role in the NHS. Then I got lucky. At the time, I lived near an industrial estate with lots of big company headquarters. One of these was Blackberry and I applied to a be temporary recruitment coordinator. I then thought, 'I can't keep doing this, I'm not any closer to being an organisational psychologist consultant.' I thought 'Maybe I'll apply for a PhD. That will give three years for the economy to sort itself out and I'll gain some skills in the meantime.' I cold called a few lecturers at different universities and a couple were interested in my research idea.

If you're interesting in becoming a self-employed independent practitioner, here is some advice based on my own doctoral research. I specifically looked at the psychological factors (competencies, personality and values) that enable women business owners to succeed in the early years of starting a coaching and training business. While my focus was on women, I think my advice can apply to others too.

- **Build and maintain relationships:** To be a successful self-employed practitioner you need to proactively reach out to people, create collaborative partnerships by working with other practitioners, know who to signpost to in the event you don't have the expertise for a client request, and maintain your pre-existing professional relationships. Every woman in my study talked about the importance of their network for their business success so once again, you can see how important relationships and your network are whether you're applying for a job or setting up on your own.

- **Self-directed learning:** This builds on an earlier section where we focused on the importance of continuous learning. To be a successful self-employed practitioner it is valuable to talk with and learn from more experienced self-employed business owners, have role models who are doing the kind of thing you want to do, make time for regular reflection on how you are doing, get a coach or mentor, proactively ask for client feedback, invest in your professional development and develop a deep self-awareness so that you can put in place tactics to overcome any issues.
- **Business planning:** This is a vital factor in succeeding as a self-employed practitioner. Still too many people make the mistake of setting up on their own without having a clear idea of what their business focuses on and what success looks like in year one, two etc. Successful self-employed practitioners make time for business planning both at the start of setting up their business but also as a standard activity once the business is up and running. This is about being clear on your business model: for example will you be a limited company or a sole trader? It's also about researching and setting out your unique selling point (USP), along with setting out the products and services you want to offer now and in the future.
- **Commercial awareness:** To be a successful independent practitioner, you need to know what you are going to charge for your services. Successful self-employed practitioners do their research, finding out what similar people charge (known as benchmarking) and finding out what your ideal client sector typically pays. It is also important to be clear on any pricing structure you might want to put in place. For example, I offer a percentage discount of my usual fees for coaching, consultancy and training for the public and charity sectors.
- **Market sector awareness:** This is an often overlooked but crucial ingredient of success in running a successful business. This is about knowing the kind of clients you do and don't want to work with, along with understanding and responding to market trends and customer issues. Successful self-employed practitioners pay regular attention to trade press, policy announcements that could affect a sector they work with, and the wider socio-economic environment. This will give you credibility when pitching for work.

HCPC registration and BPS chartership

Prior to July 2009, the British Psychological Society (BPS) was the professional regulator for psychologists in the UK, setting the criteria for accreditation and regulation of courses. The responsibility was taken over by the Health and Care Professions Council (HCPC) in 2009. Their responsibilities now include the creation of a statutory register of practitioner psychologists (with legal protection of the title 'occupational psychologist'), accreditation of courses such as the Doctorate in Occupational Psychology, and the introduction of a disciplinary procedure. The HCPC has set standards of proficiency which make clear what is considered necessary for safe and effective practice, and describe what professionals must know, understand and be able to do at the time they apply to join the HCPC Register (see Box 14.2).

Box 14.2   HCPC standards of proficiency (SOPs) for practitioner psychologists

1   Practise safely and effectively within their scope of practice.
2   Practise within the legal and ethical boundaries of their profession.
3   Look after their health and well-being, seeking appropriate support where necessary.
4   Practise as an autonomous professional, exercising their own professional judgement.
5   Recognise the impact of culture, equality and diversity on practice, and practise in a non-discriminatory and inclusive manner.
6   Understand the importance of and maintain confidentiality.
7   Communicate effectively.
8   Work appropriately with others.
9   Maintain records appropriately.
10   Reflect on and review practice.
11   Assure the quality of their practice.
12   Understand and apply the key concepts of the knowledge base relevant to their profession.
13   Draw on appropriate knowledge and skills to inform practice.
14   Establish and maintain a safe practice environment.
15   Promote and prevent ill health.

In addition, the HCPC allows the use of two generic titles – Practitioner Psychologist and Registered Psychologist – but these are only available to registrants who already hold one of the seven 'specialist' titles, such as occupational psychologist. It is an offence to use the title 'occupational psychologist' without being on the HCPC register.

The basic guidance is not to combine titles that 'belong' to the two different organisations. It is no longer permitted to use the term 'Chartered Occupational Psychologist'. The BPS title is Chartered Psychologist, and the HCPC owns the domain title 'occupational psychologist', along with the two generic titles. If you are a Chartered Psychologist **and** registered with the HCPC you are encouraged to use the titles that indicate this. For example,

- Hayley Lewis CPsychol, Occupational Psychologist; or
- Hayley Lewis, Chartered Psychologist and Occupational Psychologist; or
- Hayley Lewis, Chartered Psychologist and Registered Occupational Psychologist; or
- Hayley Lewis, Chartered Psychologist and Practitioner Occupational Psychologist.

Trainee psychologists on HCPC accredited training routes, such as a professional doctorate programme, may use 'Trainee', or 'In-Training' in combination with the domain title of occupational psychologist. For example:

- Trainee Occupational Psychologist
- Occupational Psychologist-In-Training

The BPS still retains responsibility for regulating the title Chartered Psychologist (CPsychol). Chartered Psychologist status reflects the highest standards of psychological skill, knowledge and expertise. Only those psychologists registered and recognised by the BPS have the right to use the title. The title cuts across all disciplines within the BPS and can therefore be used in conjunction with titles that are legally protected under the HCPC, such as Occupational Psychologist.

The BPS offers various services to psychologists and the public. Whether you are thinking about studying to be an organisational psychologist, or you have already graduated from your MSc, there is information on the BPS website regarding accredited courses, a portal for Continuing Professional Development (CPD), membership networks such as the Division of Occupational Psychology, information and guidelines on ethics and best practice, and access to articles and resources. For the public there is information and guidance about the use of psychology and psychological testing, along with access to a directory of chartered psychologists and expert witnesses. The BPS also publishes peer-reviewed, high-quality journals including the *Journal of Occupational and Organizational Psychology*. In the UK, there are two main ways you can become a chartered and an HCPC registered occupational psychologist. These are the Qualification in Occupational Psychology (QOP) with the British Psychological Society, or the Professional Doctorate in Organisational Psychology. The latter is currently only available at Birkbeck College, University of London.

The QOP (Stage 2)

The Qualification in Occupational Psychology (QOP) (Stage 2) is a doctoral-level qualification which takes two to four years to complete. It enables you to undertake your training while you are working in the field and acquiring valuable practical experience in a variety of settings, assessed against the four Standards expected of psychologists (see Box 14.3 in conjunction with evidencing practice at each stage of the consultancy cycle (see Figure 14.2).

Successful completion of the QOP (Stage 2) leads to Chartered membership of the BPS, full membership of the DOP, and eligibility to apply for HCPC registration as an occupational psychologist. The criteria for doing the QOP (Stage 2) are:

- Graduate Basis for Chartered membership with the BPS. This is usually obtained via an undergraduate programme or a conversion course that is accredited by the BPS and is required for many BPS-accredited post-graduate and doctoral programmes.
- BPS-accredited MSc in Occupational / Organisational Psychology.
- Access to a suitable placement (paid or voluntary) because you must be able to write up work-based projects for your QOP submissions.

During the QOP, you work closely with a supervisor (an experienced, qualified occupational psychologist) to submit a number of reports against each of the five core areas of OP. Your first submission will be one or two 6000-word reports. Your second submission

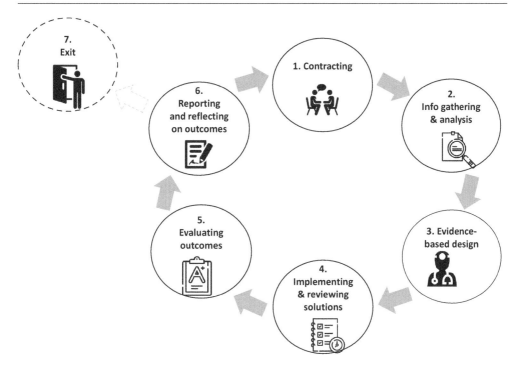

Figure 14.2 The consultancy cycle.

will be three or four 6000-word reports, depending on how many you included in the first submission. Your final submission is a research report of up to 15000 words. You then have what is called a viva examination, where a panel of experts will question you on your final research report.

The professional doctorate in occupational psychology

At present, there are not many universities that offer the professional doctorate, but this may change in the future. The professional doctorate programme takes four to five years to complete and has two parts. It is accredited by the BPS as an alternative to their QOP (Stage 2).

Part 1 is focused on excellence in professional practice and is a Master of Research (MRes) in Professional Practice in Occupational Psychology. This takes place in the first two years, with practitioners-in-training submitting six 5000-word practice logs during that time. The practice logs cover each of the five core organisational psychology areas. Each trainee is allocated a professional practice supervisor (an experienced and qualified occupational psychologist) who advises and supports them in their submission of the six evidence-based practice logs. At the end of Part 1, trainees are eligible to apply for HCPC-registered occupational psychologist status and go on the public register. Trainees can then apply to transition to Part 2.

Part 2 is focused on excellence in research and takes two to three years. During this time, practitioners undertake original doctoral-level research consisting of two empirical studies, each of publishable standard in a peer-reviewed journal. A doctoral thesis is then submitted at the end of the two to three years, usually around 50000 words, with a viva examination with academic experts in the area you have researched. Pending successful completion and examination, if you do the professional doctorate, you may use the title Doctor and apply for chartered status with the BPS.

Box 14.3   BPS standards for psychologists

Standard 1: *Ethical, reflective and legal practice*
Understand and work in accordance with the legal, ethical and professional regulations for organisational psychologists. This includes engaging in a continuous cycle of self-reflection and working with appropriate supervision to gain the required level of competence as a practitioner.

Standard 2: *Competent practice across the five core areas of organisational psychology*
Build and demonstrate competence across psychological assessment at work; learning, training and development; leadership, engagement and motivation; well-being and work; and work design, organisational change and development. Keep up to date with research, evidence and best practice.

Standard 3: *Taking an evidence-based approach*
Critically appraise psychological evidence in conjunction with consideration of wider social and policy issues. Practitioner psychologists use an evidence-based practice approach to diagnose issues effectively and inform the design of interventions.

Standard 4: *Competence in applying the consultancy cycle*
Demonstrate competence and confidence in working across all six stages of the consultancy cycle, in a range of contexts.

Benefits of chartership and registration

Investing in professional qualification may feel cost prohibitive. However, the investment can make a real impact on your career opportunities and longevity in the field. For example, if your aim is to work as a senior psychologist, at some point, in the UK Civil Service then, depending on the specific department, you will need to be chartered and registered. This is something David reflects upon:

> I chased my chartership early on in my career [before the QOP was introduced]. I was able to build up my logbook days from the sheer variety of work in my first role. Getting chartered depends on the type of roles or type of careers someone sees themselves having. There are some organisations and some roles that that have a prerequisite. For example, it is essential for some Government departments.

For many of the psychologists interviewed for this chapter, chartership and registration helped them feel more confident and able as practitioners. For Nadia, it gave her 'a stamp of approval that I've met a certain standard. It gives me automatic credibility.' While Rachel says:

> When I came out of my MSc, I had all the qualifications but intrinsically I didn't feel competent. The biggest advantage of chartership was engaging on a learning journey with my practice. Doing that work consciously to meld together my practice. By the end of chartership I felt like I'd earned that title of psychologist. It also drums into you the importance of evidence-based practice and using the evidence consistently. It makes you a better psych and a longer-lasting psych too.

While Thomas isn't yet chartered or registered, he is thinking to the future,

> My undergrad lecturer instilled in me the importance of getting chartered and therefore going for a MSc that was accredited. During my undergraduate in 2015, I physically wrote down the goal of doing chartership as my tutor had talked about the importance of doing it. Regulations could change and you could be in a job you're not qualified for. You also learn a lot through the process. It's not just the certificate at the end. I wouldn't want to be in a role but where I was surrounded by chartered and registered people, and I wasn't. You also learn a lot in terms of those standards and ethical practice.

In an increasingly competitive field, being chartered and registered can make a difference. Hannah emphasises this when she says 'I learned about the importance of evidence-based practice. This was reinforced during my chartership. You must be dedicated to put yourself through chartership and a doctorate, but it can really give you an edge.'

More than anything, chartership and registration is the quality mark of a practitioner. Not only can it give you an edge when applying for jobs, but it also protects and gives reassurance to the public. As Rachel concludes:

> I think HCPC is the kite mark. The registration process is much better understood because of the link to medical professionals. It should be the norm to go on and get your registration and chartership. Imagine if you were doing a clinical psychology degree and then didn't get registered and chartered. You just wouldn't!

Conclusion

I hope that you are feeling excited, inspired and motivated in taking your next steps toward becoming an organisational psychologist. As we head further into the 21st century, with all the uncertainty and the opportunity that societal, economic and organisational changes can bring, we need organisational psychologists even more. The work we do has a big impact on the people and world around us. That is something to be proud of. That is something to be part of.

Here's to your next step toward becoming qualified psychologist. Now go make that positive impact on the world.

Further information

Graduate membership with BPS www.bps.org.uk/graduate-membership-gmbpss

BPS Qualification in Organisational Psychology www.bps.org.uk/qualification-occupatio
nal-psychology

BPS Code of ethics and conduct www.bps.org.uk/guideline/code-ethics-and-conduct

HCPC Standards of Proficiency for practitioner psychologists www.hcpc-uk.org/standa
rds/standards-of-proficiency/practitioner-psychologists/

HCPC Standards of conduct, performance and ethics www.hcpc-uk.org/standards/standa
rds-of-conduct-performance-and-ethics/

Professional doctorate in organisational psychology www.bbk.ac.uk/courses/phd/profe
ssional-practice-in-occupational-psychology

References

Grant, A. (2013). *Give and take: Why helping others drives our success*. London: Weidenfeld &
Nicolson.

Greguletz, E., Diehl, M-R. & Kreutzer, K. (2018). Why women build less effective networks than
men: The role of structural exclusion and personal hesitation. *Human Relations*, 72, 1234–1261.

Mainiero, L.A. & Sullivan, S.E. (2005). Kaleidoscope careers: An alternative explanation for the
'opt out' generation. *Academy of Management Executive, 19*, 106–123.

Concluding remarks

Our aim to cover the whole field of organisational psychology in a mere 200 pages was no mean feat, and one thing that has struck us when putting the chapters together, and may well have struck you reading them, is how broad ranging the field is. The book is structured around the British Psychological Society's five core areas for organisational psychology: *Psychological Assessment*; *Learning, Training and Development*; *Leadership, Engagement and Motivation*; *Well-being and Work*; and *Work Design, Organisational Change and Development*. This ensures that we have covered the key topics and for those of you planning to go on and study organisational psychology further, this knowledge will provide you with a solid foundation for your next steps. The chapters in Part I offer an overview – a summary of some of the key concepts and theories, together with some ideas for the practical application of the area, but each of the five core areas really deserves a whole book of its own. There is more depth in Part II – the *In Focus* chapters each provide a more detailed look at one of the five Core Areas. We have identified five important topics for this kind of deep-dive, but had to discard dozens more, all of which would have had a legitimate place in a book such as this. We hope that the balance between breadth (in Part I) and depth (in Part II) was right for you, but if we left you wanting more, there are plenty of suggestions in each chapter for further reading.

Perhaps it's no surprise that this field is so wide ranging. Work is all about people, so any topic right across the field of psychology will be relevant to the workplace; psychological theories that address relationships, decision making, mental health and neurodivergence are as important within workplaces as outside them. Add to that the work-specific topics such as selection, career development, leadership and organisational change, and it's easy to see why organisational psychology is so extensive. This breadth can feel a little daunting but does mean that as long as you have at least some interest in people and behaviour, you are bound to find at least one aspect of organisational psychology appealing.

Across the chapters we can see some broad trends. There has been a recent increase in emphasis on the needs of the individual worker alongside the needs of the organisation. This can be seen in the growing focus on equality, diversity and inclusion – as organisations are becoming aware of the value of diverse teams and the challenges that face people in different groups. We can also see it in the awareness of psychological well-being and mental ill-heath – a growing problem within society, and one that employers know that they need to address. Organisations are increasingly aware of the value of offering work that employees find personally meaningful, and allowing ways of working that suit

DOI: 10.4324/9781003302087-18

each individual. Finally, the prominence of the individual can be seen within the field of selection, as organisations are beginning to acknowledge the importance of the candidate's experience. It feels, more than perhaps ever before, that every individual matters.

Another key theme that runs through the book is technology. This impacts every aspect of organisational life – how we work, where we work, who works and what we do – and it's not always clear how best to capitalise on technological advances. Even after some decades, we are still not entirely confident about how to manage some aspects of the internet, or how we should be using social media, and much more research is needed to offer guidance to ensure that working-from-home technology is effective for individuals and organisations. At the time of writing, developments in AI are beginning to gather pace. The potential that AI seems to have for changing the nature of our work is yet unclear, but there is no doubt that it will bring enormous, perhaps even limitless change. There will be advantages, for sure, but developments will need to be managed very carefully to ensure that we can capitalise on AI's potential for positive change without risks.

One important point that comes through in every chapter in the book is that as an organisational psychologist, you really can make a difference. As organisational psychologists we rely on evidence. This is one of our key selling points, and one of the things that marks us out as different from similar professionals in the same arena. Through our evidence-based practice, we can ensure that work conducted within organisations is based on relevant literature and theories, and we can test whether our interventions are working using the research skills that we describe in Chapter 13.

Relying on evidence really makes a difference. Throughout these chapters we have seen examples of ideas that may be intuitive but are not valid: learning styles make no difference to learning; happy workers aren't always more productive; higher salaries don't improve levels of job satisfaction. We have also seen examples of approaches that we know work, because the evidence tells us they do: acceptance and commitment therapy makes a difference to levels of anxiety; competency-based interviews lead to better employees; job crafting can make jobs more meaningful. As organisational psychologists, we know all of this. We rely on evidence rather than fashions, intuition and the latest fads: our work is well informed and therefore stands the best chance of being effective. As the organisational landscape changes, it will be increasingly important for organisational psychologists to show that our interventions have a positive impact on employees, and that the solutions we offer give value for money.

Organisational psychology is not for everyone. Perhaps reading this book has made you realise that it's not something that you want to pursue, and if that is the case, it has probably been time and money well spent. But I hope that we have managed to share some of our passion for the field. Organisational psychology can help to improve job satisfaction, increase productivity, reduce turnover and create a positive organisational culture. As the world of work continues to evolve, organisational psychologists will play an increasingly important role in ensuring that individuals and organisations thrive in a rapidly changing environment. It's an exciting time for an important profession and we wish you well, whatever path you choose to take.

Glossary

Action research: A form of research that concentrates on solving practical problems in collaboration with the people and organisations experiencing them.

Allyship: Where a member of a non-marginalised group offers their support and voice to marginalised individuals and groups.

Andragogy: A branch of constructivism which identifies and capitalises on the particular characteristics of adult learning.

Anti-racism: Taking pro-active steps to address and tackle racism.

Appreciative inquiry: An analysis and assessment approach that seeks to find what works in an organisation and to build designs from that. The results of this positively oriented process are statements that describe the future state of the organisation based on the high points and good aspects of where it has been.

Assessment centre: A process as opposed to a place. Assessment centres (ACs) take place over one or a few days where candidates are observed taking part in several different selection methods that simulate job-relevant tasks.

Assistive technology: Technology including software and digital devices that assist individuals with additional access needs as they navigate daily life and work. This can range from voice-activated software to digital bath lifts and eye-tracking software to create speech.

Asynchronous online learning: Learning that can take place at a time of the learner's choosing, based on previously devised materials such as podcasts and online quizzes.

Asynchronous video interviewing: The candidate completes the interview independently, via video, at a time and place of their choosing and the interviewer is not present when the candidate is being interviewed.

Attribute: A person's quality or characteristic.

Behaviourism: A school of psychology which focuses exclusively on observable behaviour.

Big Five Personality Traits: A well-evidenced set of five personality traits that reflect different aspects of people's behaviour and thoughts. Often known by the acronym OCEAN, they are: Openness to experience, Conscientiousness, Extraversion, Agreeableness and Neuroticism.

Causality: The ability to determine whether one variable causes the other (and the direction of this relationship).

Change agent: An internal or external facilitator whose role is to guide an organisation through a process of change.

Coaching: A series of goal-orientated, structured, client-led one-to-one conversations which aim to empower individuals to make their own choices and solve their own problems.

Coaching psychology: Coaching that is grounded in psychological theories and a rigorous evidence-base.

Cognitivism: A school of psychology which conceptualises the brain as an information processing system and focuses on processes such as memory and organisation.

Competencies: These are a person's knowledge, skills, abilities and other attributes that lead them to be successful in a job role.

Conscientiousness: One of the 'Big Five' personality traits characterised by self-control, reliability and good organisation skills.

Construct validity: This is the extent to which the selection method measures the construct in question – for example, does the interview actually measure team work or leadership skills?

Constructivism: A school of psychology that assumes that knowledge is constructed by an individual based on their experiences of the world.

Correlation: A relationship where as one variable increases, another variable either increases or decreases with it.

Criterion-related validity: Criterion-related validity examines the extent to which the predictor (e.g. a selection method) is related to a criterion (e.g. an output such as job performance). So you are asking the question: does this selection method predict job performance?

Critical Incident Technique (CIT): A qualitative research method where the researcher asks participants to describe an event when a behaviour impacted a specific outcome. CIT is often used during interviews or focus groups.

Cross-sectional design: A study which looks at the relationship between two or more variables at a single point in time.

Culture: The values, traditions, customs, stories, habits and attitudes that a group of people share that define for them their general behaviour and way of working in an organisation. A common shorthand for the definition is 'the way we do things round here'.

Cyberpsychology: The branch of psychology which is concerned with examining human interaction with digital technology, particularly the Internet.

Deductive: Research concerned with the testing of theories.

Dependent variable: The variable which is affected by change in the independent variable in an experiment.

Digital footprint: Data that is left behind and collected when users have been online.

Employee engagement: The cognitive, emotional and behavioural state that directs an employee to engage in desirable organisational action.

Epistemology: Epistemology is part of a researcher's research paradigm and seeks to answer the question, 'How can we know reality?' Common epistemologies include positivism, constructivism and pragmatism.

Ethical maturity: The increased capacity to embrace ethical complexity and to address it with appropriate respect and fairness to all partners involved.

Ethics: A set of rules or a code that directs action or governs decisions that we make.

Eudaimonic well-being: Pursuit of meaning, having a sense of purpose in your life, personal growth, focus on values and generally having a direction in life.

Experimental design: A study which is conducted in a tightly controlled environment (often a lab) where researchers manipulate one of the variables (the independent variable) in order to determine whether it affects another variable (the dependent variable).

External validity: In a research study, the extent to which the results can be generalised based on the characteristics and design of the study.

Facilitated sessions: Events or workshops orchestrated by a facilitator. Facilitators do not need to have knowledge of the content of the workshop as their skill is using their knowledge of group processes to determine approaches and techniques that help a group achieve the objectives of the session.

Focus group: A group interview, often where participants have a shared perspective, with a facilitator who guides the conversation so that the discussion revolves around a specific topic. Focus groups allow the researcher to collect information on participants' ideas and perceptions about a particular topic in a non-threatening environment.

Forced-choice questions: Questions which force test takers to choose between a set of options. For example, an example is presented with four statements or words and the test taker must choose one statement that is most like them and one statement that is least like them.

Fourth Industrial Revolution: A contemporary period of history shaped by the extensive applied use of technology throughout our personal and professional lives.

Furlough: This is a process where employees in the UK were instructed by their employer not to engage in work and the government funded a partial salary payment to enable organisations to retain workers through the COVID-19 pandemic.

Future search: A conference-style approach involving large numbers of internal and external stakeholders to guide organisation design jointly working on a design with facilitator support. Briefly, some initial questions are posed and the 'delegates' use a combination of structured activities to agree answers/solutions. This method has the benefit of generating feelings of ownership among stakeholders thus getting speedily to the implementation stage.

HARKing: Stands for Hypothesis After Results Known. This is a questionable research practice where the researcher first explores the data to find significant results, and then writes a hypothesis to support those results. This can lead to false positives and research which does not replicate.

Hedonic well-being: Includes pursuing pleasurable experiences, having high levels of positive feelings and low levels of negative feelings.

Hybrid work: A pattern of work that includes an employee working remotely (e.g. from home) for some period of time and working at organisation premises for some portion of their working time.

Hypothesis: A predictive statement based on evidence which describes the relationship or difference a researcher expects to find in a study. Hypotheses must be positively worded, logical, testable and refutable.

Incremental validity: Incremental validity is a type of validity that is used to understand whether a specific selection method increases predictive validity beyond an already-established method.

Independent variable: The variable which is manipulated in an experiment.

Inductive: Research which is focused on the generation of theories.

Internal consistency: The consistency of results across questions in an assessment that are aimed to measure the same construct / concept.

Internal validity: In a research study, the extent to which the results can be used to draw conclusions about whether one variable causes another based on the characteristics and design of the study.

Intersectionality: This refers to the way in which different identities interact to create a unique identity and often a unique experience of marginalisation or exclusionary barriers.

Interviews: A qualitative data collection method where a researcher collects information on a particular topic from a single participant at a time by verbally asking questions and receiving verbal responses. Verbal responses from participants are often recorded so the researcher can transcribe them later for analysis.

Item: An item is another word for 'question' or statement in a scale, survey or questionnaire.

Job analysis: This is a method used to analyse a specific job, and used both to identify the tasks conducted and to generate the knowledge, skills, abilities and other attributes (KSAOs) required to perform a particular job.

Knowledge work: Work where an individual's knowledge or ability to think plays the most significant part of their work. (This could include professions such as accountancy, law, project management, computing, academia and architecture.)

Large group interventions: Techniques, such as Search Conferences and Open Space, designed to work with a whole system, including organisation members, suppliers, customers and other stakeholders.

Leadership: The act of leading a group of people, often associated with taking risks and changing the status quo. An individual person can engage in leadership, or an entire group of people can collectively lead and motivate others to follow.

Likert scale: A scale with response options designed to measure the strength of a trait on a continuum. For example, a test taker is presented with a question and is asked to rate their level of agreement to the statement on a scale where 1 = Completely disagree, and 7 = Completely agree.

Management: The process of planning work for oneself or others. Management often involves creating plans of action for a group of workers, motivating them to engage in coordinated effort towards completing this plan, and measuring their performance throughout.

Mean: The average of a set of numbers.

Measures of maximum performance: Tests of specific abilities or aptitudes that have 'right' and 'wrong' answers.

Measures of typical performance: Tests that do not have 'right' or 'wrong' answers and measure how someone typically or usually behaves in a work setting or a team setting.

Mechanistic organisation: This type of organisation is highly bureaucratic. Tasks are specialised and clearly defined. This is suitable when markets and technology are well established and show little change over time.

Median: The middle number in a set of numbers.

Mentoring: A professional relationship between two people in the same field or industry, in which the mentor, usually a more experienced practitioner, offers the mentee the chance to explore and reflect on their own feelings, thoughts and behaviour and offers advice or access to opportunities.

Meta-cognition: The process of being aware of your own thought processes – thinking about your own thinking.

Mindfulness: A system of mental training intended to help individuals, groups of people and society at large overcome stress and suffering.

Motivation: The (conscious or unconscious) impetus that gives purpose or direction to behaviour.

Multilevel research: This describes how observations in empirical research can be clustered across multiple levels of analysis. Take work performance, for example: investigating individuals' specific performance contributions is using the individual level of analysis. Yet since some individuals perform better than others at different points of time, the aggregate of all individual performance contributions is not the same as the team's performance – that needs to be observed at the collective level of analysis. Hence multi-level research tends to be superior to single-level research.

Narrative interview: A type of interview where the researcher asks one or more questions, and while the participant speaks, the narrative is not interrupted. The researcher may ask for clarification or expansion after the participant's response has ended.

Neuroticism: One of the 'Big Five' personality traits characterised by a tendency towards anxiety, pessimism and depression.

Norm group: A sample of test takers who represent the intended population of people who have completed the same test or questionnaire.

Norms: Typical and accepted behaviour. **Social norms** – typical and accepted behaviour within a society; **group norms** – typical and accepted behaviour within a particular group.

Null hypothesis: The null hypothesis predicts that there is no relationship between the two variables of interest (the opposite of what our hypothesis predicts). For example, if the research hypothesis is 'There is a positive relationship between work-life balance and psychological detachment', the null hypothesis would be 'There is no relationship between work-life balance and psychological detachment'.

Null Hypothesis Significance Testing (NHST):   A type of statistical testing which looks for the probability that the null hypothesis is true. Some common types of tests which fall under the NHST umbrella are correlations, regressions, t-tests and ANOVAs. Most common statistical methods used in social sciences rely on NHST.

Ontology: Ontology is part of a researcher's research paradigm and asks the question, 'What is reality?'

Operational definition: An operational definition is a way of describing how a variable will be defined in order to make it measurable in a research study.

Organic organisation: This type of organisation is relatively flexible and relaxed. The organic style is most appropriate to unstable environmental conditions in which novel problems continually occur.

Organisation Development (OD):   The systemwide application and transfer of behavioural science knowledge to the planned development, improvement and reinforcement of the strategies, structure and processes that lead to organisation effectiveness.

Organisation development practitioner: A generic term for people practising organisation development. These individuals may include managers responsible for developing their organisations or departments, people specialising in OD as a profession, and people specialising in a field currently being integrated with OD (for example strategy or HR) who have gained some familiarity with and competence in OD.

Organisational culture: The distinctive norms, beliefs, principles and ways of behaving that combine to give each organisation its distinctive character.

Paradigm: A research paradigm represents the philosophical framework underpinning a research project, and includes the researcher's ontology, epistemology and research methodology.

Person-centred approach: A therapeutic approach that assumes that people have a biological tendency to grow and develop, and which aims to remove barriers to their development by allowing them to talk through their feelings and thoughts in a non-judgemental, confidential space.

P-hacking: P-hacking is a set of questionable research practices where the researcher manipulates quantitative data in order to make the p-value statistically significant (and be able to confirm their hypothesis, even if the data did not initially support it). This may include collecting additional data until the findings are significant, changing the way variables are structured to find a significant difference (i.e., changing a variable from a continuous set of numbers into 2 groups), or removing data points in order to make the results significant. P-hacking may contribute to research not being replicable.

Population: A population is all of the people who fall into the category of what is being studied. For example, if a researcher wanted to study employment in the UK, the population would be every employee who works in the UK.

Positive psychology: A branch of psychology pioneered by Martin Seligman and Mihaly Csikszentmihalyi which aims to produce techniques and approaches through rigorous scientific methods to help people to flourish.

Positivist research: In contrast to social constructionist research, positivist research takes the view that human behaviour, thoughts and feelings are substantially influenced by objectively measurable factors which exist independent of the researchers and people being researched.

Power tests: Tests designed to see how many questions of increasing difficulty someone can answer correctly.

Predictive validity   (see criterion-related validity)

Process consultation: A set of activities on the part of the consultant that helps the client to perceive, understand and act upon the process events that occur in the client's environment.

Prototypicality: The degree to which a member of a category maps on to what is the most representative (most typical) of the category – for example a prototypical leader is the idea of a leader who most embodies the key characteristics of leadership.

Psychological flexibility: The ability to make choices about which thoughts and feelings to focus on. It involves being aware of particular thoughts and feelings but being able to focus on the present moment rather than ruminating or fixating on unhelpful ideas.

Psychological safety: When a team experiences a working environment where they feel safe to engage in communication.

Psychometrics: Psychometric tests and assessments are tools used to measure psychological characteristics (e.g. people's motivation, personality traits and general intelligence).

p-value: A number calculated with statistics which represents the probability of finding a specific result if the null hypothesis were true. In psychology, the cut-off for p-values to be considered statistically significant is p < .05.

QRP: An abbreviation for Questionable Research Practices, which are methods researchers can engage in to make their results significant (and therefore publishable) but can lead to false positives which do not replicate. See HARKing and p-hacking.

Quasi-experiment: A quasi-experiment is an experiment which has some of the characteristics of an experimental design, but does not fulfil all the requirements to be classed as a true experiment (usually, participants cannot be randomly allocated into groups, for example, gender).

Randomised controlled trial (RCT):   An experimental design where participants are randomly allocated to either an experimental or control condition. Both groups are treated identically except one group receives treatment while the other is given a different activity of the same length. Groups then fill out the same measure for the dependent variable so the researcher can test for differences between the groups. These designs are often used to test the effectiveness of interventions.

Range restriction: Range restriction happens because the validation study sample has less variability on a score than the full population.

Reflective practice: The process of good-quality thinking about one's professional practice in order to enhance its quality.

Reliability: Reliability is the extent to which a selection method is free from error.

Remote Work: Work undertaken at a location remote from the official organisation premises, often at the employee's home.

Replication: The ability for research results to be found by other researchers / scientists with a different sample from the same population, using the same research design / measures. If results reported in a study are a true representation of a phenomenon, then most of the time, the results should be significant if other researchers attempt to repeat the research.

Research methodology: Research methodology asks the question, 'How can we go about discovering the answer to a research question?' In qualitative research, this helps researchers choose which research method is most appropriate based on their ontology and epistemology. In quantitative research, research methodology may be more based on study design.

Research question: A 'what' or 'how' question about the research topic which a study will address that guides the research process. Some examples: 'What is the relationship between work-life balance and smartphone use?' or 'How does psychological detachment affect employee well-being?'

Resilience: Being able to cope with and recover from setbacks, adapting to changing contexts or difficult situations.

Return on Investment (ROI):   When money is invested in a product or solution, the Return on Investment (ROI) is the amount of gain or profit this investment has earned.

Sample: A small subset of the population. In a research study, these are usually the people who take part in a study (participants).

Self-actualisation: The idea of an individual reaching their potential and being truly fulfilled.

Self-efficacy: The confidence an individual has in their ability to perform a specific task.

Semi-structured interview: A type of interview where the researcher asks the partici-pants a set of pre-determined questions with flexibility to ask follow-up questions or explore ideas which come up but were not in the pre-determined question set.

Social constructionist research: Research based on the assumption that there are few objective facts about the social world, and that it is therefore necessary to focus on people's subjective interpretations rather than objectively verifiable causal laws.

Social identity: The part of your identity that comes from your sense of the social groups that you belong to.

Social network: The relatively organised set of relationships that an individual or group has with others. This includes means of communication, the quality and strength of interpersonal relationships, and patterns of like and dislike between individuals. Social networks can be analysed quantitatively using social network analysis.

Speed tests: Tests that have questions that are relatively easy to complete, but are scored on how many questions are completed correctly within a strict time limit. Scoring tends to reflect the speed and accuracy with which someone answers questions.

Spurious relationship: A relationship between two variables which occurs by coin-cidence. Also, a relationship between two variables which occurs because both are related to a third variable which has not been measured.

Standard deviation: A calculation which tells us how much a set of scores varies or deviates from the mean. If a standard deviation is small, it means the scores in that variable are all similar to each other and to the mean; if a standard deviation is large, it means there is a large amount of variability between scores.

Stress: The response to a stressor.

Stressor: The thing that causes stress.

Structured interview: A type of interview where the researcher asks the participant a set of pre-determined questions without deviation or the ability to ask follow-up questions or explore ideas beyond the pre-determined question set.

Subjective well-being: The degree to which people feel that they are comfortable, healthy and happy.

Succession planning: The steps an organisation goes through to make sure that they have people ready, willing and able to take over more senior roles.

Supervision: A formal arrangement for reflecting on your professional practice collab-oratively with a colleague in order to identify ways to improve.

Synchronous online learning: Online learning that happens in real time, most often as live webinars.

Training transfer: The process by which skills and knowledge learnt through a formal training course are applied in the workplace.

Trait: A distinguishing quality or characteristic belonging to a person.

Unconditional positive regard: The psychological position in which a coach or psychologist completely supports and accepts another individual for who they are, regardless of what they say and do.

Unconscious bias: The associations, assumptions and prejudices that we associate with particular groups of people that we aren't aware we have.

Unstructured interview: A type of exploratory interview where the researcher explores an over-arching theme without a pre-determined set of questions, allowing questions to be generated from the discussion.

Validity: Validity refers to the extent to which a selection method measures what it claims to measure.

Values: Broad ideas of what matters to an individual.

Variable: Any concept, trait or characteristic which can be measured or manipulated in a research study.

Vicarious learning: The process of learning through observing others.

VUCA: A term used to describe the nature of contemporary organisations and business, referring to Volatility, Uncertainty, Complexity and Ambiguity.

WEIRD: WEIRD stands for Western, Educated, Industrialised, Rich and Democratic. It represents a sample of participants who come from cultures or countries which represent these things and are often vastly different than the majority of world cultures, which can be an issue when trying to generalise research findings.

Well-being: The degree to which people are comfortable, healthy and happy.

Index

Note: Page numbers in **bold** refer to tables, and those in *italics* refer to figures.